A Political Companion to Philip Roth

A POLITICAL COMPANION TO
Philip Roth

EDITED BY
Claudia Franziska Brühwiler
and Lee Trepanier

UNIVERSITY PRESS OF KENTUCKY

Scholarly publisher for the Commonwealth,
serving Bellarmine University, Berea College, Centre College of Kentucky,
Eastern Kentucky University, The Filson Historical Society, Georgetown College,
Kentucky Historical Society, Kentucky State University, Morehead State
University, Murray State University, Northern Kentucky University, Transylvania
University, University of Kentucky, University of Louisville, and Western
Kentucky University.
All rights reserved.

Editorial and Sales Offices: The University Press of Kentucky
663 South Limestone Street, Lexington, Kentucky 40508-4008
www.kentuckypress.com

Cataloging-in-Publication data available from the Library of Congress

ISBN 978-0-8131-6928-6 (cloth)
ISBN 978-0-8131-6930-9 (epub)
ISBN 978-0-8131-6929-3 (pdf)

This book is printed on acid-free paper meeting
the requirements of the American National Standard
for Permanence in Paper for Printed Library Materials.

Manufactured in the United States of America.

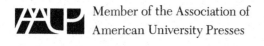 Member of the Association of
American University Presses

Contents

Series Foreword

Those who undertake a study of American political thought must attend to the great theorists, philosophers, and essayists. Such a study is incomplete, however, if it neglects American literature, one of the greatest repositories of the nation's political thought and teachings.

America's literature is distinctive because it is, above all, intended for a democratic citizenry. In contrast to eras when an author would aim to inform or influence a select aristocratic audience, in democratic times, public influence and education must resonate with a more expansive, less leisured, and diverse audience to be effective. The great works of America's literary tradition are the natural locus of democratic political teaching. Invoking the interest and attention of citizens through the pleasures afforded by the literary form, many of America's great thinkers sought to forge a democratic public philosophy with subtle and often challenging teachings that unfolded in narrative, plot, and character development. Perhaps more than any other nation's literary tradition, American literature is ineluctably political—shaped by democracy as much as it has in turn shaped democracy.

The Political Companions to Great American Authors series highlights the teachings of the great authors in America's literary and belletristic tradition. An astute political interpretation of America's literary tradition requires careful, patient, and attentive readers who approach the text with a view to understanding its underlying messages about citizenship and democracy. Essayists in this series approach the classic texts not with a "hermeneutics of suspicion" but with the curiosity of fellow citizens who believe that the great authors have something of value to teach their readers. The series brings together essays from varied approaches and viewpoints for the common purpose of elucidating the political teachings of the nation's greatest authors for those seeking a better understanding of American democracy.

Patrick J. Deneen
Series Editor

Written Remarks for the 2013 PEN Literary Gala

Philip Roth

From 1972 through 1977, I travelled to Prague every spring for a week or ten days to see a group of writers, journalists, historians, and professors there who were being persecuted by the Soviet-backed totalitarian Czech regime.

I was followed by a plainclothesman most of the time I was there, and my hotel room was bugged, as was the room's telephone. However, it was not until 1977, when I was leaving an art museum where I'd gone to see a ludicrous exhibition of Soviet socialist-realism painting—it was not until that sixth year that I was detained by the police. The intervention was unsettling, and the next day, heeding their suggestion, I left the country.

Though I kept in touch by mail—sometimes coded mail—with some of the dissident writers I'd met and befriended in Prague, I was not able to get a visa to return to Czechoslovakia again for twelve years, until 1989. In that year, the Communists were driven out and Václav Havel's democratic government came into power, wholly legitimately, not unlike General Washington and his government in 1788, through a unanimous vote of the Federal Assembly and with the overwhelming support of the Czech people.

Many of my hours in Prague were spent with the novelist Ivan Klíma and his wife, Helena, who is a psychotherapist. Ivan and Helena both spoke English and, along with a number of others—among them the novelists Ludvík Vaculík and Milan Kundera, the poet Miroslav Holub, the literature professor Zdenek Stribrny, the translator Rita Budínová-Mlynárová, whom Havel later appointed his first Ambassador to the U.S., and the writer Karel Sidon, after the Velvet Revolution the chief rabbi of Prague and eventually of the Czech Republic—together, these friends gave me a thoroughgoing education in what unstinting government repression was like in Czechoslovakia.

This education included visits with Ivan to the places where his colleagues, like Ivan stripped of their rights by the authorities, were working at the menial jobs to which the omnipresent regime had maliciously assigned them. Once they had been thrown out of the Writers' Union, they were forbidden to publish or to teach or to travel or to drive a car or to earn a proper livelihood each at his or her own calling. For good measure, their children, the children of the thinking segment of the population, were forbidden to attend academic high schools.

Some whom I met and spoke with were selling cigarettes at a street-corner kiosk, others were wielding a wrench at the public waterworks, others spent their days on bicycles delivering buns to bakeries, still others were washing windows or pushing brooms as a janitor's assistant at some out-of-the-way Prague museum. These people, as I've indicated, were the cream of the nation's intelligentsia.

So it was and so it is in the time of a totalitarian system. Every day brings a new heartache, a new tremor, more helplessness, and yet another reduction of freedom and free thought in a censored society already bound and gagged.

The usual rites of degradation: the ongoing unmooring of one's personal identity, the suppression of one's personal authority, the elimination of one's security—a craving for solidity, for one's equanimity, in the face of an ever-present uncertainty. Unforeseeableness as the new norm and perpetual anxiety as the injurious result.

And anger. The maniacal raving of a manacled being. Frenzies of futile rage ravaging only oneself. Alongside your spouse and your children, imbibing the tyranny with your morning coffee. The toll of anger.

Totalitarianism's ruthless, trauma-inducing machine cranking out the worst of everything and, over time, everything becoming more than one can bear.

One amusing anecdote from a grim and unamusing time, and then I'll sit down.

On the evening of the day following my encounter with the police, when in haste I wisely left Prague for home, Ivan was picked up from his house by the police and, not for the first time, questioned by them for hours. Only this time, they did not hector him all night about the clandestine seditious activities of Helena and himself and their cohort of troublesome dissidents and disturbers of the totalitarian peace. Instead—in a refreshing change for Ivan—they inquired about my annual visits to Prague.

As Ivan later told me in a letter, he had only one answer—one—to give them throughout their dogged nightlong inquisition about why I was hanging around the city every spring.

"Don't you read his books?" Ivan asked the police.

As might be expected, they were stymied by the question, but Ivan quickly enlightened them.

"He comes for the girls," Ivan said.

We thank Philip Roth for giving his permission to publish his written remarks. We are likewise grateful to the University of St.Gallen, Switzerland, and the Dr. h.c. Emil Zaugg-Fonds for covering the related costs. Finally, we thank Aimee Pozorski and the Wiley Agency for helping us obtain the rights to reprint this piece.

Philip Roth's Political Thought

Lee Trepanier and Claudia Franziska Brühwiler

This book looks at the political thought of one of the giants of American literature: Philip Roth. Roth's depiction of American life, which focuses on American Jewish life in Newark, New Jersey, may initially appear provincial, but his portrayal of his hometown can be seen as a microcosm of America itself: its political aspirations, its political failures, and its political self-reflection about what it means to be an American. Of course, Roth's oeuvre transcends the subject of political thought itself, raising larger questions about the role that literature, identity, and sex play in our lives. While acknowledging that Roth's writings ask us what it is to be human in the broadest and most complex sense of the term, this book will focus only on Roth's political thinking.

The political themes in Roth's works are myriad, from questions of American Jewish identity, Zionism, and American attitudes toward Israel in works like *Goodbye, Columbus, Portnoy's Complaint,* and *Operation Shylock* to the exploration of subjects such as freedom, equality, and tolerance in *Exit Ghost, American Pastoral,* and *I Married a Communist.* Roth examines not only the topics of race, class, and gender in *The Breast, The Human Stain,* and *Nemesis* but also ideas of political progress, utopia, and corruption in *The Dying Animal, Our Gang,* and *The Plot Against America.* And Roth himself was politically active as a vigorous supporter of dissident writers in Communist Czechoslovakia. Given these themes in his works and his role as a political activist, it is clear that one could categorize him as a political thinker.

Strangely, the scholarship on Philip Roth's political thought is sparse. The only monograph that explicitly addresses Roth's political thought is Claudia Franziska Brühwiler's *Political Initiation in the Novels of Philip Roth*, which focuses on the subject of political identity.[1] Simon Stow explores the question of whether Roth is a political thinker in his article "Written and Unwritten America: Roth on Reading, Politics, and Theory"; Anthony Hutchison investigates how Roth uses political ideology in the American Trilogy (*American Pastoral, I Married a Communist,* and *The Human Stain*); and Maureen Whitebrook examines Roth's use of political identity in *Operation Shylock*.[2] Finally, Michael Kimmage's *In History's Grip: Philip Roth's Newark Trilogy* indirectly addresses political issues in Roth's American Trilogy but from the vantage point of history and not political science.[3]

Except for the works cited above, the scholarship on Roth has been primarily literary in nature rather than political. Some of the most prominent works are David Gooblar's *The Major Phases of Philip Roth*, which explores Philip Roth's entire oeuvre as a literary project; Debra Shostak's *Philip Roth*, which discusses various aspects of Roth's American Trilogy; and Aimee Pozorski's *Roth and Trauma: The Problem of History in the Later Works (1995–2010)*, which appeals to a broader audience with a focus on American history.[4] Other recent publications about Roth include Aimee Pozorski's *Roth and Celebrity*, which explores Roth's public persona; David Brauner's *Philip Roth*, which focuses on the use of paradox as a rhetorical device to analyze ideological principles in his works; Pia Masiero's *Philip Roth and the Zuckerman Books*, which concentrates on Roth's recurring character, Nathan Zuckerman; Jane Statlander's *Philip Roth's Postmodern American Romance*, which discusses the impact of Roth's Jewishness on his position within American literature; and Claudia Roth Pierpont's *Roth Unbound: A Writer and His Works*, a critical biography of the person and his works.[5] Finally, there are edited collections that explore Roth's work but, again, primarily from a literary perspective: Derek Parker Royal's *Philip Roth: New Perspectives on an American Author;* Timothy Parish's *The Cambridge Companion to Philip Roth;* and Velichka D. Ivanova's *Philip Roth and World Literature*.[6]

By inviting scholars from the United States and abroad to provide an interdisciplinary and international perspective on his political thought, our book fills this void in the scholarship about Philip Roth's works. We have invited a mixture of established and rising scholars to provide an assessment of it. By engaging his major works, these contributors explore and critically evaluate the various aspects of Roth's work in a political context. Not only will this book remedy the deficiency in the scholarship about Philip Roth, but it also will provide a broader perspective about the nature and purpose of Roth's political thought for disciplines outside political science and for countries beyond the United States.

Philip Milton Roth was born on March 19, 1933, and was the second child of Herman and Bess Roth, first-generation American Jews who lived in Newark, New Jersey, a place from which Roth would draw inspiration for many of his works.[7] During Roth's childhood, Newark was a city filled with upward-striving immigrants, with the Jewish enclave being in the southwest corner of the city, known as Weequahic. His childhood was typical of an immigrant child in America during the 1930s and 1940s, with school, baseball, and listening to the radio. However, Roth also was cognizant of his Jewish identity, not only because his family attended synagogue and he went to Hebrew school but also because he experienced anti-Semitism as a child, whether listening to the tirades of Father Coughlin on the radio or observing how high his father would be allowed to climb the company ladder because he was a Jew. This sense of aspiring to be an American and not being fully accepted because of his Jewishness is a theme to which Roth constantly returns in his career as a writer. He felt that he was sharing this search for a definite sense of belonging with Saul Bellow, as Roth explained with regard to the constant labeling as an "American Jewish writer": "The book that brought him his first popular recognition, *Adventures of Augie March*, does not begin 'I am a Jew, New York–born' but rather 'I am an American, Chicago-born.'"[8]

After graduating from high school in 1950, Roth enrolled in Bucknell University and earned a degree in English.[9] He pursued graduate studies at the University of Chicago, where he received a master's degree in English literature in 1955 and worked briefly as an instructor in the university's writing program.[10] Roth also served two years in the U.S. Army (1955–1956) and, after his honorable discharge, wrote short fiction and criticism for various magazines. But it was with his first book, *Goodbye, Columbus*, that Roth entered the American literary scene with his stories about the concerns of assimilated American Jews as they depart from their ethnic enclaves for the suburban life. Although he won the 1960 U.S. National Book Award for Fiction, Roth was accused by some members in the American Jewish community of being a self-hating Jew, an accusation that was made to him directly in 1962 at a panel to discuss minority representation in American literature.[11]

Roth's next novel, *Letting Go,* published in 1962, explored the social constraints on men and women in the 1950s.[12] In the following year, Roth separated from his first wife, Margaret Martinson, whom he met in 1956 in Chicago and married in 1959. Their separation and her death in a car crash in 1968 influenced Roth's portrayal of some of the female characters in his novels, like Lucy Nelson in *When She Was Good* (1967) and Maureen Tarnopol in *My Life as a Man* (1974).[13] After *When She Was Good*, Roth's *Portnoy's Complaint* was published in 1969, a novel that not only made Roth a public figure but also sparked a storm of controversy over its explicit treatment of sexuality, such as detailed depictions of masturbation.[14] Roth followed *Portnoy's Complaint* with a satire of the Nixon administration in *Our Gang* (1971) and *The Breast* (1972), which features David Kepesh, who also appears as the protagonist in *The Professor of Desire* (1974) and *The Dying Animal* (2001).[15] In this trilogy, Kepesh is depicted as a literature professor who is able to gratify his sexual desires but unable to emotionally connect with others, with him at one point being transformed into a 155-pound breast.[16]

Further demonstrating his versatility as a writer, Roth wrote the satirical *The Great American Novel* (1973), which is about a Communist conspiracy to eliminate the history of a baseball league, and the nonfiction *Reading Myself and Others* (1975), an anthology of essays, interviews, and criticism that assesses his work at that time in a conversation with other American authors and critics.[17] But it was *My Life as a Man* (1974) that introduced the protagonist Nathan Zuckerman that Roth would employ in his later works.[18] Zuckerman is not only the protagonist in Roth's last novel of the 1970s, *The Ghost Writer* (1979), but also dominates in the following novels: *Zuckerman Unbound* (1981), *The Anatomy Lesson* (1983), *The Prague Orgy* (1985) (with these four books later referred to as *Zuckerman Bound*), *The Counterlife* (1986), *American Pastoral* (1997), *I Married a Communist* (1998), *The Human Stain* (2000), and *Exit Ghost* (2007). With Zuckerman, Roth creates a fictional alter ego who explores the relationship between art and life, religious and national identity, and the consequences of the choices one makes in life in family, career, and sexual partners.[19]

Roth also visited Prague in the 1970s, with his first visit in 1972 introducing him to Czech history, culture, and politics and inspiring him to write stories about Kafka that were republished in *Reading Myself and Others*. Roth continually returned to Prague to visit Czech writers like Ivan Klíma, Milan Kundera, and Václav Havel until 1977, when he was declared persona non grata.[20] During these trips, Roth smuggled money into the country to support these writers, which eventually led to PEN taking over these arrangements, and he helped get their works published in the United States.[21] Roth's experiences in Prague had a lasting effect on him as a writer and political activist to the extent that he dedicated *The Ghost Writer* to Milan Kundera, a novel that imagines a life for Anne Frank if she had survived the Holocaust.[22]

Besides his trips to Prague, Roth also travelled regularly to Paris, where Milan Kundera had managed to relocate, in the late 1970s, and, by the early 1980s, he also traveled to Israel. Roth began a relationship with the English actress Claire Bloom and rented a writing studio in London where he stayed in the winters and also renewed and made new friendships with members of the British literary and cultural crowd.[23] Roth and Bloom married in 1990 but separated in 1994, with Bloom writing a memoir, *Leaving a Doll's House* (1996), that describes the marriage in detail with an unflattering portrayal of Roth.[24]

During the 1980s, Roth again produced a series of a novels that employed his fictional alter ego, Nathan Zuckerman: *Zuckerman Unbound* (1981) is about Zuckerman's confronting infamy for the success of *Carnovsky*, a *Portnoy*-like book; *The Anatomy Lesson* (1983) is a reflection about the protagonist in pain and in middle age, contemplating enrolling in medical school; *The Prague Orgy* (1985) recounts Zuckerman's journeys to Prague to obtain a manuscript of unpublished Yiddish stories; and *The Counterlife* (1986), which includes Nathan's brother, Henry, presents multiple accounts of their lives that contradict one another in their search for meaning in marriage, family, and the role that Israel plays in the lives of Jews.[25] Roth concluded the decade with a nonfictional book, *The Facts: A Novelist's Autobiography* (1988), which traces his life from childhood to becoming a successful and respected novelist, and in which Roth and Zuckerman write letters to each other.[26]

In *Deception* (1990) Roth gave his own name to a protagonist who has conversations with his married English lover about their loveless, upper-middle-class marriages held together, in her case, only by a child.[27] This book was followed by *Patrimony: A True Story* (1991), a memoir about the life and death of Roth's father from a brain tumor. In 1993 the revised *A Philip Roth Reader* (originally published in 1980) was issued, which included selections from Roth's first eight novels as well as stories like "Novotny's Pain" and "Looking at Kafka."[28] But it was *Operation Shylock: A Confession* (1993), *Sabbath's Theater* (1995), *American Pastoral* (1997), and *I Married a Communist* (1998) that returned Roth to prominence in American literature. *Operation Shylock*, which was awarded the 1994 PEN/Faulkner Award in 1994, is about the character Philip Roth's journey to Israel, where he discovers that his identity has been appropriated by someone proclaiming Diasporism, a counter-Zionist ideology; *Sabbath's Theater*, winner of the 1995 National Book Award, centers on an elderly former puppeteer whose loss of his partner, Drenka, precipitates a crisis in his life; *American Pastoral*, which was honored with the 1998 Pulitzer Prize, recounts the tragic fate of Seymour "Swede" Levov during the tumultuous 1960s; and *I Married a Communist* follows the life of the Communist Ira Ringold, whose success as a radio star is destroyed by wife, daughter, and others close to him.[29]

During the 2000s, Roth wrote *The Human Stain*, which was awarded the 2001 PEN/Faulkner Award, a story about the African American Coleman Silk, who passes himself off as white and Jewish; *The Dying Animal* (2001), the last novel of the David Kepesh's trilogy; *The Plot Against America* (2007), a counterfactual history of the United States with a fascist government; *Exit Ghost* (2007), the last book that features Nathan Zuckerman; and a collection of previously published interviews with important twentieth-century writers entitled *Shop Talk* (2001).[30] Roth also published four books in this decade on the theme of "four men of different ages brought down low": *Everyman* (2006), which won the PEN/Faulkner Award, follows the life of an ordinary person's reflection on life and death; *Indignation* (2008) tells the story of Marcus Messner, whose atheism leads to his expulsion from college and enlistment in the U.S. Army; *The Humbling* (2009) narrates the life of Simon Axler, an actor who compensates for his stage fright with a sexual relationship with a younger woman; and *Nemesis* (2010), the most recently published book of Roth's career, which recounts the effects of the polio epidemic in the Jewish neighborhood of Newark.[31]

Philip Roth is one of the most honored American writers: his books have thrice won the PEN/Faulkner Award; twice received the National Book Award and the National Book Critics Circle Award; and also have been awarded the Pulitzer Prize, the Man Book International Prize, and the National Humanities Medal, as well as international prizes such as the Spanish Prince of Asturias Award and an award by the German newspaper *Welt*.[32] He is only the third living American writer to have his works published by the Library of America, an honor previously bestowed on Eudora Welty and Saul Bellow. Along with John Updike and Saul Bellow, Roth is considered one of the greatest American authors of the second half of the twentieth century. He has played a central role in American letters during his lifetime and consequently deserves attention not only as a writer but also as a political thinker.

This volume is targeted at a diverse audience of scholars interested in literature, philosophy, intellectual history, religious studies, and the social sciences. Given the number of novels, short stories, essays, and works of nonfiction that Roth has written, we have restricted ourselves to what we think are key developments in Roth's political thought. We also have limited ourselves to analyzing Roth's works themselves as opposed to adopting a comparative analysis of his work with that of authors who have inspired him. Although we believe such a comparison is a worthy endeavor for a future project, we think that Roth's political thought must first be presented and understood on its own terms.

Roth's writing directly engages some of the major social and political events in twentieth-century America: the Great Depression; World War II and the Holocaust; the Vietnam and Korean Wars; the quiz show scandals and anti-Communist hysteria of the 1950s; the civil rights and radical revolutionary movements of the 1960s; the corruption of the Nixon administration and political repression of Communist Czechoslovakia in the 1970s; the rise of conservatism in the 1980s and political correctness in the 1990s; the Lewinsky scandal and the War on Terror; and the prejudice and assimilation of Jewish Americans into mainstream American society as well as the ethnic, social, and economic stratification of the United States in general. These and other key events and developments in America serve as the political template for Roth's works. With America as his canvas, Roth illuminates how the personal lives of ordinary Americans are affected and in turn affect the public events of national life—as he said himself: "America is the place I know best in the world. It's the only place I know in the world. My consciousness and my language were shaped by America. I'm an American writer in ways that a plumber isn't an American plumber or a miner an American miner or a cardiologist an American cardiologist. Rather, what the heart is to the cardiologist, the coal to the miner, the kitchen sink to the plumber, America is to me."[33]

Although Roth's own political position is clear, as a New Deal liberal or Clinton Democrat, his fiction is not written from this vantage point, and the pieties of American liberalism are exposed for their faults and contradictions. He explores the tension between the American aspiration for perfection and the limitations, whether due to politics, prejudice, or his characters' own poor choices, that thwart that desire. Opposed to moral absolutism of any kind, Roth's writings serve a bulwark against the political extremism and fanaticism that sometimes haunts America. Without this critical scrutiny, perhaps even provocation, from Roth's works, American democracy would not be able to examine itself and therefore be able to pull itself back from the brink of political madness to which it has from time to time succumbed.

This volume opens with a reprint of Philip Roth's remarks at the 2013 PEN Literary Gala, in which Roth speaks about his experience of traveling to Prague to assist the Czech writer Ivan Klíma. Roth describes how the Czech intelligentsia who did not conform to the Communist regime were marginalized in society and had to perform menial jobs in order to survive. For Roth, totalitarianism was a regime that suppressed one's identity in "rites of degradation," causing an unbearable anger at oneself, one's family, and one's community. Yet, in spite of the humiliation the government inflicted upon its citizens, people were able to discover that they still had a reservoir of self-respect, dignity, and even humor to cope in those difficult times.

The first of our collected essays, "'An ear in search of a word': Writing and the Politics of Listening in Roth's *I Married a Communist*," argues that literature can play a role of being a witness to atrocities and take actions to make suffering transformative. In her analysis of *I Married a Communist*, Aimee Pozorski understands the novel as an account not only of the anti-Communist agenda in the United States that affected Roth both as a writer and as a citizen but also of how this experience formed his public life, such as in the elegy he published in the *New York Times* that celebrated his former mentor, and the speech he delivered at the 2013 PEN Literary Gala. According to Pozorski, listening is not a passive activity but an active one that records events for a public record in the hope that it will be used to change minds, lives, and even history itself.

In "Serving His Tour as an 'Exasperated Liberal and Indignant Citizen': Philip Roth, a Public Intellectual?," Claudia Franziska Brühwiler shows that, in spite of his constant assertions that he is not a public intellectual, Roth is a stellar example of one. Although Americans writers are not held to the same standard as public intellectuals as their European counterparts, Roth's writing still provokes political discussion, whether it is a defense of artistic freedom, a response to charges of misogyny, or criticizing presidential politics. But perhaps it is his support of dissident writers in Czechoslovakia that demonstrates that Roth is a public intellectual in both word and in deed.

Simon Stow looks at how Roth's novels can help democratic citizens better understand American politics in his essay, "The Politics and Literature of Unknowingness: Philip Roth's *Our Gang* and *The Plot Against America*." Stow uses the concepts of "unknowing" and "knowing" to explain how literature can either prompt citizens to reflect upon their political beliefs ("unknowing") or merely reinforce what they already believe ("knowing"). By comparing *Our Gang*, which is characterized by "knowing," with *The Plot Against America*, which is a work that is "unknowing," Stow shows how Roth succeeds in one case and fails in another, suggesting how literature can provoke critical political reflection rather than being didactic.

The theme of the political ideologies of perfectionism, Zionism, and progress characterize the next three essays. In "Four Pathologies and a State of Sanity: Political Philosophy and Philip Roth on the Individual in Society," Michael G. Festl illuminates how the aspirations of the characters in Roth's American Trilogy are actually pathologies that plague these characters. Rather than reconciling themselves to the reality in which they live, these characters aspire to "perfection," which leads to death and destruction. Festl spells out a typology of a lack of reconciliation (Merry Levov and Lester Farley), partial reconciliation (Eve Frame), and overreconciliation (Swede, Coleman, and Ira) with tragic results. Only William Orcutt III, the lover of the Swede's wife, is perfectly reconciled to American society, a civilized savagery that is unbearable to the reader and thereby indicts American society with its ideology of perfectionism.

Louis Gordon examines a different type of ideology, Zionism, in "Three Voices or One? Philip Roth and Zionism." In this essay Gordon compares the Zionist views of Philip Roth the author in *The Facts,* Philip Roth the character in *Operation Shylock,* and the character Nathan Zuckerman in *Counterlife.* What Gordon discovers is that very little divergence exists among these three voices on the question of Zionism: all of them adopt a political progressive stance toward Israel and Zionism that is similar to the Israeli Civil Rights and Democracy Movement.

The final ideology that is examined is the American myth of progress, a faith in the infinite advancement that has continuously informed in various degrees America's understanding of itself. In "Roth at Century's End: The Problem of Progress in *The Dying Animal,*" Matthew Shipe argues that this myth is critiqued by David Kepesh's struggle to find meaning in the political and cultural changes that he has experienced in his lifetime. When the apocalypse never materializes in the new millennium, Kepesh, unlike his American compatriots, does not accept an optimistic future of an ever-expanding global capitalism and liberal democracy. He instead resigns himself to the limitations of what he can comprehend about the future as well as the past for himself and his country.

The final set of essays explores the role that the body plays in the political themes of race, class, gender, and religious identity. In "'Novotny's Pain': Philip Roth on Politics and the Problem of Pain," Till Kinzel reveals to us the connection between the Novotny's pain and the body politic of the American republic in the middle of the twentieth century, signaling the nontragic nature of liberal democracy: Novotny's alienation from war and military life ceases to have any significance for him once he continues with his life. His pain consequently serves as a nonverbal bodily sign of disagreement with the noncontroversiality of the Korean War and the government proclamations that Americans are "fighting for freedom" to arouse public support.

Yael Maurer continues this theme of the body in her essay, "The Body Politic: Philip Roth's American Men," where she focuses on the Jewish male body as a site of political anxiety and possible heroic liberation in *Portnoy's Complaint, I Married a Communist,* and *Nemesis.* Whereas in *Portnoy's Complaint,* Roth's comical presentation of the body as both personal and political precludes the reader from feeling the protagonist's pain when he falls from his ideals, the other two novels provide us protagonists who are just as youthful as Alexander but the negation of their personal and political bodies have tragic consequences. Bucky's and Ira's fates leave them, and the reader, to try to make sense of their past, their ideals, and of history itself.

Debra Shostak's "Philip Roth and Life as a Man" also focuses on the body but from both the male and female perspectives. She also concentrates on Roth's later novels, as Roth scholarship already has explored these themes in the works of his early to mid-career. In her essay, Shostak shows how the ideological discourses of gender and sexuality deform what it means to be a human being in Roth's works. Paying attention to manhood as a type of moral achievement and bodily performance, Shostak argues that the struggles of women, in response to men, have made them grotesque human beings, too. Contrary to some claims, Shostak suggests that the place of the feminine in Roth's works recuperates Roth to some degree from the repeated accusations that he offers misogynistic representations of women.

In "The American Berserk in *Sabbath's Theater*," Brett Ashley Kaplan includes race and anti-Semitism with gender in her study of victimization and perpetration. For Kaplan, Jewish anxiety is about not only the fear of being a victim but also a dread of being a perpetrator of racism and sexism. *Sabbath's Theater* expresses this anxiety, the confusion between victimization and perpetration, through Sabbath's sexuality, especially when he compares himself to Benito Mussolini or imagines himself being buried next to a Holocaust survivor. Thus, Sabbath fears not only being a victim but also being a perpetrator of the very things that repulse him.

In the last essay of this book, "Philip Roth and the American 'Underclass' in *The Human Stain*," Andy Connolly examines the role that class plays, along with race and identity politics, in *The Human Stain*. Connolly looks at Faunia Farley's status as a maligned "white underclass" and how her social position contrasts with Coleman Silk's committed belief that he has transcended the historical boundaries established by his racial origins. Through a detailed examination of Faunia's life, Connolly shows that her inescapable sense of belonging to the underclass provides a new way of understanding the limitations that Coleman believes he has overcome.

Besides our contributors, we want to thank Stephen Wrinn and his staff at the University of Kentucky Press for guiding us through this process as well as the anonymous referees and Patrick Deneen, the series editor. We also want to express our gratitude to the University of St.Gallen and the Dr. h.c. Emil Zaugg-Fonds for providing us funds to reprint Roth's 2013 PEN

Literary Gala Remarks, as well as to Aimee Pozorski and the Wiley Agency for helping us obtain the rights to do so. Finally, we would like to thank our parents, our spouses—PD Dr. iur. Daniel Häusermann and Dr. MiJung— and our friends for their continual and enduring love and support while we worked on this project.

Ultimately what we will discover in Roth's work is a depth, complexity, and richness that relates not only to politics and political thought but also to what it means to be a human being. With some of the best-known as well as rising Roth scholars contributing to this volume, we hope it will engage and serve as a valuable resource for both scholars from a variety of fields and the general public. The brilliance of Roth's work, along with the sheer volume of it, secures his place in American letters. It will take several years to unravel his impact not only in literature but in politics, philosophy, religion, and other disciplines. We imagine this volume not as the definitive account of Roth's political thought but rather as a starting point for our exploration of it. We look forward to future books, articles, and essays on this topic.

Notes

1. Claudia Franziska Brühwiler, *Political Initiation in the Novels of Philip Roth* (New York: Bloomsbury Academic, 2014).

2. Simon Stow, "Written and Unwritten America: Roth on Reading, Politics, and Theory," *Philosophy and Literature* 30 (2004): 410–23; Anthony Hutchison, *Writing the Republic* (New York: Columbia University Press, 2007); Maureen Whitebrook, *Identity, Narrative and Politics* (London: Routledge, 2001), 43–63. Catherine Morley also dedicates one chapter of her book to Roth's American Trilogy: *The Quest for Epic in Contemporary American Literature: Paul Auster, Don DeLillo, Philip Roth* (London: Routledge, 2009).

3. Michael Kimmage, *In History's Grip: Philip Roth's Newark Trilogy* (Palo Alto: Stanford University Press, 2012).

4. David Gooblar, *The Major Phases of Philip Roth* (New York: Bloomsbury, 2011); Debra Shostak, *Philip Roth: American Pastoral, The Human Stain, The Plot Against America* (New York: Bloomsbury, 2011); Aimee Pozorski, *Roth and Trauma: The Problem of History in the Later Works (1995–2010)* (New York: Bloomsbury, 2011).

5. Aimee Pozorski, *Roth and Celebrity* (Lanham, MD: Lexington Books, 2012); David Brauner, *Philip Roth* (Manchester: Manchester University Press, 2007); Pia Masiero, *Philip Roth and the Zuckerman Books* (Amherst, NY: Cam-

bria Press); Jane Statlander, *Philip Roth's Postmodern American Romance* (New York: Peter Lang, 2010); Claudia Roth Pierpont, *Roth Unbound: A Writer and His Books* (New York: Farrar, Straus and Giroux, 2013).

6. Derek Parker Royal, ed., *Philip Roth: New Perspectives on an American Author* (Westport, CT: Praeger, 2005); Timothy Parish, ed., *The Cambridge Companion to Philip Roth* (Cambridge: Cambridge University Press, 2007); Velichka D. Ivanova, ed., *Philip Roth and World Literature: Transatlantic Perspectives and Uneasy Passages* (Amherst, NY: Cambria Press, 2014). For more about Roth's scholarship, refer to *The Philip Roth Society's* website at www.philiprothsociety.org/#!bibliography/c1sah.

7. Pierpont, *Roth Unbound*, 13–14.

8. Philip Roth, *Reading Myself and Others* (New York: Vintage International, 2001), 104.

9. Ibid., 23–27

10. Ibid., 28–30, 35–36, 75. Until 1991, when he retired from academia, Roth continued to teach creative writing and comparative literature at such places like the University of Iowa, Princeton University, and the University of Pennsylvania.

11. Ibid., 7–14.

12. Pierpont, *Roth Unbound*, 34–36.

13. Ibid., 36–45.

14. Ibid., 53–68.

15. For more about *Our Gang*, see ibid., 69–75.

16. For more about *The Breast, Dying Animal,* and *Professor of Desire,* see ibid., 104–7.

17. For more about *The Great American Novel,* see ibid., 76–77; about *Reading Myself and Others,* see ibid., 70, 282.

18. For more about *My Life as a Man,* see ibid., 81–85.

19. Ibid., 111–12.

20. Ibid., 86–88, 91, 95, 98.

21. Ibid., 92–93, 96–97.

22. For more about *The Ghost Writer,* see ibid., 108–21.

23. Ibid., 99–100, 141–42.

24. For more about Claire Bloom's relationship to Roth, see ibid., 99–101, 121–22, 143, 152, 99–101, 121–22, 143, 152, 167–70, 226–29.

25. For more about *Zuckerman Unbound,* see ibid., 124–27; about *The Anatomy Lesson,* 128–37; about *The Prague Orgy,* 137–40; about *The Counterlife,* 143–57.

26. For more about *The Facts,* see ibid., 160–62, 166, 176, 203, 323.

27. Ibid., 168–70.

28. For more about *Patrimony,* see ibid., 171–73; about Novotny's Pain," 29, 119.

29. For more about *Sabbath's Theater,* see ibid., 189–25; about *I Married a Communist,* 230–38, and its relationship to Claire Bloom, 226–29; about *Operation Shylock,* 137–88. *Operation Shylock* incorporates the temporary side-effects Roth experience of the sedative halcion, 186–88.

30. For more about *The Dying Animal,* see ibid., 23–27, 260–69; about *Human Stain,* 245–58; about *The Plot Against America,* 271–79; about *Exit Ghost,* 289–95; about *Shop Talk,* 111, 157, 273.

31. Ibid., 319. For more about *Everyman,* see ibid., 248–89; about *Indignation,* 296–302; about *The Humbling,* 309–11; and about *Nemesis,* 311–19.

32. Claudia Franziska Brühwiler, "A Reluctant Public Intellectual: Philip Roth in the German-Speaking Media," *Philip Roth Studies* 10 (2014): 77–90.

33. Roth, *Readings,* 110.

1

"An ear in search of a word"

Writing and the Politics of Listening in Roth's I Married a Communist

Aimee Pozorski

> I don't want to be on the side of the good.
> I want to be on the side of the good sentence.
> —Philip Roth, 2013

When asked how he felt that his contemporary Joseph O'Neill reads him with "ethical trust, a trust that remains unbroken," Philip Roth quipped, "I don't want to be on the side of the good."[1] Such a sharp rejoinder reminds us that, ultimately, Roth seeks to appear to care far more about style than about ethics, goodness, or even politics—that what drives his craft is just that, *craft,* rather than simply the sentiment of the day or the national debates that seem either to unify or divide us. And yet, as I shall later show, he does engage national debates too, but through a writing style that perpetually emphasizes his commitment to "the good sentence" over and against goodness in the form of ethics, morality, and politics.

This commitment to the life of the writer—a craftsman securely positioned on the side of the "good sentence"—has only been reinforced by the perception that, ever since buying his farmhouse in western Connecticut, he has retreated from public life completely. However, I would argue that, for as much as he seems to reject a relationship with the outside world, he and—crucially—his fiction dwell very much within it. My first impulse is consistently to reject the thought that Roth is a "political" writer in any form; but a close reading of *I Married a Communist* (1998) as well as nonfiction published after his retirement in 2012 reminds us that there are many ways to be political, or—more precisely—to be a political writer. The word "politics" for many denotes a theory of government. Surely, political scientists have a more complex theory of politics, whereas I see myself intervening in a more conventional understanding.

Yet I would like to recast an understanding not only of Roth here but also of politics. *I Married a Communist* can be read beyond the denotative definition of politics and can be read beyond its representation of the story of Ira Rinn, the public (and political!) figure central to the novel. The novel, in other words, does not only reject Communism or anti-Communism as theories of government, but also, more subtly, it offers a politics of listening in its place, a political model that comes from trauma theory's insistence on listening to witnesses of atrocity and taking actions to make their suffering transformative.

In the essay that follows, I engage the crucial conversation begun by several literary scholars who read *I Married a Communist* in terms of its engagement with the anti-Communist agenda in the United States that clearly affected Roth as both a writer and a citizen. I use the method of close reading informed by a theory of trauma first to engage Roth's novel but then also to situate that reading in the larger view of his public life. In considering Roth's public life, I look particularly at the elegy he published in the *New York Times* celebrating the life of a former mentor and teacher, and, later, in terms of a public speech he delivered at the 2013 PEN Literary Gala in response to receiving the PEN Literary Service Award, remarks published in this volume.

In my reading of *I Married a Communist,* I contend that a closer look at the narrative frame of the novel reminds us that its present is set during six long nights of conversation between Nathan Zuckerman and Ira's brother, Murray, and that these conversations open an alternative understanding of Roth and his politics, an understanding of politics closer to "Actions concerned with the acquisition or exercise of power, status, or authority."[2] Although this use of "politics" is "frequently derogatory,"[3] Roth represents the writer figure embodied by Zuckerman as able to listen and to use his status as a writer for the good, to be on the side of the good, as well as on the side of the good sentence. Roth, in other words, is very much a political writer, if we understand his investment in how leaders acquire power and how that power is used.

It may seem paradoxical that a leader who listens seems not to be a leader at all. Listening cannot be leading because it is associated with inaction, with passivity, with compliance. But as these conversations between Murray and Nathan reveal, listening becomes a means to an end, with that end being a written document, a public record, a novel, or a speech or even an obituary used to change minds, to change lives, to change history.

The unique position of the writer allows him ideally to have it both ways: to be engaged politically, especially in the sense of the latter definition offered above, and to write as an intellectual writes, to bring to life specific stories, to communicate difference and complexities. As Nathan remarks late in *I Married a Communist,* he is, indeed, has always been, "an ear in search of a word"—a phrase that evokes a disembodied ear in search of the magic word to make it whole.[4] And yet there is something serious here, too: In seeing himself as a vessel to take in language, to listen, in the very act of writing—the complete manuscript of *I Married a Communist* is the perfect literary example here—he conveys the ways in which one can be both on the side of the good (politically speaking) and on the side of the good sentence.

In the three texts I take up here, the novel, the obituary written on the occasion of the death of Bob Lowenstein (the inspiration for the character of Murray Ringold), and the 2013 PEN Gala speech collected here for the first time, we see instances of both sides of an engaged writer—the literary, on the one hand; the political, on the other—and both sides come from the life and mind of the writer, the listening ear who depicts the world's truths and complexities. As Nathan asks, rhetorically, in *I Married a Communist:* "was I from the beginning, by inclination as much as my choice, merely an ear in search of a word?" (222).

I would argue, then, that Roth's apparent retreat to the woods during his most prolific writing years provides evidence that one can paradoxically retreat and also be more engaged with the world than ever. However, the headlines seem only to emphasize the vision of Roth as an introvert who rarely engages—in any sense—the public world. Characteristic of this public conception of Roth is a piece by Celestine Bohlen, written in Paris in

2011, which declares: "Philip Roth is known to be a difficult interview. He says himself he doesn't like doing them, and obliges only at the request of his publishers."[5] Of course, he does retreat, but he does so as a writer rather than a participant. Or, rather, he participates through writing, as does Zuckerman, who is not disengaged at all. But can one be literary and also political? We must not, especially with Roth, try to choose one over the other, even if Roth directs us to do so.

Roth's Politics in Context

Following almost immediately on the heels of his announced retirement, Philip Roth entered the public arena with a scathing account of his experience with "the Soviet-backed totalitarian Czech regime."[6] For an author so careful about his craft, this account, delivered publicly at the 2013 PEN Gala in Manhattan, seemed both surprising but also in keeping with what we know about Roth's personal beliefs. This essay offers a close reading of Roth's remarks in the context of his 2013 *New York Times* obituary for his homeroom teacher, Bob Lowenstein, an obituary that heralds Lowenstein's dignity in the face of the anti-Communist movement in the United States. In the obituary, Roth tells us that this beloved teacher is the model for a major character in *I Married a Communist:* "Murray Ringold, by the way, undergoes an education of his own. So too did Bob, of course, when, impaled suddenly on his moment in time, caught in the trap set to ruin so many promising careers of that American era—a casualty like thousands of others of the first shameful decade in his country's postwar history."[7] With this statement in mind, and against the backdrop of Roth's recent nonfiction, we might read *I Married a Communist* as inherently political—as political as it is literary. The novel, structured as it is around numerous lectures, speeches, and rants, seems to embody the relationship between politics and aesthetics, leading me ultimately to return to the age-old questions: Can aesthetics be political? Is not literary fiction also political in its way?

Despite Roth's protests to the contrary, it is difficult not to note the anti-Communist politics in *I Married a Communist,* set as it is against the backdrop of the McCarthy era and the Red Scare. As such, many critics have traced its political connections, particularly the intersections among politics, history, and the myth of America as represented through the narrative of Ira and his personal and public decline as a radio star.[8] In terms of

their understanding of the significance of the novel for its political importance—reading politics in the novel in terms of a representation of a theory
or practice of government—such critics as Ira Nadel, Mark Shechner, and
Bonnie Lyons are exemplary in this regard.

According to Nadel: "Eve Frame in *I Married a Communist* emphasizes the politics of the cinema, a theme that becomes increasingly more
persistent in Roth's novels as he develops the idea of film as a form of personal or political propaganda."[9] Likewise, in his focus on Ira, Shechner suggests: "Ira is Roth's stick to beat the old Stalinist left. . . . Though Roth
encountered Stalinism in Prague, American Stalinism is only a reflex of a
history that Roth knows as a reader of the liberal anti-Communist journals
of his time."[10] Lyons interprets the significance of the Ira figure in terms of
Roth's interest in exposing "the betrayals and hypocrisies of the McCarthy
era in America."[11] All three of these readings, then, consider Roth's focus on
politics in terms of the central couple in the novel, actors Eve Frame and Ira
Rinn, who fall victim in one form or another to the values of the McCarthy
era, suffering both personal and professional consequences.

Even the reviewers from more popular venues such as the *New York
Times* have gotten in on the fun, trapped, I would argue, by the red her-
ring of the Ira tale, and therefore criticize Roth for being too political, for
losing focus in a polyphonic whip of voices in American history. According to Michiko Kakutani, "The bulk of *I Married a Communist* . . . is less
concerned with Nathan than with his childhood mentor, Ira Ringold. Like
Swede Levov in *American Pastoral,* Ira is meant to be a representative
man, another American innocent sucked up, spun around and spit out by
the great whirlwind of American history."[12] Robert Kelly also values the
novel's tracking of the rise and fall of Ira Rinn, agreeing that readers are
able to "watch the way in which Ira's personal life distorts and trivializes the
Marxist agenda in which he more and more stridently believes, and which
he even clamorously advocates in a dangerous time, while that compassion-
ate concern for others that is radical to the Marxist worldview gives way in
him to murderous revenges. Ira, in his own small way, seems to come to
represent the Stalins of our century."[13]

For the purposes of this essay, however, I am more interested in the ways
the novel *frames* Ira's story, particularly in the exchanges between Murray,
Ira's brother, who tells the story, and Zuckerman, the dutiful student who
listens to Murray for six consecutive nights on his back porch beneath the

stars. In focusing on these conversations—conversations between a longtime English teacher and the longtime writer, Nathan, we are able to see
another side of Roth's politics, a politics of listening that emerges despite,
or perhaps because of, the writer's retreat from the world. In so doing, I am
more in conversation with such scholars as Ross Posnock and Pia Masiero—
and to some extent, David Brauner and David Gooblar—who have read the
tension between Zuckerman's retreat as a writer, on the one hand, and the
novel's warning against political retreat, on the other.

Yet I propose that Roth's depiction of Zuckerman reveals how a responsible writer may be at once political and reclusive, may be poetical and provocative at the same time. What emerges in conversation between the two
literary-minded men is a recognition that the way to do that, paradoxically,
is through listening—to be engaged and to show engagement through listening—to be the ear, as Zuckerman says, to capture what the voice seeks
to convey. As such, Roth's novel asks: What would it mean to think about
politics not as about rhetoric, about speaking a message, but about listening
to a message—about channeling that message not through language at the
podium but through language at the end of a pen?

It is with this logic in mind that I contend that the "retreat versus
engagement" political dichotomy is false—that when Murray warns Nathan
of the dangers of retreat, he is also worrying about Nathan's disengagement
from the world.[14] But the very fact of the book, the very book Nathan produced as a result of his listening ear, shows that the writerly retreat might
sometimes be the most significant form of engagement after all. Posnock
seems to align political and social retreat with the Communist political
agenda when he writes:

> The aging Nathan Zuckerman, living alone in the Berkshires, seems to
> have embraced this venerable solitude by the end of *I Married a Com-
> munist* (the trilogy's second volume) despite the warning to "beware"
> that his old teacher Murray Ringold proffers near the end of the novel.
> . . . One of the book's pointed ironies is that this "utopia of the shack in
> the woods . . . an impregnable solitude"—the emblem of Thoreauvian
> integrity and of the elusive "real thing" that lures the protagonists of
> the trilogy's first two volumes—is not simply an American preoccu-
> pation but is shared by the alleged collectivist antidote to such bleak
> autonomy—Communism.[15]

Murray warns Nathan that holing up in the woods in a shack, like Thoreau, can be dangerous. For Murray, retreat is not only selfish but also politically dangerous: the individual in the woods is no more responsible than a group misguided by a misunderstanding of political theory.

In reading Roth's narrative framing through the lens of narratology, Pia Masiero seems most closely aligned with my thinking here, in seeing the significance in the exchange between Nathan and Murray—the exchange of their dialogue, but, most notably, in Nathan's willingness to listen. According to Masiero: "Nathan's seclusion is not, strictly speaking, the story here, but it is nevertheless crucial to his being a writer. Isolation and silence are more and more overtly the ingredients amplifying Nathan's capacity to resonate with the presence of other voices and to evoke the past. The present of writing is nicely circumscribed in the four years spent out in the woods."[16]

Seclusion helps with the writing, the writing of this book about politics. But the writing is always already the focus—for Zuckerman, since 1979's *The Ghost Writer*. The isolation brings forth the voices—listening to the voices becomes Zuckerman's own form of politics, a form, frankly, more reparative and productive than totalitarian groupthink. In his reading of *I Married a Communist*, Derek Parker Royal has also emphasized the profundity of the voices and the centrality of listening to his art. For Royal, Nathan's "understanding is inspired through listening. . . . . [T]he godlike ability of the artist to be in full control of the medium, and creating something from nothing, becomes displaced by the 'godliness' of aural omnipresence."[17]

It is in their connection between listening and writing, then, that I position my argument alongside Masiero and Royal and try to move further in the provocative claim that Zuckerman's listening, contrary to Ira's shouting, is itself a form of politics—a writerly politics of listening that, while appearing at first glance the craft of the narcissistic recluse, actually becomes the most effective form of engagement in national dialogue.

The Politics of Listening: *I Married a Communist*

The values and phrasing behind the term "politics of listening" has its origin in trauma theory but has found most use in feminist discourses and literatures of underrepresented minority groups. Such authors as Laura Tunbridge, Jennifer Lynn Stoever, and Beverly Weber all have used the phrase "politics of listening" in their work, and all approach their topics from an ethical standpoint in the face of historical or cultural crisis.[18] Feminist publications such as *Signs* and *differences* are the best-known journals with essay titles taking on the topic.

For example, Marianne Hirsch and Valerie Smith in their guest-edited issue of *Signs* (Autumn 2002) with a special focus on "Feminism and Cultural Memory" include a section entitled "Dis/Identifications" composed of essays that "define the relationships between primary and secondary witnessing, envisioning a feminist politics of listening and warning against the pitfalls of appropriation."[19] Looking further back, to the work of Wendy Hui Kyong Chun on the 1989 Montreal Massacre, we see the phrase "politics of listening" in a connection between politics and the question of witness, especially in the wake of a traumatic event.

In this essay originally published in *differences: A Journal of Feminist Cultural Studies,* Chun cites Cathy Caruth's *Unclaimed Experience,* where Caruth reads Tasso's story of Tancred and Lucinda as "the story of the way in which trauma may lead, therefore, to the encounter with another, through the very possibility and surprise of listening to another's wound."[20] Drawing also on the work of Shoshana Felman and Dori Laub, Chun concludes her essay thus: the "contract of listening must be accompanied by a politics that understands acts of violence not as 'representative of' or 'suitable for' each other, but by a politics that sees these acts as forceful because they recall other events, because they open up the self to others. Such a contract of listening would allow for history" (140).[21] In this formulation of an ethical politics, Chun understands listening as a way of bringing witnesses together with their interlocutors, as well as bringing our various, repeating, and often-traumatic histories together so we may build a new history out of the loss of the past.

On the one hand, I cannot help but to wonder whether it is ironic to read Roth through the lens of feminist political theory, given the scorn with which he treats his literary feminist scholars and professors in the novels—Marcia Umanoff and Delphine Roux from *American Pastoral* and the *Human Stain* respectively. Yet, when considering *I Married a Communist* (which, incidentally, is the only novel of this American trilogy that does not feature a high-minded and liberal woman professor), it is not a stretch to understand the past that Murray discusses as traumatic in its own right. It is difficult for him to speak not only of Ira's history but of his own as well: the loss of his beloved wife, Doris, the Newark Riots of the 1960s within which he lived and worked, his own fate at the hands of the anti-Communist forces in the United States.

Setting aside the Ira and Eve Frame narrative for a moment, then, I would like to cast attention on the poignant conversations between Nathan and Murray, when the story of Ira has been told and all that remains is the bond between two old friends, student and mentor, Nathan and Murray. In what follows, I will closely read three important sections from the novel—sections when only Murray Ringold speaks to Nathan: the introduction of Murray; two hundred pages in when reflecting on the effects of listening to Murray; and the conclusion, saying good-bye to Murray—all sections that crucially establish a narrative framework, even when one would otherwise want to read the novel as about Ira and Eve, actors, accomplices, ultimate mutual enemies. In the readings that follow, the novel emerges as equally about the relationship between Murray and Zuckerman, and a new kind of politics established between them: a politics that involves not simply taking a stand but rather leaving open the question, acknowledging unknowability, listening and listening, features, as we have seen, of a good writer and a good student, features of both Nathan and Roth, both writers, both students of literature and of life.

When looking at the first sentence of the novel, it becomes clear why readers might want to focus on the drama between Ira and Eve, and would perhaps lose sight of the role Murray plays throughout. Generally, readers consider the novel Ira's and Eve's story—or, when read biographically, Roth's and Bloom's—but the real focus is on the exchange between Murray and Nathan, with the first line reminding us of that fact: "Ira Ringold's older brother, Murray, was my first high school English teacher, and it was through him that I hooked up with Ira" (*Communist*, 1).

Ira is the first mention, but Murray is central to the narrative and the thematic aspects of the novel. The passivity here is striking and surprising—"it was through him" and "hooked up with"—until one realizes that the sentence has been constructed to begin and end with Ira, with Murray literally in the center of the sentence, central, yes, but also buried within the center, hidden.

The novel continues:

Along with the brawn and conspicuous braininess, Mr. Ringold brought with him into the classroom a charge of visceral spontaneity that was

a revelation to tamed, respectabilized kids who were yet to comprehend that obeying a teacher's rules of decorum had nothing to do with
mental development. . . . Maybe Mr. Ringold knew very well that what
boys like me needed to learn was not only how to express themselves
with precision and acquire a more discerning response to words, but
how to be rambunctious without being stupid, how not to be too well
concealed or too well behaved, how to begin to release the masculine
intensities from the institutional rectitude that intimidated the bright
kids the most. (*Communist,* 1–2)

Murray is immediately introduced via his mental and physical toughness;
key words are "charge" and "spontaneity"—he carries an electrical current
into the classroom. His goal, Nathan learns, is not to teach students how
to obey but to teach students, in many ways, how not to obey and how to
question authority. The students who are his charges here are described as
"respectabilized"—not a standard adjective as I know it, yet it nonetheless
communicates the fact that although they have been raised to be respectable kids, respectful kids, this socialization process nonetheless has been
done unto them. It is not a state they have chosen.

The key skills Murray must teach on the way to questioning authority,
it seems, are communication and comprehension. As with later moments
in the novel, Nathan realizes that his education requires him to break free
from institutional thought, even school. Paradoxically, what he learns in
school from Mr. Ringold is how to reject what is learned in school. The
repetition of the prefix "in," as with the words "intensities," "institutional,"
and "intimidated," focuses on the inside, calling to mind the necessity at the
end of the day, of serving as socially engaged insiders—a necessity for both
Murray and Nathan.

By way of introducing this man central to his story, Nathan recalls:

Not that the impression his bold classroom style left on my sense of
freedom was apparent at the time; no kid thought that way about
school or teachers or himself. An incipient craving for social independence, however, had to have been nourished somewhere by Murray's
example, and I told him this when, in July 1997, for the first time since
I graduated from high school in 1950, I ran into Murray, now ninety
years old but in every discernible way still the teacher whose task is

realistically, without self-parody or inflating dramatics, to personify for his students the maverick dictum "I don't give a good goddamn," to teach them that you don't have to be Al Capone to transgress—you just have to think. "In human society," Mr. Ringold taught us, "thinking's the greatest transgression of all." (*Communist*, 2)

Once again, Ringold is aligned with "social independence," with a value for reading beyond the rhetoric of the time or even the governing social values. What is interesting is that Nathan recognizes he was not ready for such a message, a hidden message as it were, as a kid, looking as he was for protection inside school. For Murray, thinking is transgressive—a way to be transgressive without being a hardened criminal or even, as one would hope, at odds with the law. The sheer length of the sentence about social independence alone reveals that, as a writer, Nathan/Roth has been happy to break with writing convention, covering six or seven typed lines in one inflated thought.

A few paragraphs later, we learn what happened not only to Murray and his career but to Ira, the center of the novel. Nathan recalls learning that

In '55, almost four years after Ira was blacklisted from radio for being a Communist, Murray had been dismissed from his teaching job by the Board of Education for refusing to cooperate with the House Un-American Activities Committee when it had come through Newark for four days of hearings. He was reinstated, but only after a six-year legal struggle that ended with a 5–4 decision by the state supreme court, reinstated with back pay, minus the amount of money he had earned supporting his family those six years as a vacuum salesman. (*Communist*, 4)

Again, the focus is on how, why, and when Ira was blacklisted, but Murray, too, ran into trouble, albeit a different kind of trouble, with slightly different authorities. He was dismissed from the Board of Education—his very employer, one tasked with teaching communication and critical thinking to the students—for a refusal to engage with a process with which he disagreed. Here, as before, public education becomes an institution to rail against, even if one must attend to learn how to do that from an English teacher.

So it is with this introduction in mind that we turn to a place in the novel when Nathan again considers from where he has come, where he considers his education at the feet of Murray, an education that takes place both in the present of the novel and the past:

> Occasionally now, looking back, I think of my life as one long speech that I've been listening to. The rhetoric is sometimes original, sometimes pleasurable, sometimes pasteboard crap (the speech of the incognito), sometimes maniacal, sometimes matter-of-fact, and sometimes like the sharp prick of a needle, and I have been hearing it for as long as I can remember: how to think, how not to think, how to behave, how not to behave, whom to loathe and whom to admire; what to embrace and when to escape; what is rapturous, what is murderous, what is laudable, what is shallow, what is sinister, what is shit, and how to remain pure in the soul. Talking to me doesn't seem to present an obstacle to anyone. This is perhaps a consequence of having gone around for years looking as if I needed talking to. But whatever reason, the book of my life is a book of voices. When I ask myself how I arrived at where I am, the answer surprises me: "Listening." (*Communist,* 222)

The fact that this long paragraph ends with a single word following a colon—"listening"—strikes a chord and becomes, for me, the one-word mantra of the text. The sheer length of it also carries with it a certain irony, as Nathan seems quite willing to talk about how much he listens.

The anaphora again about an education of how to be in the world—"how to think, how not to think, how to behave, how not to behave"—recalls what Nathan said he learned from Murray in the beginning of the book. He has been listening, learning, hearing, a repository, for his whole life. The self-deprecating quip about appearing as if he looked like he "needed talking to" registers as a recognition that he may have been a troublemaker, or easily swayed by troublemakers, but ultimately suggests only that people wanted to speak to him, to have his focused attention while they talked. When he says, "the book of my life is a book of voices," we think not only about the book in our hands, the very book he has written as a result of his conversations with Murray, but also about his entire life spent listening to the voices, values, stories of others who deliver up various levels of speech and rhetoric in his very presences.

And yet, this thorough observation does not mark the end of Nathan's reflection. He continues to question the effect of listening and politics on his entire life, as though he cannot let go of this topic:

> Can that have been the unseen drama? Was all the rest a masquerade disguising the real no good that I was obstinately up to? Listening to them. Listening to them talk. The utterly wild phenomenon that is. Everyone perceiving experience as something not to have but to have so as to talk about it. Why is that? Why do they want me to hear them and their arias? Where was it decided that this was my use? Or was I from the beginning, by inclination as much as my choice, merely an ear in search of a word? (*Communist*, 222)

Here, Nathan aligns teenage rebellion with listening; "the real no good that I was obstinately up to" may refer back to the intergenerational conflict between Nathan and his father, to his seeking out as mentors Communists, writers, propagandists, actors. His knowledge of acting life, his having been invited into Ira's inside circle, even attending a rally at which Paul Robson speaks, clarifies his word choice, "drama." The novel is a drama; Nathan's life is a drama; he has been given access to the acting life of Ira and Eve. Suddenly, he thinks of his own story as a drama and masquerade.

But that leads him to a second thought: listening seems not to have been such a bad thing, has served him well, in fact. He wonders why him, why he must receive all the stories, until he observes that he indeed has chosen this fate—that he is an ear waiting to hear, searching out the word, the message, for his fiction and his life.

At this point, the transition to the ideas of one of his literary mentors seems striking, as we are suddenly thrown into a memory of what the proletariat writer and leader Leo Glucksman told him:

> Politics is the great generalizer . . . and literature the great particularizer, and not only are they in an inverse relationship to each other—they are in an *antagonistic* relationship. To politics, literature is decadent, soft, irrelevant, boring, wrongheaded, dull, something that makes no sense and that really oughtn't be. Why? Because the particularizing impulse *is* literature. How can you be an artist and renounce the nuance? But how can you be a politician and *allow* the nuance?

> As an artist the nuance is your *task*. Your task is *not* to simplify. Even
> should you choose to write in the simplest way, a la Hemingway, the
> task remains to impart the nuance, to elucidate the complication, to
> imply the contradiction. Not to erase the contradiction, not to deny
> the contradiction, but to see where, within the contradiction, lies the
> tormented human being. To allow for the chaos, to let it in. You *must*
> let it in. Otherwise you produce propaganda, if not for a political party,
> a political movement, then stupid propaganda for life itself—for life as
> it might itself prefer to be publicized. (*Communist*, 223)

I quote this passage at length because it at once seems the least relevant
digression at this moment and the most relevant message about how to read
the entire novel. At the very least, the passage, through the voice of Leo,
highlights the received dichotomy between literature and politics, arguing
the position that politics is reductive and that literature embodies chaos,
contradiction. Literature, as Leo has it, or as Nathan remembers Leo saying, focuses on nuance, the particulars. For literary scholars and writers
alike, this is what makes literature special: It does not have to be political,
not in the sense that it takes a side or becomes involved in the rhetoric and
decision making of a nation. In this way, it is a nice self-referential moment,
as the very existence of *I Married a Communist* seems to reject clarity and
generalizations in favor of the messiness and chaos of life. Again, this is
what the novel does self-reflexively and often, as the case with Kakutani,
what it is punished for in reviews.

Ultimately, ironically, Leo's message is crystal clear, solidified, as at the
end of a Shakespearean speech, in very simple language in case you missed
it the first time: "You do not have to write to legitimize Communism, and
you do not have to write to legitimize capitalism. You are out of both. If you
are a writer, you are as unallied to the one as you are to the other" (*Communist*, 224). And here is the final message: writers are independent from
politics. But as we have seen and will see in conversation with Murray, there
is another way to be an ally, to write a literary novel, to depict the suffering
of another, to reject simplicity for the chaos and complexity of human life,
the life of Ira, for example, and of Murray, of the Swede before them, of
Coleman Silk after him. A writer is not, therefore, political. But is listening—listening to the stories of these individuals and then retreating to the
woods in order to tell them?

The novel ends as it begins: with Nathan reflecting on his relationship with Murray, and particularly on the six nights they had together talking and listening under the stars. When it is time to leave, Nathan presents himself as a guide to Murray in the dark, with the dark being as literal as figurative, signaling that after all of those nights, hours, and pages depicting thoughtful discussion, there is no more clarity than when they began. Nathan recalls:

> I helped Murray down the deck's three steps and guided him in the dark along the path to where my car was parked. We were silent as we swung along the curves of the mountain road and past Lake Madamaska and into Athena. When I looked over I saw that his head was back and his eyes were shut. First I thought he was asleep, and then I wondered if he was dead, if, after his having remembered the whole of Ira's story—the will to go on had lost its grip even on this most enduring of men. (*Communist*, 313)

This is the moment when one realizes the gravity of the language shared between them, the horror of the story Murray had to tell and the difficulty of taking it in, of being that listening ear. While this may be a projection, we know from the beginning that Murray is quite old, that all of the stress of recalling could possibly kill him, or at least this is Nathan's fear as he interprets a sleeping man as a dead man in his car.

As is typical of Nathan, the present reality hurls him into the past, and yet again he reminds us of when he first met Murray, the poignant scenes in the classroom, where Nathan the dutiful student learns in the presence of a wiser man:

> And then I was recalling him again reading to our high school English class, sitting on the corner of his desk, but without the minatory blackboard eraser, reading scenes to us from *Macbeth*, doing all the voices, not afraid to be dramatic and perform, and myself being impressed by how manly literature seemed in his enactment of it. I remembered hearing Mr. Ringold read the scene at the end of act 4 of *Macbeth* when Macduff learned from Ross that Macbeth has slain Macduff's family, my first encounter with a spiritual state that is aesthetic and overrides everything else. (*Communist*, 313–14)

Here, too, literature trumps politics: Nathan is listening to the voices—
what is so lovely (but also political, in looking back to T. S. Eliot and Charles
Dickens) is the mention that Murray does them all—and discovering,
indeed, "encountering" the "spiritual state that is aesthetic." For Nathan,
the aesthetics that literature offers, particularly the great literature of
Shakespeare, is more important than social commentary, politics, any physical reality beneath the spiritual. To say that aesthetics "overrides everything
else" is to say that the beautiful, poetic, nuanced, chaotic, affective dimensions of language are what drive him here. It is something we have known
about Zuckerman from the moment we met him in 1979, and it stays with
him consistently until his departure in *Exit Ghost.*

As it happens, as we have already guessed, Murray is not dead but simply resting his eyes, giving time for Nathan to reflect, and he opens his eyes
and his mouth in order to underscore Nathan's politics of listening. Nathan
recounts:

> By the time we got into Athena, Murray's eyes were open and he was
> saying, "Here I am with an eminent ex-student and I never let the guy
> speak. Never asked him about himself."
>
> "Next time."
>
> "Why do you live up there, alone like that? Why don't you have the
> heart for the world?'"
>
> "I prefer it this way," I said.
>
> "No, I watched you listening. I don't think you do. I don't think for a
> moment the exuberance is gone. You were like that as a kid. That's why
> I got such a kick out of you—you paid attention. You still do. But what
> is up here to pay attention to? You should get out from under whatever's
> the problem. To give in to the temptation to yield isn't smart. At a cer-
> tain age, that can polish you off like any other disease. Do you really
> want to whittle it all away before your time has come? Beware the uto-
> pia of isolation. Beware the utopia of the shack in the woods, the oasis
> defense against rage and grief. An impregnable solitude. That's how life
> ended for Ira, and long before the day he dropped dead." (*Communist,*
> 315)

What is somewhat curious is that Murray knows Nathan to be a listener—
"No, I watched you listening," he says—and yet believes this rather intro-

verted character should be in the world to listen more. Nathan says, "I prefer it this way," as if to indicate it is the best way to live in order to record the conversations, the insights gained from listening. The ability to "pay attention"—both as a kid and as a grown writer—for Murray signals that Nathan ought to be out in the world and reject his shack in the woods. In his most foreboding tone, Murray's lines, "Beware the utopia of isolation. Beware the utopia of the shack in the woods," sound remarkably close to "Beware the Ides of March," the latter a warning that it pays to heed. But I continue to posit here that one can be engaged with rage and grief within one's solitude, which is not "impregnable" at all really when one carries with him the voices of so many others.

When Nathan returns home from this good-bye with Murray, he returns to the deck, to the glow of the candle:

On the deck, the citronella candle was still burning in its aluminum bucket when I got back, that little pot of fire the only light by which my house was discernable, except for a dim radiance off the orange moon silhouetting the low roof. As I left the car and started toward the house, the elongated wavering of the flame reminded me of the radio dial—no bigger than a watch face and, beneath the tiny black numerals, the color of a ripening banana skin—that was all that could be seen in our dark bedroom when my kid brother and I, contrary to parental directive, stayed up past ten to listen to a favorite program. The two of us in our twin beds and, magisterial on the night table between us, the Philco, Jr., the cathedral shaped table radio we'd inherited when my father bought the Emerson console for the living room. The radio turned as low as it would go, though still with the volume enough to act on our ears the most powerful magnet. (*Communist*, 320)

The citronella candle seems significant here, burning as it does in an aluminum bucket—a realistic detail but also indicating a fending off of annoyances, mosquitoes that might otherwise disrupt the peaceful moment under the stars, and also pointing to more figurative annoyances that buzz around the head of a writer on even a good day. The flame of the candle reminds Nathan of the light of the radio dial and the radio, another instrument that trains him in listening to the voices of history. They listen, despite what the authorities say. The focus on listening and ears here—the volume turned up to "act on our ears the most powerful magnet"—shows that what Murray says is true, Nathan was always a listener, was indeed compelled by the voices of others. The radio also speaks to the history of Ira and his early fame, as Nathan undoubtedly has spent many hours listening to Ira speak as well.

To blow out the candle, then, is to blow out the memory of the radio, again hurling Nathan to the present tense, to what his six nights with Murray also mean to him:

> I blew out the candle's scented flame and stretched myself across the chaise on the deck and realized that listening in the black of a summer's night to a barely visible Murray had been something like listening to the bedroom radio when I was a kid ambitious to change the world by having all my untested convictions, masquerading as stories, broadcast nationwide. Murray, the radio: voices from the void controlling everything within, the convolutions of a story floating on air and into the ear so that the drama is perceived well behind the eyes, the cup that is the cranium a cup transformed into a limitless globe of a stage, containing fellow creatures whole. How deep our hearing goes! Think of all it means to understand from something that you simply hear. The godlikeness of having an ear! Is it not the least *semi*divine phenomenon to be hurled into the innermost wrongness of a human existence by virtue of nothing more than sitting in the dark, listening to what is said? (*Communist*, 320–21)

Blowing out the candle leaves Nathan in the dark, with nothing to see or smell, but only to hear—the sound of Murray talking, barely visible, as he recounted the history of Newark in the 1950s and 1960s and beyond. Listening to Murray in the present, Nathan says, is listening to the radio in the past—crucially, during both times, "ambitious to change the world." A politics of listening allows for one to change the world. The stories, the voices float "into the ear," transforming the brain to a stage, yet another reference to drama and to show business that led to Ira's career. And here is where Nathan becomes his most philosophical, his most political, I might say, in defense of an ethics of listening. "How deep our hearing goes," he revels—deep into the ear but also into writing, into politics, transformed into language to tell a particular and personal history. "Think of all it means"—this listening, this having an ear. Nathan links it to divinity, or semidivinity, as the human listener becomes close to God in his ability to come into contact with the "innermost wrongness of human existence" by nothing more and nothing less than listening to what is said.

The phrase "innermost wrongness" is touching here, as even in his very celebration of hearing and of listening, Nathan realizes that what is heard is not often about the rightness of human existence, is not often reparative. What we are left with is a writer in the dark, thinking of all he has heard about humanity's wrongness, thinking too of his own wrongness, burdened to put it all down in from the protection or confinement of his shack in the woods.

A Political Elegy for Bob Lowenstein

Although many close to Roth knew of the connection between the character of Murray Ringold and Roth's past as a student at Weequahic High, it wasn't until the summer of 2013, when Bob Lowenstein, the model of Roth's Murray character, died that we came to understand how Roth was able to depict Murray so lovingly, with such humanity. In a heartfelt obituary written for Lowenstein, Roth reveals: "Bob was my homeroom teacher. This meant that I saw him first thing in the morning, every single day of the school year. I was never to take a language course with him—had Mademoiselle Glucksman for French and Señorita Baleroso for Spanish—but I didn't forget him. Who at Weequahic did? Consequently, when it came his turn to be mauled in Congress's anti-Communist crusade of the 1940s and 1950s, I followed his fate as best I could in the stories that I had my parents clip from the Newark newspapers and mail to me" ("In Memory of").

As with the history of Ira and Murray, Bob Lowenstein was destroyed not by politics but by the anti-Communist sentiment and propaganda that brought down so many free thinkers. When Roth remembers running into Lowenstein after a long absence, he remembers, first and foremost, listening, listening as he did when he was a student in high school when Lowenstein was his teacher. Roth writes: "We talked over lunch—we talked all afternoon long. He had, as usual, a lot to say, and I believe I listened to all that he said no less attentively than I listened in that 8:30 homeroom at the Hawthorne Avenue Annex when he read out the announcements for the school day" ("In Memory of"). Roth, like Nathan, prides himself on being an attentive listener as well as learner in the company of someone older, wiser.

Roth makes this connection in the obituary when he recalls: "In *I Married a Communist,* the narrator Nathan Zuckerman says, 'I think of my life as one long speech that I've been listening to.' For me, Bob's is one of the persuasive voices I can still hear speaking. The tang of the real permeated his talk. Like all great teachers, he personified the drama of transformation through talk" ("In Memory of"). Roth, like Nathan, also sees listening as a kind of access to "drama" and "performance": things come alive through the exchange of conversation, which results in its own kind of political movement. Roth's phrase "tang of the real" also conveys the sharp sense of realism Lowenstein's voice carried. His synesthesia—mixing an abstract concept like "real" with the quality of taste, "tang," emphasizes how singular and transformative was his voice. In this sense, listening requires the witness not only to transcribe but also to remake the world. It also helps us understand Nathan's own paradoxical speech, as he, too, wants his talk to be transformative.

But there are also moments in the obituary, as I am sure there are moments in the novel, when Roth turns from one sense of the political to the next in his employment of slanted language to protest a movement he still sees as despicable: "Bob was the model for a major figure in my novel *I Married a Communist,* a book I published in 1998 recalling the anti-Communist period I mentioned earlier and that savage, malicious mauling that people like Bob suffered in those years from the teeth and the claws of the scum then in power" ("In Memory of"). On the one hand, this is awfully literary language, personifying the anti-Communist witch-hunters as predatory lions with teeth and claws and power. The line "the teeth and the claws of the scum then in power" is perfectly parallel, perfectly rhythmic, perfectly slanted rhetoric with which the majority of his readers nonetheless largely agree.

In the obituary, Roth positions Lowenstein as a kind of Daniel in the lion's den, recalling how "Bob had iron in him and he resisted the outrage of the injustice with extraordinary courage and bravery, but he was a man, and he felt it as a man, and so he suffered too" ("In Memory of"). That Roth heralds Lowenstein as a survivor in the face of injustice is no surprise— even in *I Married a Communist,* he emerges, although quietly, as the true hero of the book, one who fought with courage but nonetheless lost almost everything.

Even in this obituary, Roth seems to toggle between the two positions: the life of the writer who lives by a politics of listening, on the one hand, and, on the other, the political tyranny that is always stronger. For on this note Roth writes: "I hope that in my novel I have given ample recognition to the qualities of our late, legendary and noble friend, who understood, as did the poet Charles Péguy, that 'tyranny is always better organized than freedom.' I don't know how Péguy found this out, but Bob learned it the hard way" ("In Memory of"). But even so, I do not think Roth, or Zuckerman, would choose the side of tyranny. Freedom must reign for the work of the writer, as true political change is not possible any other way.

A few months before Roth wrote this obituary, he revealed anti-Communist sentiments in the remarks delivered at the 2013 PEN Literary Gala on April 30, 2013, upon receiving the PEN Literary Service Award. Here, too, unlike most of his fiction, an absolute commitment to the necessary freedoms of the writer and intellectual, and the necessary political freedom the nation must offer its artists is on display in unequivocal terms. On some level, I wonder if Roth experienced a kind of freedom from writing fiction in order to be a political writer, political in the sense of engaging with theories of forms of government rather than working on the individual and communal level of promoting change.

Yet, on another level, I see this kind of commitment to freedom in the very style of his writing from his 1969 *Portnoy's Complaint* and beyond. A similar literary style is on view here—lyrical, poetical, and provocative—but also it carries with it, as with the obituary, a kind of urgency in the face of experienced censorship at the hands of anti-Communist movements. Crucially, it is not until these 2013 remarks are read alongside his fiction that it becomes clear just how like the anti-Communist witch-hunters were like the totalitarian governments they sought to condemn. This is where Roth is at his most political, but also his most nuanced, most literary, most on the side of the good (sentence).

Roth's Politics Recognized and Unmasked

Ultimately, what emerges in Roth's 2013 remarks on the occasion of receiving a literary service award—an award that in itself reflects the effects of his writing—is a new way of understanding listening as a necessary activity. In my reading of Roth's remarks, listening *to* another speaker crucially combats listening *in,* in the sense of spying and heavy-handed governmental oversight. In light of these remarks I wonder: What does it mean to use listening necessary for the enterprise of writing as a countermeasure to the totalitarian forces that use listening to revoke rights?

The speech begins by setting the context: "From 1972 through 1977, I traveled to Prague every spring for a week or ten days to see a group of writers, journalists, historians, and professors there who were being persecuted by the Soviet-backed totalitarian Czech regime" ("Written Remarks"). Here, Roth refers importantly to Communist Czechoslovakia (1948 to 1989) as well as to his involvement with the Writers from the Other Europe series that epitomized his engagement with the critical and literary minded, the literate, the intelligentsia of Eastern Europe. After being detained in his sixth year, he left the country and did not return until Václav Havel's democratic government was unanimously elected to power.

When he returned in 1989, he writes, he received "a thoroughgoing education in what unstinting government repression was like in Czechoslovakia" ("Written Remarks"). The education came from friends and colleagues led by Ivan and Helen Klíma, who spoke of their realities under the totalitarian regime. To me, this political statement and reference to the "unstinting government repression" sets up what is to follow in an exemplary political speech. Perhaps, for Roth, after retirement, such moments are called for, even necessary. On the one hand, there is a huge gap between his literary fiction and his nonfiction writing. On the other hand, as we can see in *I Married a Communist,* in reading that work retroactively, there exists in that novel many of the same sentiments: a worry, in the United States, about the Red Scare and what the national government did in the name of national security.

He continues by stating: "Once they had been thrown out of the Writer's Union, they were forbidden to publish or to teach to or travel or to drive a car or to earn a proper livelihood each at his or her own calling. For good measure, the children of the thinking segment of the population, were forbidden to attend academic high schools" ("Written Remarks"). Such a sentence, I might argue here, is as literary as his novels from the parallelism to the repletion, the cataloguing necessary to make a point about life in a Communist country. Further, Roth writes, incensed, his friends who compose "the cream of the nation's intelligentsia" are reduced to manual labor rather than using their writing and thinking to be heard ("Written Remarks").

In a further political turn, then, Roth writes, toward the end of the speech: "So it was and so it is in the time of a totalitarian system. . . . . The usual rites of degradation: the ongoing unmooring of one's personal identity, the suppression of one's personal authority, the elimination of one's security—a craving for solidity, for one's equanimity, in the face of an ever-present uncertainty" ("Written Remarks"). His use of anaphora here tells me this might as well be a poem as, for emphasis, "unmooring of one's" turns to "suppression of one's," turns to "elimination of one's," each phrasing more violent than the next.

Finally, at the end, this government is once again personified—just as Roth personifies the McCarthy movement in the United States in his Lowenstein obituary. In this way, he writes: "totalitarianism's ruthless trauma-inducing machine cranking out the worst of everything, and, over time everything becoming more than one can bear" ("Written Remarks"). The use of internal rhyme is effective here: machine/everything, with "everything" repeated, uses sound to reinforce the sense of totality—everything is taken over by the government, even one's personal thoughts and writings.

Such a history is nearly unimaginable now, even though such regimes have threatened the freedoms of artists and citizens throughout the twentieth and twenty-first centuries. But I am struck in looking back to Roth's 1960 writing about the responsibility of a writer, the responsibility of a writer who listens, in this uncanny reflection on the ways in which American and global history works: "the American writer in the middle of the twentieth century has his hands full in trying to understand, describe, and then make *credible* much of American reality. It stupefies, it sickens, it infuriates, and finally it is even a kind of embarrassment to one's [own] meager imagination. The actuality is continually outdoing our talents, and the culture tosses up figures almost daily that are the envy of any novelist."[22] Culture, clearly, tosses up the good as it tosses up the bad. As Roth's nuanced creative fiction shows, for every McCarthy there is a Lowenstein—both of whom find a place in Roth's writing. Likewise, for every Stalin there is a Klíma, both of whom also find their way into Roth's writing. He has listened to Klíma and written of his history from the safety of his cabin in the woods of western Connecticut.

On the one hand, it may seem ironic that the most garrulous living writer would be associated with listening, with a politics of listening as I have laid out here. Maybe the focus is on the listening that takes place in the world, the listening in of an intellectual mind, in order to be able to put it all down on paper—not in order to determine right from left, good from bad, conservative from liberal, Communist from capitalist—but in order to show the complexity of human life that would ideally be at the heart of all politics. He listens so that his characters and his friends may speak about listening, about ethical and political engagement outside of binary oppositions, outside of divisive and reductive truth claims about the world.

Notes

1. Aimee Pozorski, "On Philip Roth: Ethics and Elegy after the Holocaust," *Philip Roth*, ed. Pozorski (Ipswich, MA: Salem, 2013), 6.
2. "Politics," in *Oxford English Dictionary* (Oxford: Oxford University Press, 2014).
3. Ibid.
4. Philip Roth, *I Married a Communist* (Boston: Houghton Mifflin 1998), 222; hereafter cited parenthetically as *Communist*.
5. Celestine Bohlen, "Rare Unfurling of the Reluctant Philip Roth," *New York Times*, September 15, 2001, www.nytimes.com.
6. Philip Roth, "Written Remarks for the 2013 PEN Literary Gala," in *Roth and Politics*, ed. Claudia Franziska Brühwiler and Lee Trepanier (Lexington: University Press of Kentucky, 2015); hereafter cited parenthetically as "Written Remarks."
7. Philip Roth, "In Memory of a Friend, Mentor, Teacher," *New York Times*, April 20, 2013; hereafter cited parenthetical as "In Memory of."
8. See especially Philip Abbott, "'Bryan, Bryan, Bryan, Bryan': Democratic Theory, Populism, and Philip Roth's American Trilogy," *Canadian Review of American Studies* 37, no. 3 (2007): 431–52; Laura Arce, "Conspiracy and Betrayal in the Shade of McCarthy's America: Philip Roth's *I Married a Communist*," *ES: Revista De Filologia Inglesia* 32 (2011): 27–42; Anthony Hutchinson, "'Purity as Petrefaction': Liberalism and Betrayal in Philip Roth's *I Married a Communist*," *Rethinking History* 9, no. 203 (2005): 315–27; Michael Kimmage, "The Mechanics of History in Philip Roth's American Trilogy," in *Philip Roth*, ed. Aimee Pozorski, 150–63 (Ipswich, MA: Salem, 2013); Catherine Morley, "Bardic Aspirations: Philip Roth's Epic of America," *English: The Journal of the English Association.* 57, no. 218 (2008): 171–98; Sorin Radu-Cucu, "'The Spirit of the Common Man': Populism and the Rhetoric of Betrayal in Philip Roth's *I Married a Communist*," *Philip Roth Studies* 4, no. 2 (2008): 171–86; Larry Schwartz, "Philip Roth's *I Married a Communist*: Re-Thinking the Cold War," *Cultural Logic: An Electronic Journal of Marxist Theory and Practice* (2004); and Simon Stow, "Written and

Unwritten America: Roth on Reading, Politics, and Theory," *Studies in American Jewish Literature* 23 (2004): 77–87.

9. Ira Nadel, "Philip Roth and Film," in *Roth and Celebrity*, ed. Aimee Pozorski (Lanham, MD: Lexington, 2012), 50.

10. Mark Shechner, "Roth's American Trilogy," in *The Cambridge Companion to Philip Roth*, ed. Timothy Parrish (Cambridge: Cambridge University Press, 2007), 149.

11. Bonnie Lyons, "Philip Roth's American Tragedies," in *Turning Up the Flame: Philip Roth's Later Novels*, ed. Jay L. Halio and Ben Siegel (Newark: University of Delaware Press, 2005), 128.

12. Michiko Kakutani, "Manly Giant vs. Zealots and Scheming Women," *New York Times*, October 6, 1998, www.nytimes.com.

13. Robert Kelly, "Are You Now or Have You Ever Been?" *New York Times*, October 11, 1988, www.nytimes.com.

14. David Gooblar and David Brauner are excellent examples of this scholarship. For Gooblar: "What Murray recognizes is that Zuckerman's isolation, ostensibly a retreat from the expenditure of energy that self-making in the world requires, is just another utopian attempt at total self-determination" (Gooblar, *The Major Phases of Philip Roth* [New York: Continuum, 2001], 145). Brauner argues that Murray "initiates Zuckerman the schoolboy into the mysteries of literature and it is he who has to warn Zuckerman the old man of the dangers of forsaking life for literature, of subscribing to another version of the pastoral myth with which Ira deluded himself and eluded his history" (Brauner, *Philip Roth* [Manchester, UK: Manchester University Press, 2007], 154).

15. Ross Posnock, *Philip Roth's Rude Truth: The Art of Immaturity* (Princeton, NJ: Princeton University Press, 2006), 46.

16. Pia Masiero, *Philip Roth and the Zuckerman Books: The Making of a Storyworld* (Amherst, NY: Cambria, 2011), 168–69. For Masiero: "The exertion of the writer's responsibility is, rather plainly, writing. What Nathan *could* do with the material he has been entrusted with is rather obviously what is being read."

17. Derek Parker Royal, "Pastoral Dreams and National Identity in *American Pastoral* and *I Married a Communist*," in *Philip Roth: New Perspectives on an American Author*, ed. Derek Parker Royal (Westport, CT: Praeger, 2005), 200.

18. See Stoever, "The Contours of the Sonic Color-Line: Slavery, Segregation, and the Cultural Politics of Listening," *Dissertation Abstracts International*, Section A: The Humanities and Social Sciences 68, no. 10 (2008); Tunbridge, "Singing Translations: The Politics of Listening between the Wars," *Representations* 123 (2013): 53–86; and Weber, "Beyond the Culture Trap: Immigrant Women in Germany, Planet-Talk, and a Politics of Listening," *Women in German Yearbook: Feminist Studies in German Literature and Culture* 21 (2005): 16–38.

19. Marianne Hirsch and Valerie Smith, "Feminism and Cultural Memory: An Introduction," *Signs: A Journal of Women in Culture and Society* 28, no. 1 (2002): 14.

20. Cathy Caruth, *Unclaimed Experience: Trauma, Narrative and History* (Baltimore: Johns Hopkins University Press, 1996), 8; Wendy Hui-Kyong Chun, "Unbearable Witness: Towards a Politics of Listening," *Differences: A Journal of Feminist Cultural Studies* 11, no. 1 (1999): 133.

21. Caruth, *Unclaimed Experience*, 137–39; Chun, "Unbearable Witness," 140.

22. Philip Roth, "Writing American Fiction," in *Reading Myself and Others*, by Roth (New York: Vintage, 2001), 167–68.

2

Serving His Tour as an "Exasperated Liberal and Indignant Citizen"

Philip Roth, a Public Intellectual?

Claudia Franziska Brühwiler

"I'm a novelist, but I'm not Émile Zola."[1] This is one phrase that could squash this essay's premise, namely that Philip Roth should be considered as a public intellectual, as part of a category of writers that became known thanks to Zola's battle in defense of Alfred Dreyfus, who had been unjustly convicted for treason in 1894. "I'm not Émile Zola" was thus Roth's justification for declining to get involved in the case of Kathy Boudin, a member of the Weather Underground who had been imprisoned for her role in a holdup in which two policemen were killed in 1981.[2] Roth refuses to be categorized as a public intellectual because he finds the term "pompous," as if he were winding a laurel wreath for himself.[3] Not feeling like another Zola and refusing to allow others to bestow laurels on him, however, does not spare Roth from being perceived as a potential Zola. This perception is not just wishful thinking by the public and critics but is actually grounded in Roth's writing and activities, particularly during the first part of his career.

As I have argued elsewhere,[4] German-speaking media are particularly prone to treat Roth as a public intellectual, in that they tend to interview him about political issues and ask him about the responsibility of writers. Although one can explain away this line of interviewing as a German pre-occupation, as a reflex of cultural critics and journalists in search of U.S. counterparts of the Nobel laureates Heinrich Böll and Günter Grass, Roth once indeed did take upon the role of a public intellectual by giving Eastern Europeans a platform on our side of the Iron Curtain. Even earlier, he used literature in ways he claims are incompatible with literature's purpose, by mocking the presidency and unmasking its erstwhile incumbents. More-over, he stood up for artistic freedom from the very outset of his writing life, which includes for him the right to refuse any alleged political responsibility and moral standards imposed by certain parts of society. In other words, I would argue that Roth has reached out to the public either in the pages of his novels or personally to speak out as a writer-intellectual, even though he would reject that label. It seems that his experience of seeing literature, and particularly his own work, on trial made Roth shy away from claiming a public purpose for either writers or their work as such.

In the following, I will first outline the general understanding of the term "public intellectual" and why Roth believes that writers should not strive to be so categorized. I will then turn to his early battles in defense of artistic freedom and the right to provocation, which he claimed for his cru-sade against Richard Nixon as well. Finally, we will turn to his most public engagement, namely his support for dissident writers in Czechoslovakia.

Writers as Public Intellectuals—And the American Exception

When Roth claimed not to be Zola, he referred to the man who was first called an "intellectual," though the term was meant to be derogatory. The French novelist Maurice Barrès denounced the thinkers who joined forces with the writer Émile Zola in the Dreyfus affair as "*intellectuels.*" In French diction, the term still does not require the adjective "public," as it had, from its coinage, a public connotation, rendering the English word usage pleonastic.[5] In the U.S. context, it was C. Wright Mills (1957) who first spoke of "public intellectuals," a term that was finally popularized by the historian Russell Jacoby (1987). True to the spirit of Zola and his follow-ers, "public intellectuals" are "*engagés*" thinkers who use their intellectual (and thus social) capital to get involved politically and express their ideas, beliefs, and convictions to a wide spectrum of the public.[6] In a normative reading, public intellectuals should act as "critical guardian[s] of humane and universal values"[7] and speak "the truth to power."[8]

A particular subspecies of these treasured public intellectuals are Nobel Prize laureates, who enjoy increased public interest in spite of their oftentimes highly complex research that is usually unintelligible to the average news follower. Accordingly, Frédéric Lebaron describes the Nobel Prize as a "process of social construction of public intellectuals,"[9] since the laureates are suddenly exposed to public attention that reaches beyond their fields of expertise. The same applies to writers who receive this honor, as Edward Said observed astutely: "The easiest way of demonstrating that is simply to list the names of some recent Nobel Prize winners, then to allow each name to trigger in the mind an emblematized region, which in turn can be seen as a sort of platform or jumping-off point for that writer's subsequent activity as an intervention in debates taking place very far from the world of literature."[10]

The Dreyfus affair, in a sense the founding moment of the idea of publicly engaged intellectuals, shows that writers did and do act as public intellectuals irrespective of a Nobel award. For instance, in central and Eastern Europe, writer-intellectuals assumed high political offices such as Czechoslovakian president Václav Havel, who was at first primarily known as a playwright and dissident,[11] and Arpad Göncz, translator of John Updike's oeuvre and former president of Hungary.[12] In Germany, writers mainly became an immediate political force with Willy Brandt's ascendance to the post of chancellor. Once in power, he sought Günter Grass's advice and thus broke down the "traditionally asserted opposition between the life of the mind and the world of power."[13] Yet, earlier in German history we can already find writers who used their public exposure in support of political ideas; for instance, the playwright Bertolt Brecht or the novelist Thomas Mann.

According to Philip Roth, American writers are hardly visible as public intellectuals. In an interview with a German journalist in 1983, he concurred that American writers only rarely spoke out publicly compared with their European colleagues, and he explained this perceived reluctance as a matter of tradition: "You have a famous example: Grass. And Böll as well. Here, there is no such tradition. That my phone should ring and a senator ask for my opinion: unimaginable. I would faint."[14] Perhaps emboldened by the belief that his words would not reach an American audience or playing with European beliefs of superiority, Roth later told the same interviewer that there might be yet another explanation for why U.S. authors remained mute in the public realm: "This is an expression of our cultural limitations. It would not occur to anyone to ask a writer."[15] In yet another conversation with the German press, however, Roth conceded that it was less a problem of the media asking *a* writer than one of asking *an American* writer. Agreeing with the novelist John Irving that the U.S. media criticize American writers fiercely when they express their opinion on politics, Roth modified his claim and pointed out that the *New York Times* indeed seeks the opinions of writers, though of European ones:

> The *Times* asks European, but not American writers. For instance: when Bill Clinton had a few problems with an intern, I was hoping that someone in this country would call John Updike. He wrote brilliant books about sex and power; one could even say he's an authority in that field. It would have been obvious to let him write about the Lewinsky affair. Didn't happen. Millions of words have been written about Monica Lewinsky—but not by any writers.[16]

With lack of status come certain advantages, however: liberty, for instance, and the privilege of playing rather than arguing. In an interview with a Swedish newspaper, Roth suggested that what had made the American novel particularly successful and popular was this: "Writing that is uncontaminated by political propaganda—or even political responsibility."[17] Yet in the very next sentence, Roth lists the political realities that nourish an American writer's imagination and constantly feed his or her stories:

> Very little truthfulness anywhere, antagonism everywhere, so much calculated to disgust, the gigantic hypocrisies, no holding fierce passions at bay, the ordinary viciousness you can see just by pressing the remote, explosive weapons in the hands of creeps, the gloomy tabulation of unspeakable violent events, the unceasing despoliation of the biosphere for profit, surveillance overkill that will come back to haunt us, great concentrations of wealth financing the most undemocratic malevolents around, science illiterates still fighting the Scopes trial 89 years on, economic inequities the size of the Ritz, indebtedness on everyone's tail, families not knowing how bad things can get, money

being squeezed out of every last thing—that frenzy—and (by no means new) government hardly by the people through representative democracy but rather by the great financial interests, the old American plutocracy worse than ever.[18]

In spite of his awareness of these issues, Roth stubbornly claims to be nothing more than "an ordinary citizen,"[19] only a writer, and writers are, thus his lament, not important, since "Americans don't read anymore":[20]

There are always exceptions, but nobody here would listen for even thirty seconds to what a writer has to say. Who is that anyway, people would wonder. There is no special respect for writers. . . . They have no greater moral authority than a plumber. . . . Yes, it is as if a plumber were suddenly to make a statement about the state of the world; everyone would be astounded.[21]

Contrary to Roth's statement, however, one of his later novels did provoke a discussion of his political views. Repeated interpretations of *The Plot Against America* (2004) as an allegory of the administration of George W. Bush even prompted Roth to write an article for the *New York Times* titled "The Story behind *The Plot Against America*" and to share his motivation for writing the novel.[22] He stressed that the novel was "neither an allegory nor a metaphor nor a didactic tract; *The Plot* is about what it is about, which isn't now but then" ("Story behind *The Plot*"). In a later interview with Hermione Lee for the *New Yorker*, Roth declared that he was "not out to make fiction into a political statement."[23] Roth's denial of any political intention behind his works accords with his belief that, with reference to Sinclair Lewis, "repeating . . . 'It can happen here,' does little to prevent 'it' from happening."[24] Roth claims that he does not assume any political responsibility in writing fiction, does not succumb to any political purpose, however much he might agree with it: "However much I may loathe anti-Semitism . . . my job in a work of fiction is not to offer consolation to Jewish sufferers or to mount an attack upon their persecutors" (*Reading*, 109).

In Roth's eyes, writers would misjudge their role if they delivered propaganda and supported a political cause in their writings. Or, to put it into the blunt words of Ernest Hemingway, as imagined by Roth in *The Great American Novel* (1973): "If I have a message, I send it Western Union."[25]

Creating fiction should not serve a political idea but rather only art, thus Roth's belief. The same claim is reiterated by one of Roth's characters, the scholar Leo Glucksman, who is sought out by the ever-recurrent Nathan Zuckerman in *I Married a Communist* (1998). The novel is just as much about betrayal in the McCarthy era as it is about the coming of age of a writer, Zuckerman, who first has to find his voice. On this quest, Glucksman challenges, to put it euphemistically, one of the budding novelist's central premises of writing:[26] "Art is taking the right *stand* on everything? Art as the advocate of good things? Who taught you this? Who taught you art is slogans? Who taught you art is in the service of *'the people'*? Art is in the service of *art*—otherwise there is no art worthy of *anyone's* attention. What *is* the motive for writing serious literature, Mr. Zuckerman? To disarm the enemies of price control? The motive for writing serious literature is *to write serious literature.*"[27]

Roth would reiterate Glucksman's position, as we saw earlier, yet he learned at the outset of his writing life that some critics and readers did indeed expect art to be "the advocate of good things"—and they certainly did not want fiction to be turned into an artistic playground to mock stereotypes and take delight in offense, obscenity, and provocation.

"What Is Being Done to Silence This Man?"—Roth against Political Correctness

Roth experienced very early on what it meant to scandalize his readership, namely with one of his short stories, "Defender of the Faith," that was first published in the *New Yorker* and then reprinted in Roth's début book, *Goodbye, Columbus* (1959). The short piece is set in the American military and depicts a Jewish sergeant struggling to reconcile his authority and duty with the appeals of his soldiers to their mutual religious background. His subordinates increasingly take advantage of his goodwill and seek different excuses to receive favorable treatment for ostensibly religious reasons. In the same collection of short stories, Roth also captures the extramarital affairs of an otherwise respectable Jewish family father in his late fifties, and in yet another story he lets a young Jewish boy disrupt his bar mitzvah class to coerce his rabbi and other members of the community to declare themselves believers of Immaculate Conception and Jesus Christ.

By casting Jews as common sinners or ridiculing repetitive bar mitzvah lessons, Roth had gone too far in the eyes of many Jewish readers, and had even betrayed his roots and community. One of his readers accused Roth of "hav[ing] done as much harm" with a single story "as all the organized anti-Semitic organizations have done to make people believe that all Jews are cheats, liars, connivers."[28] A rabbi even wrote to the Jewish Anti-Defamation League, inquiring: "What is being done to silence this man? Medieval Jews would have known what to do with him" (*Reading*, 216). Finally, when Roth appeared in 1962 at Yeshiva University in New York to discuss his writing, he got to experience the full wrath of his community. During the question-and-answer session, he tried to react calmly to accusations masked as questions like this one: "Mr. Roth, would you write the same stories you've written if you were living in Nazi Germany?"[29] As Roth explains in his playful attempt at autobiography, he could no longer hold back when he saw not only his own work but literature as such on trial: "You were brought up on anti-Semitic literature!" "Yes," I hollered back, "and what is that?"—curious really to know what he meant. "English literature!" he cried. "English literature is anti-Semitic literature!" (*Facts*, 129).

Roth had thus established the reputation of a "self-loathing Jew," the author of anti-Semitic literature in service of goyshe prejudices. Even in Israel, readers took note of his peculiar story lines and characters, which dismayed a notable literary critic of *Haaretz,* Gershom Scholem. Scholem related in one of his articles in 1967 that one of his "hobbies is following anti-Semitic literature. On a recent trip abroad, one of them handed me Roth's latest book and laughingly commented: 'Perhaps this too belongs to your life-time interest.' And, indeed, my friend was right."[30] Scholem's remark predated the one novel that would catapult Roth to international limelight and bolster his reputation as a Jewish writer who is mainly preoccupied with his Judaism: *Portnoy's Complaint* (1969).

Although the incidents at Yeshiva University had disheartened Roth to the extent that he swore to "never write about Jews again" (*Facts*, 129), he set off to create a character whose thoughts and troubles revolve around only two things—his insatiable sexual appetite and his Judaism. Alexander Portnoy is a young Jewish man living with his family in Newark, where he tries to hide his constant lusting for shikses from his domineering mother. At the same time, he seeks to free himself from the constant demands of his Jewish heritage, the expectations of his community to be just another good Jewish boy: "Jew Jew Jew Jew Jew Jew! It is coming out of my ears already, the saga of the suffering Jews! Do me a favor, my people, and stick your suffering heritage up your suffering ass—*I happen also to be a human being!*"[31]

Written as the confession of Portnoy to his psychoanalyst, the tale of his adolescent angsts and yearnings is explicit in language, without fear of obscenity and with a biting humor, all of which captivated thousands of readers. In the year of its publication, *Portnoy's Complaint* stayed at the top of the *New York Times* best-seller list for fourteen consecutive weeks.[32] As Roth observed, however, the novel was "at once such a hit and such a scandal" because "a novel in the guise of a confession was received and judged by any number of readers as a confession in the guise of a novel" (*Reading*, 218). Indeed, notable critics like Marie Syrkin and Irving Howe harshly criticized the novel for its depiction of Jews as well as for its obscenity.[33] *Haaretz* critic Scholem felt confirmed in his earlier judgment of Philip Roth's oeuvre and described *Portnoy* as "the book for which all the anti-Semites have been praying."[34] Scholem saw in the character of Alexander Portnoy an epitome of racist Jewish stereotypes, down to the obsession with the Gentile woman, the shikse. He solemnly predicted that every Jew would have to pay for the book except for the author himself: "Here in the center of Roth's revolting book . . . stands the loathsome figure whom the anti-Semites have conjured in their imagination and portrayed in their literature, and a Jewish author, a highly gifted if perverted artist, offers all the slogans which for them are priceless."[35]

In addition to his reputation as an enemy of his own religious community, Roth with time became labeled as a misogynist. Former Booker Prize juror Carmen Callil's criticism of Roth is far from new, as one of his earliest novels, *When She Was Good* (1967), was repeatedly branded as misogynist for its unsympathetic depiction of the female protagonist,[36] who is the only female character at the center of a Rothian novel. Reviewers and literary scholars criticized Roth's female characters as being too stereotypical, farcical, or sexualized, functioning mainly as props to male fantasies, decorative additions to an otherwise male-centered universe. Roth's ex-wife, the British actress Claire Bloom, seemed to confirm this perception in her memoir *Leaving a Doll's House* (1996), published, ironically, by Callil's Virago Press. Bloom depicts a domineering and at times eccentric husband who gets caught up in his anxieties and would even sacrifice their relationship to his art. According to her account, Roth had originally planned to name the wife of his eponymous philandering hero in the short novel *Deception* (1990) "Claire," but he described the supposedly fictional Claire in a way that his actual wife considered insulting and revolting. He eventually dropped this reference for the publication of the book; still, their marriage ended in 1995 in divorce.

Fittingly, *Deception* contains one of many examples of how Roth uses his own scandals, or the way critics and scholars try to turn his works into literary scandals, and how he enriches his fiction by playing with the arguments of his opponents. In bed with "Philip Roth," the unnamed lover starts subjecting him to a trial, accusing him of sexism and misogyny: "You are out of order! It is not for you to interrogate the court but to answer the questions of the court. You are charged with sexism, misogyny, woman abuse, slander of women, denigration of women, defamation of women, and ruthless seduction, crimes all carrying the most severe penalties. People like you are not treated kindly if found guilty, and for good reason. . . . Why did you publish books that cause women suffering? Didn't you think that those writings could be used against us by our enemies?"[37]

The defendant's answer could be passed on to all of those critics of Philip Roth who constantly remind him of what is proper: "I can only reply that this self-styled equal-rights democracy has aims and objectives that are not mine as a writer" (109–10).

Roth's retort to Claire Bloom's memoir was, however, a little more, though not totally subtle. To the unassuming reader, the character of Eve Frame in *I Married a Communist* is just what narrator Nathan Zuckerman makes her out to be—a famous actress struggling with her Jewish roots who marries the novel's main character, the radio actor Ira Ringold, and who worships her highly musical daughter from a first, unhappy marriage. Hurt and embittered after yet another unsuccessful relationship, Frame aims to destroy Ringold after their divorce by denouncing him for his political affiliations—*I Married a Communist*, exclaims the title of her memoirs. If one reads the tale of Ira and Eve side by side with the one of Philip and Claire, the parallels are unavoidable, beginning with Eve's and Claire's profession, the musically gifted daughter who is hardly tolerated by her stepfather, and the vengeful memoirs. The *Guardian* reviewer Linda Grant thus judged the novel as "a howl of rage about fact, which has bullyingly usurped the self-appointed task of fiction to tell the truth"[38]—a scandal used to produce yet another, though indeed only minor, literary scandal. It probably did not have a great impact on Roth, at least not if we may assume that he faces and responds to such criticism with the same presumptions that his writer-protagonist Zuckerman does. Earlier, in *The Anatomy Lesson* (1983), Roth had let his Nathan Zuckerman feel what it means to be considered a misogynist: "From what he'd read of the reviews in the feminist press, he could expect a picture of himself up in the post office, alongside the mug shot of the Marquis de Sade, once the militants took Washington and began guillotining the thousand top misogynists in the arts. He came off no better there than with the disapproving Jews. Worse. They had put him on the cover of one of their magazines. WHY DOES THIS MAN HATE WOMEN?"[39]

Although Roth's mockery of feminist critics was relatively tame and rare, the charges of anti-Semitism would become a recurring theme, not only in his autobiography *The Facts* (1988) and in his many nonfictional contributions collected in *Reading Myself and Others* (1976) but also in his fiction. He chose his constant literary companion or alter ego Nathan Zuckerman to project his own torments as a young writer accused of exploiting his family's stories and tarnishing the Jewish community's reputation. *The Ghost Writer* (1979) is Zuckerman's failed Bildungsroman, his quest to become a serious writer with the aid of his idol, the reclusive writer E. I. Lonoff. During his stay with Lonoff, he reminisces about the struggles with his parents, particularly with his father, who felt insulted and ridiculed in one of his son's short stories. Echoing arguments Roth had heard after the publication of *Goodbye, Columbus*, a judge and friend of the family admonishes Zuckerman to consider the consequences for the Jewish community should his story ever get published. To help Zuckerman see the implications of his work, the judge sends him a questionnaire that is suggestive of Roth's "trial" at New York's Yeshiva University:

1. If you had been living in Nazi Germany in the thirties, would you have written such a story? . . .
10. Can you honestly say there is anything in your short story that would not warm the heart of a Julius Streicher or a Joseph Goebbels?[40]

As Roth further follows Zuckerman's life in subsequent novels, the reader learns that Zuckerman, very much like his creator, did not let himself be influenced by societal demands of propriety, but gains fame and notoriety as the author of a novel tellingly titled *Carnovsky*. In *Zuckerman Unbound* (1981), the writer-protagonist shares how life changed for him after this giant success: "The only book that seemed to exist was his own. And whenever he tried to forget it, someone reminded him."[41] As Roth had said of many people's reaction to *Portnoy*, Zuckerman complained that his readers often mistook "impersonation for confession and were calling out to a character who lived in a book" (10). Zuckerman consequently received mail addressed not only to himself but also to his fictional character "Gilbert Carnovsky" as well as letters "addressed simply to 'The Enemy of the Jews'" (58). Roth's readers thereby experience the paranoia of the haunted writer, the absurdity of certain claims and the farcical situations he undergoes simply because the written and the unwritten world merge for some of Zuckerman's/Roth's readers. At the same time, Zuckerman has to recognize how his family is suffering due to his success, being just as much victims of their son's literary scandal as he is. He pays for his fictional brazenness by being called "Bastard" (193) by his dying father. His brother Henry would finally erase any doubt that their father might not have intended to say what he did: "*Of course* he said 'Bastard.' He'd seen it! He'd seen what you had done to him and Mother in that book!" (217).

Following the buzz, scandal, and accusations, Zuckerman falls into depression and becomes increasingly wary of his individuality. The scandal and the subsequent illness seem to have a transforming effect on him: "Yes, illness had done it: Zuckerman had become Carnovsky. The journalists had known it all along" (*Anatomy*, 102). Ironically, his personal crisis coincides with the Watergate hearings, which instill, for the only time, compassion in him for the diminishing President Nixon: "He almost felt for him, the only other American he saw daily who seemed to be in as much trouble as he was" (*Anatomy*, 10). Zuckerman would in later novels set out to reclaim the dignity of Coleman Silk, defend Ira Ringold against the defamatory book by his wife, and explore the scandals of others rather than his own. In his last appearance in *Exit Ghost* (2007), Roth even lets him pass up the chance to expose a scandalous truth about his one-time mentor, E. I. Lonoff. A young upcoming writer seeks in Zuckerman a mentor who would support his endeavor to write a Lonoff biography. Roth once let a writer envision the plight of a Lonoff biographer in *Deception*, mockingly dismissing the thought that a literary hermit like Lonoff might "in secret [have] the remissive history of Jean Genet" (*Deception*, 98), which let the biographer scorn the Lonoff family and its desire for a "pious monument" (98) to the deceased. Now, however, Zuckerman shows sympathy for similar wishes, in spite of reminders of his former self, that he, Zuckerman, had once also been brash and rash in his writing. Roth's alter ego is finally tired of scandals, even political ones: "I've served my tour as exasperated liberal and indignant citizen. . . . I don't wish to register an opinion, I don't want to express myself on "the issues"—I don't even want to know what they are. It no longer suits me to know, and what doesn't suit me, I expunge."[42]

Against the "Armor of Dignity": Satirizing Presidents

Before becoming tired of "serving his tour as an exasperated liberal" citizen, Roth experimented with satire, not only for the fun and to gain a feel for the genre but also motivated by actual political anger. During his college years at Bucknell University, he headed the magazine *Et Cetera* and used it as a platform for his satiric exploits,[43] which would later find a more prominent readership. His irony-laden essay "Positive Thinking on Pennsylvania Avenue" (1957/1996) in the *Chicago Review* showed the satirical potential of a president's quirks, with Roth taking delight in Dwight Eisenhower's "chummy tone" in his good-night prayers, a means to unburden his presidential shoulders and pass the chances of failure to the Lord. But, as Roth stated in an interview, it was only in the 1960s and 1970s that he had found a truly compelling reason to try his hand at satire again: "Why have I turned to political satire? In a word: Nixon" (*Reading*, 41).

Roth eyed Nixon's rise to power early on with a mixture of fear and disgust. Having grown up as the son of an ardent New Dealer who believed in "the sanctity of F.D.R. and the Democratic Party" (*Facts*, 31), Roth took pride in the fact that "Richard Nixon was known as a crook in our kitchen some twenty-odd years before this dawned on the majority of Americans as a real possibility" (*Reading*, 9–11). Roth saw in Nixon a man "transparently fraudulent, if not on the edge of mental disorder" (*Reading*, 11), whose changing viewpoints could not be explained reasonably. In the fall of 1971, Roth drafted a piece that was intended for the pages of the *New York Times*, which rejected it as "tasteless."[44] Therein, he marvelled how Nixon could be "positively gaga over his trip to Red China, as he used to call it," and refer to the country as the People's Republic of China "as easily as any Weatherman": "Doesn't he stand for *anything*? It turns out he isn't even anti Communist. He never even believed in *that*" (*Reading*, 41).

With his satirical closet drama *Our Gang* (1971), Roth thus set out "to destroy the protective armor of 'dignity' that shields anyone in an office as high and powerful as the Presidency" (*Reading*, 40)—and thereby show the *New York Times* what "tasteless" really could amount to.[45] Focusing on President Trick E. Dixon, the play decries not only "the fine art of government lying" (*Reading*, 49) but also the ineffectiveness of the president's entourage and those believed to be primary watchdogs, namely the media. Even though it would be the media that—sometime after the publication of Roth's vitriolic play and thanks only to the tenacity of the *Washington Post's* journalists[46]—would unveil the illegal machinations in the Nixon administration, they are, in Roth's eyes, only to be relied on "to cloud the issue and miss the point" (*Reading*, 49).

Roth lifts the curtain on Nixon's character with an actual quote from April 3, 1971, which observers considered exemplary of the president's struggles with language: "From personal and religious beliefs, I consider abortions an unacceptable form of population control. Furthermore, unrestricted abortion policies, or abortion on demand, I cannot square with my personal belief in the sanctity of human life—including the life of the yet unborn. For, surely, the unborn have rights also, recognized in law, recognized even in principles expounded by the United Nations"[47]

Our attention then turns to Tricky, as Dixon is henceforth only called, discussing the massacre of My Lai with a citizen who is troubled not by the deaths of the civilians but by the possibility that one of them might have been a pregnant woman. In the exchange, Roth on the one hand condemns the bigotry and reverse morals he ascribes to Nixon and his supporters. On the other hand, he incessantly spoofs Nixon's rhetoric, letting Tricky remind his interlocutor of his background as a lawyer by directly speaking of the "tradition in the courts of this land" (5) and of what "good lawyers" (6) should do, as well as by introducing new absurd hypotheses and discussing their consequences. He carries his arguments for the rights of the unborn further in the next scene, a press conference populated by reporters with names that already convey the nature of their questions: Mr. Asslick, Mr. Daring, Mr. Fascinated . . .

Roth likewise graces Tricky's staff as well as Vice President-What's-his-name, Spiro Agnew, with such telling names. As we encounter all the coaches in the third scene, Tricky is in the midst of a crisis, one to add to his *Six Hundred Crises,* as Roth renames Nixon's biographic book *Six Crises* (1962). None other than the Boy Scouts are rioting in the capital, because they have taken offense at what they took to be the president's propagation of intercourse. A serious situation, as Tricky reminds his staff: "Gentlemen, you can go to war without Congressional consent, you can ruin the economy and trample on the Bill of Rights, but you just do not violate the moral code of the Boy Scouts of America and expect to be reelected to the highest office in the land!" (28). The unusual riot and Dixon's earnest response ironically echo Clinton Rossiter's description of the president as someone expected "to go through some rather undignified paces by a people who think of him as a combination of scoutmaster, Delphic oracle, hero of the silver screen, and father of the multitudes" (247). Pondering on how to deal with the rioters and the public, the "spiritual coach" advocates a new version of the Checkers speech, whereby he literally refers to Nixon's actual speech as Dwight D. Eisenhower's running mate.[48]

Meanwhile, the "political coach" is sure that the team has "used the truth some time or other in the past, too" (36), and the "highbrow coach," a caricature of Henry Kissinger, suggests blaming everything on a former baseball player. Incidentally, the latter has left the country for Copenhagen, the—as the highbrow coach puts it—"pornography capital of the world" (64), against which Tricky Dixon subsequently wages war. Roth lets Tricky deliver his "Something is Rotten in the State of Denmark" speech (83), wherein he lets his antihero imitate structure and expressions from Nixon's Checkers speech. Fortunately, Tricky cannot return to presidential business as usual, as he is assassinated in a bizarre manner in the penultimate chapter. Yet for a comeback artist of Dixon's/Nixon's quality, neither death nor the arrival in hell puts an end to his career: in his final appearance, he addresses his "fellow Fallen" (185) in hell and tries to oust Satan from his dominating position, for "despite my brief tenure in the 'White' House, I firmly believe that I was able to maintain and perpetuate all that was evil in American life when I came to power" (191).

With its escalations, absurd twists, and unrealistically one-dimensional characters, *Our Gang* is an over-the-top satire that some consider ineffective due to its hyperbolic nature:[49] its tone, thus the argument, becomes too bitter, too vitriolic to remain humorous, pungent, and strike a chord. A reviewer with the *New York Times* considered the satire "far-fetched, unfair, tasteless, disturbing, logical, coarse and very funny—I laughed out loud 16 times and giggled internally a statistically unverifiable amount."[50] Nixon himself heard of *Our Gang* thanks to his chief of staff, Bob Haldeman, as could be later learned thanks to the recordings from the White House. Upon hearing that a satire had been published that vilified him, Nixon simply asked whether the author was a Jew.[51]

Yet I think the play does achieve its aim of destroying "the protective armor of 'dignity' that shields anyone in an office as high and powerful as the Presidency" (*Reading*, 40) and does not allow the reader to dismiss it as outlandish and irrelevant. It makes the reader wary by mimicking Nixon's rhetorical ticks and his meandering way of speaking, which brings the fictional Tricky at times uncomfortably close to the original. Tricky's still latent hatred for "Jack Charisma" (59) and his preoccupation with his own perspiration are just two of many instances, apart from the character's very name, in which Roth blatantly points at Nixon. One might find Roth's satirical methods crude and uninspired, a reminder of his predilection for the burlesque, yet they do not fail to leave a mark. Roth had Nixon descend to hell even prior to the publication of the Pentagon Papers. This gives the play not only a prophetic aftertaste and Roth a Cassandra-like status but also underlines Roth's notion that the actual scandal of Watergate was the only type of scandal the media understood as such and that they had missed the actual scandal all along: Nixon's rise to power.

Watergate itself would not inspire Roth to focus yet again on the hated president, but Nixon would continue to haunt the pages of Roth's novels, though mainly through the lens of the media. For instance, in *The Anatomy Lesson* (1983), Roth's writer-protagonist Nathan Zuckerman follows Watergate on TV, "our President's chicanery the dummy gestures, the satanic sweating, the screwy dazzling lies" (10). Nixon would also bring back the political reflexes of Zuckerman senior, the man "famous for fanatical devotion" (*Zuckerman Unbound*, 190) for liberal icons. As mother Zuckerman reports: "Mr. Metz . . . says Daddy seems to follow perfectly. He can tell by how angry he gets whenever he hears Nixon's name" (104). And, in *American Pastoral* (1997), Nixon would be an outlet for Roth's Lou Levov, a reason to let go of decorum:

> "That skunk!" the Swede's father said bitterly. "That miserable fascist dog!" and out of him, with terrifying force, poured a tirade of abuse,

vitriol about the president of the United States. . . . Get Nixon. Get the
bastard in some way. Get Nixon and all will be well. If we can just tar
and feather Nixon, America will be America again, without everything
loathsome and lawless that's crept in, without all the violence and malice and madness and hate. Put him in a cage, cage the crook, and we'll
have our great country back the way it was![52]

In contrast to his character Lou Levov, Roth did not need Nixon as an
excuse to abandon propriety, as he had repeatedly bathed his work in alleged
obscenity. But for him, Nixon was likewise liberating in that the despised
presidential figure gave Roth not only the needed material to experiment
with satire and the grotesque but also, by serving as a counterfigure to the
idealized and revered Franklin Delano Roosevelt, another constant political point of reference in his works.

Against Kafkaesque Nightmares: Eastern Europe—and America

In only a few instances, Roth left the confines of fiction to reflect on political
issues and acted in the manner of a public intellectual, though maybe a bit
more discreetly than others. What led him to political engagement was a
literary obsession, namely the desire to see the hometown of one of his idols,
Franz Kafka. Already his first visit to Prague in 1972 turned into more than
a writer's pilgrimage, for his then-partner, Barbara Sproul, established con-
tacts with political dissidents in the country, acting on behalf of Amnesty
International.[53] Getting a sense for the oppressive political circumstances
and their effect on Czechoslovakian writers, Roth would later no longer
be just the cover for his partner's human rights engagement and began to
organize financial aid for authors through PEN.[54]

Although the financial flow to Prague petered out in 1977, when PEN
no longer wanted to focus solely on Czechoslovakian dissident-writers, Roth
embarked on an additional support project that lasted from 1974 until the
end of the Cold War. For Penguin, he edited the series "Writers from the
Other Europe" (*Shop Talk,* 78), which featured many of the artists he had
met in Prague, such as Ivan Klíma, as well as writers for whom he hoped to
get greater attention, for instance Bruno Schulz, whom he even referenced
in *The Prague Orgy* (1985). Roth thus gave Eastern European authors,

some of whom had not yet been translated into English, a prominent platform to present their writing to an English-speaking readership that could hardly imagine the risks these writers took in pursuit of their calling. Roth kept visiting his colleagues until he was denied a visa in 1976 and had to depend on couriers to stay in touch with them and to get manuscripts across the border (*Shop Talk,* 44). In addition to editing the series for Penguin, he then also reflected on his Prague experience in the Zuckerman novel *The Prague Orgy,* which gives the reader an impression of the limitations on an artistic life in a country in which one half "is employed spying on the other half."[55] The story of Zuckerman wandering around Prague in search of a lost manuscript further shows how literature can gain a different status under a totalitarian regime that leads to a situation in which "nothing goes and everything matters; here everything goes and nothing matters" (*Shop Talk,* 53). As Zuckerman observes: "Here where the literary culture is held hostage, the art of narration flourishes by mouth. In Prague, stories aren't simply stories; it's what they have instead of life. . . . Storytelling is the form their resistance has taken against the coercion of the powers-that-be" (*Prague Orgy,* 64).

Roth would later use his influence once more to help a writer abroad, when the Congolese novelist Emmanuel Dongala and his wife were unable to escape the civil war ravaging their country. Thanks to Roth's intervention, President Bill Clinton made sure that they would be granted a visa to come to the United States.[56] Ironically, Clinton himself would also receive moral support of a special kind from Roth. Although he does not appear as a character in *The Human Stain* (2000), he and his much-debated extramarital affair are on the reader's mind throughout the novel, as Roth reflects the president's predicament and society's hypocrisy. The actual focus, though, is on a character inspired by Roth's longtime friend Professor Melvin Tumin:[57] Coleman Silk, a professor of classics at a fictional liberal arts college, Athena.

"Does anyone know these people? Do they exist or are they spooks?"[58] The double meaning of the term "spooks" leads to the allegation of racism—the ghosts he was looking for are African American students. Silk becomes the victim of political correctness enforced at the expense of common sense. After his wife's death, he finds consolation in an affair with Faunia Farley, one of the college's janitors and in her mid-thirties, who is married to a violent and traumatized Vietnam veteran. This relationship seems to give rise to yet another minor scandal, as Silk receives an anonymous letter that he can attribute to his prim former colleague, a female French professor: "Everyone knows," her note reads, "you're sexually exploiting an abused, illiterate woman half your age" (38).

Coleman Silk becomes the victim of "the persecuting spirit" (2), as Roth's narrator Zuckerman calls it in reference to Nathaniel Hawthorne. The puritans antagonizing Silk are the same that turn the summer of 1998 into "the summer of an enormous piety binge, a purity binge, when terrorism—which had replaced communism as the prevailing threat to the country's security—was succeeded by cocksucking, and a virile, youthful middle-aged president and a brash, smitten twenty-one-year-old employee carrying on in the Oval Office like two teenage kids in a parking lot revived America's oldest communal passion, historically perhaps its most treacherous and subversive pleasure: the ecstasy of sanctimony" (2).

While the nation seems to delight in its disgust and finger-pointing, Zuckerman is alienated and appalled by the purifying zest around him and dreams "of a mammoth banner, draped Dadaistically like a Christo wrapping from one end of the White House to the other and bearing the legend A HUMAN BEING LIVES HERE" (3). The actual scandal, however, would only be revealed to Zuckerman after Silk's burial, namely that he was of African American descent and had denied his roots, committing a virtual matricide: "His crime exceeded anything and everything they wanted to lay on him. He said 'spooks,' he has a girlfriend half his age—it's all kid stuff" (355)

Such is also Zuckerman's—and, we may infer, Roth's—assessment of Clinton's "crime" against propriety: kid stuff, an assessment emphasized by his comparison of the adulterous president and his intern to "two teenagers in a parking lot" (2). Again, the media are only to be trusted "to cloud the issue and miss the point" (*Reading*, 49) by focusing on the incidental rather than the substantial. As in the case of Silk, we find Clinton's true crime elsewhere, indeed, even in a part of Roth's American Trilogy preceding *The Human Stain* and linking him to Richard Nixon. Murray Ringold, one of the central characters of *I Married Communist* (1998) and a survivor of the Red Scare era, relates to Nathan Zuckerman how he watched Nixon's funeral in 1994. Disgustedly, Ringold recalls each scene shown on television, each scene and each speaker: "Then the realists take command, the connoisseurs of deal making and deal breaking, masters of the most shameless ways of undoing an opponent, those for whom moral concerns must always come last, uttering all the well-known, unreal, sham-ridden cant about everything but the dead man's real passions. Clinton exalting Nixon for his 'remarkable journey; and, under the spell of his own sincerity, expressing hushed gratitude for all the 'wise counsel' Nixon had given him" (278).

In his final speech in hell, *Our Gang*'s Tricky Dick tells his "fellow fallen" that it is "our whole lives that you should be judging here tonight" (200)—as Clinton claimed to do in Nixon's case, as David Greenberg pointed out.[59] Yet Bill Clinton's verdict was, in Zuckerman's reading, unjust. In both Silk's and Clinton's cases it is not what guardians of public morals and propriety label as scandalous that infuriates Zuckerman; it is rather society's sanctimony and blindness to the actual crime that disgust him. Silk committed a virtual matricide by cutting all ties to his family; Clinton cried over the nation's loss of Nixon, against his better judgment. The purity binge of 1998 is for Roth and his narrator Zuckerman only the point of departure to uncover America's actual crimes: its history of race relations, its obsession with purity and propriety, the resulting hypocrisy.

Conclusion: Declining the Laurels . . . to Little Effect

Philip Roth has still not received the Nobel Prize, the award that forces even the most reluctant intellectuals into the public. Whether he will receive it one day is up to the committee in Stockholm, in which he has little faith—to a French journalist he marveled that his turn might come once a writer from the Trobriand Islands had been honored.[60] Irrespective of any awards, Roth will remain on the radar of those seeking a critical voice who speaks as bluntly on American affairs as he defends artistic freedom. Roth may think this only to be the case in Europe, where cultural critics further such intuitions by claiming that it "is now easier to find on the newsstands of *la France profonde* than in the convenience-store equivalents of the American heartland."[61] Having chronicled America's plights in the twentieth century, unmasked the country's lies but also highlighted those traits that set it apart from Europe, Roth will, though *nolens volens*, retain an important place in the country's cultural and political conscience.

Notes

An earlier draft of this chapter was presented at the American Political Science Association's Annual Meeting in Washington, DC, in 2014, as part of the panel

"The Artist as Public Intellectual and Political Leader" that was sponsored by the McConnell Center. I thank Professor Lee Trepanier for the invitation, and I am indebted to all the panel participants for their valuable comments, in particular to discussant Professor Rebecca LeMoine.

1. Claudia Roth Pierpoint, *Roth Unbound: A Writer and His Books* (New York: Farrar, Straus and Giroux, 2013), 225.

2. Elizabeth Kolbert portrayed Kathy Boudin in 2001 for the *New Yorker*, providing insight into Boudin's initiation to far-left terrorism, her actual involvement in the holdup, and her later atonement by improving the lot of HIV-positive prisoners (see Kolbert, "The Prisoner," *New Yorker*, July 16, 2001, 44–57). Her defense team thought that Roth might be sympathetic to her cause due to the way *American Pastoral* discussed the Weather Underground.

3. Anthony Palou, "Philip Roth chez lui," *Le Figaro*, October 8, 2009, 40.

4. Claudia Franziska Brühwiler, "A Reluctant Public Intellectual: Philip Roth in the German-Speaking Media," *Philip Roth Studies* 10, no. 1 (2014). The article includes general observations on public intellectuals that are covered here as well and focuses on the way Roth is portrayed in the German-speaking media.

5. Edward W. Said, "The Public Role of Writers and Intellectuals," in *The Public Intellectual,* ed. Helen Small (Oxford and Malden, MA: Blackwell, 2002), 22; Eleanor Townsley, "The Public Intellectual Trope in the United States," *American Sociologist* (2006): 39; Susan Rubin Suleiman, "The Literary Significance of the Dreyfus Affair," in *The Dreyfus Affair: Art, Truth, and Justice,* ed. Norman L. Kleeblatt (Berkeley: University of California Press, 1987), 120.

6. Jonathon Lane, "Loyalty, Democracy and the Public Intellectual," *Minerva* 43 (2005): 74; Pascal Ory and Jean-François Sirinelli, *Les intellectuels en France: De l'affaire Dreyfus à nos jours,* 3rd ed. (Paris: Armand Colin, 2002), 10.

7. Matthew A. Kemp, "French Intellectuals and the Iraq War," *Modern & Contemporary France* 17, no. 2 (2009): 199.

8. Said, "The Role," 25.

9. Frédéric Lebaron, "'Nobel' Economists as Public Intellectuals: The Circulation of Symbolic Capital," *International Journal of Contemporary Sociology* 43, no. 1 (2006): 88.

10. Said, "The Role," 25.

11. The situation in post–Cold War Czechoslovakia even led Roth to ask: "Have there ever before been so many translators, novelists, and poets at the head of anything other than the PEN club?" (Philip Roth, *Shop Talk: A Writer and His Colleagues at Work* [New York: Vintage International, 2002], 46; hereafter cited parenthetically).

12. Wolf Lepenies, *Aufstieg und Fall der Intellektuellen in Europa* (Frankfurt am Main and New York: Campus Verlag, 1992), 54.

13. Frank Brunssen, "'Speak Out!'—Günter Grass as an International Intellectual," *Debatte: Journal of Contemporary Central and Eastern Europe* 15, no. 3 (2007): 325.

14. Volker Hage, *Philip Roth: Bücher und Begegnungen* (Munich: Hanser, 2008), 20, my translation. Original passage: "Sie haben doch ein berühmtes Beispiel: Grass. Und Böll ja auch. Das hat bei uns keine Tradition. Dass bei mir das Telefon klingelt und ein Senator mich um meine Meinung bittet: unvorstellbar. Ich würde vor Schreck umfallen."

15. Hage, *Philip Roth*, 55, my translation. Original passage: "Das ist Ausdruck unserer kulturellen Beschränktheit. Einen Schriftsteller zu fragen, fällt hier einfach niemandem ein."

16. Martin Scholz, "Ich bin nicht mehr so verrückt," *Frankfurter Rundschau,* October 12, 2009, www.fr-online.de, my translation. Original passage: "Die Times fragt Europäer, aber keine amerikanischen Schriftsteller. Ein Beispiel: Als Bill Clinton ein paar Probleme mit einer Praktikantin hatte, hoffte ich, dass irgendjemand in diesem Land mal bei John Updike anrufen würde. Er hat brillante Bücher über Sex und Macht geschrieben, man könnte sagen: Er war die Autorität auf diesem Gebiet. Da hätte es doch nahe gelegen, ihn über die Lewinsky-Affäre schreiben zu lassen. Ist nicht passiert. Es wurden Millionen Wörter über Monica Lewinsky geschrieben—aber nicht von Schriftstellern."

17. Daniel Sandstrom, "My Life as a Writer," *New York Times,* March 2, 2014, www.nytimes.com/2014/03/16/books/review/my-life-as-a-writer.html?_r=0.

18. Ibid.

19. Nils Minkmar, "Der Tag, als Philip Roth anrief," *Frankfurter Allgemeine Sonntagszeitung,* August 7, 2005, 2.

20. Martin Scholz, "Ich kann den Hass auf Amerika nicht ernst nehmen," *Frankfurter Rundschau,* October 15, 2005. Also published in *Der Standard,* October 7, 2005, http://derstandard.at. My translation. Original passage: "Die Amerikaner lesen gar nichts mehr."

21. Minkmar, "Der Tag," 2, my translation. Original passage: "Es gibt immer Ausnahmen, aber hier würde niemand auch nur dreissig Sekunden hinhören, was ein Schriftsteller zu wagen hat. Wer ist denn der, würde man fragen. Es gibt keinen besonderen Respekt für Schriftsteller, keiner versteht, was sie genau machen. Sie haben keine grössere moralische Autorität als der Klempner. . . . Ja, es ist, als würde der Klempner plötzlich Statements zur Weltlage abgeben, da würden sich auch alle wundern." Clearly, Roth could not envisage the rise of a plumber during the presidential race in 2008.

22. Philip Roth, "The Story behind *The Plot Against America,*" New York Times, September 19, 2004, www.nytimes.com/2004/09/19/books/review/19ROTHL .html?pagewanted=all&module=Search&mabReward=relbias%3Ar%2C%7B%221%22%3A%22RI%3A5%22%7D&_r=0; hereafter cited parenthetically.

23. Arda Collins, "Age Makes a Difference," New Yorker, October 27, 2007, www.newyorker.com/magazine/2007/10/01/age-makes-a-difference.

24. Philip Roth, Reading Myself and Others (New York: Vintage International, 2001), 207; hereafter cited parenthetically as *Reading.*

25. Philip Roth, *The Great American Novel* (London, Vintage, 2006), 46.

26. I have covered Roth's perception of the relationship between literature and politics more extensively and with a detailed discussion of Glucksman's position in *Political Initiation in the Novels of Philip Roth* (London and New York: Bloomsbury Academic, 2013), 41–54.

27. Philip Roth, *I Married a Communist* (London: Vintage, 1999); hereafter cited parenthetically as *Communist*.

28. David Gooblar, *The Major Phases of Philip Roth* (London and New York: Continuum, 2011), 13.

29. Philip Roth, *The Facts: A Novelist's Autobiography* (New York: Vintage International, 1997), 127; hereafter cited parenthetically as *Facts*.

30. Yitzhak Laor, "Von Exodus bis Operation Shylock: Wer ist Philip Roth in Israel? / From Exodus to Operation Shylock: Who Is Philip Roth in Israel?," *Du* 740 (2003): 78.

31. Philip Roth, *Portnoy's Complaint* (London: Vintage, 1999), 76.

32. Gooblar, *Major Phases,* 33.

33. In "Roth, Rushdie, and Rage: Religious Reactions to Portnoy and the Verses" (*Journal of Ecumenical Studies* 43, no. 1 [2008]: 33–37), David J. Zucker gives an overview of the many criticisms *Portnoy's Complaint* provoked.

34. Alan Cooper, *Philip Roth and the Jews* (Albany: State University of New York Press), 110.

35. Cooper, *Philip Roth,* 110.

36. Nicole Peeler, "The Woman of Ressentiment in *When She Was Good,*" *Philip Roth Studies* 6, no. 1 (2010): 31.

37. Philip Roth, *Deception* (London: Vintage, 2002), 109; hereafter cited parenthetically.

38. Linda Grant, "The Wrath of Roth," Guardian.com, October 3, 1998.

39. Philip Roth, *The Anatomy Lesson* (London: Vintage, 2005), 171; hereafter cited parenthetically as *Anatomy.*

40. Philip Roth, *The Ghost Writer* (London: Vintage, 2002), 103–4; hereafter cited parenthetically.

41. Philip Roth, *Zuckerman Unbound* (New York: Vintage International, 1997), 50; hereafter cited parenthetically.

42. Philip Roth, *Exit Ghost* (London: Jonathan Cape, 2007), 36–37; hereafter cited parenthetically.

43. Roth Pierpoint, *Roth Unbound,* 23.

44. Ibid., 71.

45. Ibid.

46. See, for instance, David Greenberg, *Nixon's Shadow: The History of an Image* (New York: Norton, 2003), 158–62.

47. Philip Roth, *Our Gang: (Starring Tricky and His Friends)* (London: Vintage, 2006), 2; hereafter cited parenthetically.

48. Richard Nixon gave the Checkers speech on September 23, 1952, on NBC. He therein defended himself against allegations of corruption that had been raised

by a *New York Post* article on September 18. The article alleged that some Nixon supporters had established a private fund to cover his expenses (see, for instance, Greenberg, *Nixon's Shadow*). "Checkers" refers to the "little cocker spaniel dog" sent from a "man down in Texas" for the Nixon kids (Richard Nixon, "Checkers Speech," September 23, 1952, American Rhetoric, www.americanrhetoric.com/speeches/richardnixoncheckers.html).

49. Daniel Frick, *Reinventing Richard Nixon: A Cultural History of an American Obsession* (Lawrence: University Press of Kansas, 2008).

50. Dwight McDonald, "Our Gang," *New York Times*, November 7, 1971, www.nytimes.com/books/98/10/11/specials/roth-gang.html.

51. Willi Winkler, "Lebenslänglich," *Süddeutsche Zeitung* April 23, 2011, 3. This was also picked up by the French press: Emmanuel Hecht, "N le maudit," *L'Express*, April 16, 2014, 92; Marion Cocquet, "Quand Philip Roth mettait Nixon en rage," *LePoint.fr*, January 31, 2014, via factiva.

52. Philip Roth, *American Pastoral* (London: Vintage, 2005), 299–300; hereafter cited parenthetically.

53. Roth Pierpoint, *Roth Unbound*, 86.

54. Ibid., 91–92.

55. Philip Roth, *The Prague Orgy* (New York: Vintage International, 1996), 33.

56. Roth Pierpoint, *Roth Unbound*, 235.

57. Philip Roth, "An Open Letter to Wikipedia," *New Yorker*, September 12, 2012, www.newyorker.com.

58. Philip Roth, *The Human Stain* (London: Vintage, 2001), 2.

59. Greenberg, *Nixon's Shadow*, 346.

60. "Philip Roth: 'Je sais que la mort vient,'" *Le Point*, September 27, 2012, 108–12, via factiva.

61. Charles Holdefer, "France and American Literature," *World Literature Today* 77, no. 2 (2003), 2, via factiva.

3

The Politics and Literature of Unknowingness

Philip Roth's Our Gang *and* The Plot Against America

Simon Stow

"A novel," observed Milan Kundera in a 1980 interview with Philip Roth, "does not assert anything; a novel searches and poses questions. . . . I don't know which of my characters is right. I invent stories, confront one with another, and by this means I ask questions. The stupidity of people comes from having an answer for everything. The wisdom of the novel comes from having a question for everything. . . . The novelist teaches the reader to comprehend the world as a question. There is wisdom and tolerance in that attitude. In a world built on sacrosanct certainties the novel is dead."[1] Much of what Roth himself has written and said about the reading and writing of fiction suggests that he shares Kundera's view about the importance of literature's interrogative function. Indeed, while acknowledging the significance of Franz Kafka's work to the political protests in Czechoslovakia in the 1960s, Roth nevertheless asserted that "whatever changes fiction may appear to inspire have usually to do with the goals of the reader and not the writer."[2] His claim is not that literature leaves everything as it is but rather that the author's role is not to advocate or pontificate but to problematize in the written world of the text, the people, places, and things of the unwritten world in which that text is produced.[3] Chekhov, Roth notes, "makes a distinction between 'the solution of the problem and a correct presentation of the problem'—and adds, 'only the latter is obligatory for the artist'" (*Reading*, 16). In any struggle between Chekov and Norman Mailer—about whom, Roth observed in 1960, "he has become an actor in the cultural drama"—Roth would clearly side with the Russian (*Reading*, 170).

Paradoxically, however, politics and/or political readings of the author's work have stalked Roth since the beginning of his career. He notes that the heroine of the ostensibly apolitical *When She Was Good*—written during what Roth called the most "politicized" years of his life—employed language that echoed, in its duplicity, that of the American government's justification for its war in Vietnam (*Reading*, 10); and Derek Parker Royal argues that several of the author's early and "lesser-known" works took on "history and contemporary politics, and aggressively so."[4] Among those works that Royal identifies as directly engaging with politics is, of course, Roth's 1971 satire *Our Gang*, a ferocious attack on the person and administration of Richard M. Nixon. Likewise, many readers have understood Roth's 2004 novel *The Plot Against America,* depicting an alternate history in which the aviator Charles A. Lindbergh becomes the president of a quasi-fascist United States, to be the author's commentary on the person and administration of another president—George W. Bush—whom Roth once reviled as "unfit to run a hardware store."[5]

Drawing a distinction between "knowing" and "unknowing" texts and readings—between texts and readings that articulate a position and those that interrogate our practices—this essay considers what *Our Gang* and *The Plot Against America,* novels from either end of Roth's career, might reveal about the potential role for literature in the democratic "political."[6] Despite Roth's suggestion that the political impact of novels has little to do with the aims of the author, it will be argued that when those aims are interrogative or problematizing (what is here being called "unknowing") rather than expressive of a specific position (what is here being called "knowing"), literature is likely to generate greater critical political reflection in the reader and, as such, to have a more positive impact upon democratic politics. This does not, of course, commit the essay to the view that this is Roth's intention, simply to the idea that literature's value to democracy lies in the potential cultivation of unknowingness in its audience rather than in the knowing expression of preexisting political positions. In this, the argument stands in contrast to other, more dominant, theories of the relationship between literature and democracy. Unlike the "classical" account, it does not suggest that certain authors have special insight into human behavior that can only be made clear in a literary form, though it does not rule out such a possibility.[7] Likewise, it does not claim that certain kinds of texts and readings can alert us to particular kinds of suffering that will lead its readers to be more aware of their biases, and thus, to be more tolerant about specific kinds of behaviors that they might otherwise find abhorrent, though, once again, it does not rule this out.[8] Rather, it argues that literature's value to democracy lies in the possibility that it might serve, in Arthur C. Danto's words, to "transfigure the commonplace."[9] It might do so, it suggests, in ways that lead its readers to recognize the contingency and precariousness of their values—and those of the world around them—in ways that cultivate a critical attitude valuable to democratic politics, one outlined in the work of William Connolly and others.[10] It offers, that is, the possibility of an ethos of openness and contingency appropriate to the democratic citizen.[11]

The value of Philip Roth's work to this exercise is to show how a commitment to unknowingness in the author might serve to cultivate the same in the reader. Likewise, it suggests that knowingness in the author is unlikely to generate unknowingness in an audience. Roth is, however, not just a hook on which to hang a theoretical discussion, for it will be suggested—though the argument does not rely on the veracity of this claim for its plausibility— that this commitment to cultivating unknowability in his readers is central to Roth's work and that this work is successful as literature to the extent that he is able to achieve it. In this, the essay is an attempt to reflect upon both a long-standing debate about politics and literature and to identify the ways in which Roth's work succeeds and sometimes fails as literature: goals that suggest that the democratic and the literary might ultimately be inseparable.

The essay proceeds, first, by setting out Roth's distinction between knowing and unknowingness. It identifies the ways in which the written world of literature is, on Roth's account, inadequate to capture the totality of the unwritten world, and it reflects his obvious frustration at attempts to conflate the former with the latter by seeking unwritten-world referents for his literary creations. At the heart of this objection, it suggests, is Roth's commitment to unknowingness as a literary strategy. The essay then identifies the various literary devices that Roth employs toward achieving his goal. Second, suggesting that Roth's commitment to unknowingness is all but abandoned in his political satire of Richard Nixon, the essay argues that *Our Gang* is an example of knowing writing and that, as such, it fails both as literature and as a possible political intervention. It nevertheless suggests that the novel is an *instructive* failure, one that reveals much, not only about the failings of knowing literature but also about how and why unknowing literature might affect its audience in democratically productive ways. Turning to Roth's 2004 novel *The Plot Against America*, the essay notes the ways in which this book, despite the author's protests, has also been subject to—politically motivated—knowing readings of the sort that Roth abhors. It nevertheless suggests that unlike with knowing writing, the blame for knowing reading cannot always be laid at the author's door. It identifies the ways in which the text embodies unknowingness and seeks to achieve this in its audience. The essay concludes by returning to the novel's opening line. Focusing on a hitherto overlooked aspect of its formulation that suggests, contrary to Roth's objections, that the novel offers the possibility of critical reflection on our contemporary polity, but not the critical parallel that is most often ascribed to it. In this, it suggests, *The Plot Against America* may ultimately be a deeply unknowing and deeply political text that demonstrates the connection between these two values.

Knowing and Unknowing Texts, Knowing and Unknowing Readings

In an interview concerning *The Great American Novel* where, in a typical act of narrative playfulness, Roth serves as his own interlocutor, the author praises the value of a certain kind of unknowingness by contrasting it with the notion that the unwritten world can be understood in its totality. "I don't claim to know," he writes, "what America is 'really like.' *Not* knowing, or no longer knowing for sure, is just what perplexes many of the people who live and work here and consider this country home. That is why I invented the paranoid fantasist Word Smith—the narrator who calls himself Smitty— to be (purportedly) the author of *The Great American Novel*. What he describes is what America is really like to one like him" (*Reading*, 79). To claim to know the world is, Roth suggests, to be a paranoid fantasist. Even as he makes this claim, however, Roth undercuts it by making the paranoid fantasist an author, thereby destabilizing and making contingent his own authorial pronouncements on the world outside the text.[12] In this, perhaps, Roth embraces a certain kind of Socratic irony, one so thoroughgoing that it is never quite clear when he is being serious and when he is not. There are some for whom such an attitude bespeaks frivolity or frustration—Goethe is said to have observed that whoever could say when Socrates was being serious and when he was joking would be doing humanity a great service[13]—but for Roth, as for Socrates, it is a way of acknowledging the limitations on his own understanding. Indeed, the inability of the author to capture the totality of the unwritten world in the written world of the text is a persistent theme in Roth's work, both creative and critical. Speaking at Stanford in 1960, Roth observed that the "American writer in the middle of the twentieth century has his hands full in trying to understand, describe, and then make *credible* much of American reality. It stupefies, it sickens, it infuriates, and finally it is even a kind of embarrassment to one's meager imagination. The actuality is continually outdoing our talents, and the culture tosses up figures almost daily that are the envy of any novelist" (*Reading*, 168).

It is no surprise, therefore, that Roth has sought to resist knowing readings of his work, those that seek to make the written world of literature correspond directly to the unwritten world in which it is written.[14] For even though Roth once declared that "every writer learns over a lifetime to be tolerant of the stupid inferences that are drawn from literature and the fantasies implausibly imposed upon it," over the course of his career he has expressed differing levels of frustration over such readings.[15] While he seemed merely bemused by the reader who admonished him for the depiction of his sister in *Portnoy's Complaint*—despite his not having a sister (*Reading*, 35)—Roth appeared far more frustrated by the reluctance of the website Wikipedia to correct an inaccuracy in its entry on *The Human Stain*. At stake was the assertion that the novel's central protagonist, Coleman Silk, was based upon the writer Anatole Broyard. Balking at this suggestion, Roth sought to correct the record but was told that he was not "a credible source" because the website required additional citations. In a letter to Wikipedia published in the *New Yorker*, Roth observed that novel writing is "for the novelist a game of let's pretend," and was at pains to differentiate the life of Broyard from that of Silk. At the heart of his protest was Roth's account of his unknowingness.

Having outlined key details of the fictional Silk's biography, Roth asked: "As for Anatole Broyard, was he ever in the Navy? The Army? Prison? Graduate school? The Communist Party? Did he have children? Had he ever been the innocent victim of institutional harassment? I had no idea. He and I barely knew each other." Likewise, he noted, "I knew nothing of Anatole Broyard's mistresses or, if he ever had any, who they were"; "I knew nothing at all of Broyard's private life—of his family, parents, siblings, relatives, education, friendships, marriage, love affairs"; "I've never known, spoken to, or, to my knowledge, been in the company of a single member of Broyard's family. I did not even know whether he had children." Roth concluded the account of his unknowingness by contrasting it with what he did know:

> I knew everything about Coleman Silk because I had invented him from scratch, just as in the five-year period before the 2000 publication of "The Human Stain" I had invented the puppeteer Mickey Sabbath of "Sabbath's Theater" (1995), the glove manufacturer Swede Levov of "American Pastoral" (1997), and the brothers Ringold in "I Married a Communist" (1998), one a high-school English teacher and the other a star of radio in its heyday. Neither before nor after writing these books was I a puppeteer, a glove manufacturer, a high-school teacher, or a radio star.[16]

It is something of an irony, perhaps, that *The Human Stain* should precipitate this dispute given that a key incident in the novel—the use of the word "spooks"—turns on a knowing reading: one in which the speaker's intent is ignored in favor of what the listeners "know" to be true. Indeed, that the most destructive act in the text—the anonymous letter sent to Coleman Silk by his antagonist Delphine Roux—is built upon a claim that "Everybody knows" further suggests Roth's distaste for "knowingness." As Royal observes: "This not knowing, the question mark that lies at the very center of being, is for Roth one of the indelible 'stains' of existence. And it is something that should never be denied."[17]

Roth identifies a major source of literary knowingness in the conflation of author and characters. It takes two forms. First, in an assumption that the details of his or her characters' lives are simply thinly veiled accounts of events in the author's own. Second, in the view that one or more of the characters is a mouthpiece for the author's opinions. In response to the first, Roth's reply to the interviewer who asked him about the relationship between the death of Zuckerman's father to that of his own—Roth offered the interviewer his father's telephone number[18]—suggests the myriad of problems of the roman à clef assumption. His response to the second assumption is more complex. In a 2014 interview with the *New York Times*, Roth identified a question that "any number of" journalists "cannot seem to ignore," that "goes something like this: 'Do you still think such-and-such? Do you still believe so-and-so?' and then they quote something spoken not by me but by a character in a book of mine." In reply, Roth observed: "Whoever looks for the writer's thinking in the words and thoughts of his characters is looking in the wrong direction. Seeking out a writer's 'thoughts' violates the richness of the mixture that is the very hallmark of the novel."[19] Much earlier in his career, however, Roth offered a far less temperate and possibly more revealing rejoinder to such knowingness in response to Diana Trilling's review of *Portnoy's Complaint*. Addressing Trilling directly, Roth observed: "If I may, I'd like to distinguish for you between myself and 'Mr. Roth,' the character in your review who is identified as the 'author of *Portnoy's Complaint*'" (*Reading*, 22). Roth seemed most offended by the suggestion that his novel was about "fortifying a position," that he had offered "a farce with a thesis" (*Reading*, 26–27). "Obviously," Roth noted, "I am not looking to be acquitted, as a person, of having some sort of view of things, nor would I hold that my fiction aspires to be a slice of life and nothing more. I am saying only that, as with any novelist, the presentation and the 'position' are inseparable, and I don't think a reader would be doing me (or even himself) justice if, for tendentious or polemical purposes, he were to divide the one into two, as you do with 'Mr. Roth'" (*Reading*, 26). He concluded by seeking to undo Trilling's knowing conflation of himself with the 'Mr. Roth' she had constructed. "'Mr. Roth's' view of life," he suggested, "is more hidden from certain readers in his wide audience than they imagine, more imbedded in parody, burlesque, slapstick, ridicule, insult, invective, lampoon, wisecrack, in nonsense, in levity, in play—in, that is, the methods and devices of Comedy, than their own view of life may enable them to realize" (*Reading*, 28). It is, perhaps, for this reason that Roth has so often sought to play with, and thereby destabilize, knowingness in his readers. His most persistent mechanism here is the use of multiple literary doppelgängers in, and across, texts.

"The habit of presenting the author as a fictional character in his own books is," writes Paul Berman, "an old trick of Roth's, not to say a mania."[20] In *Operation Shylock*, for example, the narrator, "Philip Roth," encounters another "Philip Roth," who may, or may not, be an imposter. Neither is, however, necessarily the "Philip Roth" who wrote the novel in which these other Roths appear. Likewise, there is "Philip Roth" the narrator of *The Plot Against America* who shares much, including many family members and a childhood residence, with the "Philip Roth" who wrote the text. So pervasive are Roth's identity games that his publisher has taken to using the subheading "Roth Books" to refer to some—but not all—of the author's tomes in the list of his works in his books. These include—the possibly ironically titled—*Deception* and *The Facts*. This game of literary cat and mouse is further complicated by the role of Roth's frequent narrator, Nathan Zuckerman. Zuckerman shares many biographical details with his creator, and Roth's publisher ascribes nine novels to him beginning with the tellingly titled *The Ghost Writer* and ending with the spirit's departure in *Exit Ghost*.[21] What Berman identifies as Roth's mania may, however, be the author's attempt to disrupt knowing readings: to undermine the certainty about what the text and/or the author might "mean." It is in such uncertainty—such unknowing—that critical thinking begins. As such, Roth's playfulness might show us how mistaken Goethe was to believe that the person who identified when Socrates was being serious and when he was joking would be doing humanity a great service.

In employing what Claudia Roth Pierpont identifies as *Maskenfreiheit*—"the freedom conferred by masks"[22]—to destabilize his readers, and thus, knowing readings, Roth offers a further opportunity for literary-critical reflection: the potentially illuminating juxtaposition of written and unwritten worlds: one that is simply unavailable when the two worlds are conflated. In this, Roth's work echoes that of Plato in *The Republic* or John Rawls in *A Theory of Justice*, where the creation of an alternate fictional reality—be it the Ideal City or the Original Position—creates the possibility of critical leverage on the structures and values of the reality in which it was created.[23] That such literary juxtapositions are not always successful is, of course, suggested by the many literal readings of *The Republic* that see Plato as a protototalitarian.[24] Indeed, it might be argued that Roth's exploitation of the freedom conferred by masks simply serves to encourage those prone to knowing readings to conflate the various Philip Roths and other narrators in ways that prove self-defeating: that Roth might be thought to bring the very knowing readings that he reviles upon himself.[25] In these circumstances, perhaps, Roth's protestations concerning the tendency of his readers to see his life and views in his novels and characters might be considered somewhat disingenuous. Indeed, when readers as sophisticated as John Updike and J. M. Coetzee see political purpose in Roth's writing,[26] it may be that the author's protestations about his belief that literature is unsuited to the task of changing the world should not be taken at face value: that knowing readings are more to his liking than he appears to suggest.[27] A further problem here is also that even though Roth has decried and played with knowing readings, he has also been guilty of knowing *writing*. One of the reasons why *The Human Stain* might be considered less successful, or at least less compelling, than the other two volumes in his American Trilogy is, perhaps, Roth's palpable anger at the sort of knowing readings practiced in the text.[28] Roth's knowing writing finds its fullest expression, however, in his 1971 novel, *Our Gang*, a text so deflated by knowing anger and purpose as to be incapable of producing anything but knowing responses.

Not So Tricky Dicky

In a volume dedicated to the work of, and thus likely to be read by scholars and devotees of a particular author, it is perhaps unwise to point out that one of that author's texts is a failure. *Our Gang* is, nevertheless, a failure on every level: it fails as literature, it fails as satire, its fails as comedy, and it even fails as agitprop. This is, no doubt, one of the reasons why it is the most overlooked text in Roth's canon, drawing remarkably little critical commentary and even less praise.[29] Calling the novel "demonstrably wretched," Jonathan Yardley identified much that is wrong with the text in two sentences. "*Our Gang* is," he wrote, "a satire of Richard Nixon and his administration, written before Watergate, during a period when Nixon had taken stands not to Roth's liking on abortion and other matters. It takes its epigraphs from Jonathan Swift and George Orwell, but the only resemblance it bears to the work of these writers is that it, too, is written in English."[30] Given that the aim of this essay is to praise Roth, not to bury him, it is perhaps necessary to note that although *Our Gang* is a failure, it is an instructive failure, one whose shortcomings reveal much about the strengths of Roth's other work, both as literature and as an engagement, intentional or otherwise, with the political.

In an interview aimed at assuaging concerns expressed by his publisher about the vulgarity of a text depicting Nixon's assassination,[31] Roth argued that vulgarity is essential to satire, a genre whose goal is "to dislocate the reader and get him to view a familiar subject in ways he may be willing or unaccustomed" (*Reading*, 42). It is, however, precisely this possibility— Danto's "transfiguration of the commonplace"—that is destroyed by know- ing reading. One of the reasons why *Our Gang* fails, both as literature and as a potential source of political-critical reflection, is that some of the key elements of Roth's other work aimed at disrupting knowing readings—such as narrative playfulness and manipulation of the written/unwritten-world distinction—are largely absent from this text.[32] Certainly, there is never any doubt about the identity of the author of this work; his views of Richard Nixon; or his reasons for writing. "*Our Gang*," Roth asserted, "is out to destroy the protective armor of 'dignity' that shields any one in an office as high and powerful as the Presidency" (*Reading*, 40). In a remark that reveals much about both the knowingness of *Our Gang* and the sources of unknowingness in his other texts, Roth observes: "[A]side from the Nixon satire, I have never written anything determinedly and intention- ally destructive. Polemical or blasphemous assault upon the powers that be has served me more as a *theme* than as an overriding purpose in my work" (*Reading*, 8). In *Our Gang*, by contrast, the theme of the novel is its very purpose.

Although it is always possible that knowing writing might—under cer- tain circumstances[33]—produce unknowing reading, the odds would seem to be against it: in the absence of any effective mechanisms of transfigura- tion, such texts can generally only invite "straight" readings.[34] As such, that Roth's stated of aim of dislocating the reader and getting him or her to look differently at a familiar subject should be frustrated seems inevitable. Cer- tainly, it is hard to imagine anybody coming away from the novel with a dif- ferent attitude toward Nixon than they brought to it. Employing Socrates's distinction between the speaker who acts as a servant to his audience by giving them what they want, and the speaker who acts as physician by giv- ing them what they need, the Roth of *Our Gang* clearly belongs to the for- mer category.[35] It is no surprise, therefore, that the most charitable reading of the novel was offered by a former editor of the *Partisan Review*—and sometime Trotskyite—Dwight McDonald. "'Our Gang' is," he wrote, "a political satire that I found far-fetched, unfair, tasteless, disturbing, logical, coarse and very funny—I laughed out loud 16 times and giggled internally a statistically unverifiable amount. In short, a masterpiece."[36]

Laughter is, of course, in the belly of the beholder: what some find uproariously funny leaves others cold. There is, nevertheless, a trait seemingly peculiar to Americans in which, upon hearing a humorous joke, remark, or anecdote, they observe, "That's funny," without ever laughing; as if they were committed to identifying rather than experiencing comedy.[37] This is, perhaps, what might be called "knowing laughter"—that which emerges from the confirmation of a preexisting belief rather than the reconfiguration of a worldview. This may be the way in which *Our Gang* is funny: conceptually funny, or funny in the abstract. Certainly there is something forced and peculiar about McDonald's account of his *Our Gang* experience—one wonders whether he kept track of his guffaws with a pad and pencil or just totted them up in his head—and indeed, about the notion that his internal giggles were beyond statistical verification.[38] Till Kinzel, one of the few critics who seems to share McDonald's view of the text, identifies: "Roth's hilariously absurd choice of Denmark as an external enemy [that] is complemented by the equally absurd internal enemy in the form of the Boy Scouts of America under the pernicious influence of the baseball player Charles Curtis Flood."[39] There is, nevertheless, something of E. B. White's observation that dissecting a joke is like dissecting a frog—that neither survives the experience—about such analysis. Being told that, or why, something is funny is not the same thing as experiencing the transfiguring possibilities of a joke.[40]

One of the main problems, then, with *Our Gang* is that it is a largely unfunny satire. One wonders, for example, what Christopher Buckley, among others, might have done with the same material. Many of the constituents of humor are present—ostensibly funny names, absurd situations, and buffoonish characters—yet these constituents never quite coalesce into a decent joke.[41] As Roth notes, however, "[p]olitical satire isn't writing that lasts. Though satire, by and large, deals with enduring social and political problems, its comic appeal lies in the use made of the situation of the moment . . . subtleties of wit and malice are wholly lost over the years" (*Reading*, 37). Roth's defenders might argue that, devoid of its historical context, *Our Gang*'s humor inevitably falls flat. It is, nevertheless, hard to imagine the circumstances, historical or otherwise, in which the novel's asinine nomenclature—"Mr. Asslick," "Mr. Shrewd," "Miss Charmin',", "Senator Joseph McCatastrophy," "Governor George Wallow," "Mr. Catch-Me-In-A-Contradiction," and "Trick E. Dixon"—would be considered funny, let alone transfiguring of anybody's experience as a reader or citizen. As Roth himself has acknowledged, the names in this novel are precisely the sort of one-to-one written- to unwritten-world referent that he denies and deplores elsewhere (*Reading*, 49). In this, one is, perhaps, forced to agree with Nixon's chief of staff, H. R. Haldeman, who called *Our Gang* "a very childish book."[42] Indeed, it is telling that one of the most common descriptions of the novel's humor in *Our Gang* is "sophomoric."[43] Even Roth's friend and biographer, Claudia Roth Pierpont, suggests that the humor is "overextended and strained" and "too often suited to a frat night skit."[44] Inadvertently, perhaps, Roth acknowledges just such a pedigree for *Our Gang.* "At Bucknell University, where I went to college and edited a literary magazine," he observed in an interview concerning the novel, "I spent nearly as much time writing satire as I did trying to write fiction" (*Reading*, 43). Even more telling, perhaps, is Roth's account of his earliest literary-political foray—a clear precursor to *Our Gang*—that he described as "a long angry free-verse poem about McCarthyism [written] for the college magazine" (*Reading*, 10).

A further problem with *Our Gang*, both as literature and as political satire, is, then, that the author's views are not, as Roth had suggested in his response to Trilling, "hidden," but all too clearly on show. Indeed, Trilling's description of *Portnoy's Complaint* as "a farce with a thesis" concerned with "fortifying a position" seems far more applicable to *Our Gang* than it does to *Portnoy.* Although Roth has decried authors who seek social or political change through their work or otherwise—"My own feeling is," he writes, "that times are tough for a fiction writer when he takes to writing letters to his newspaper rather than those complicated, disguised letters to himself, which are stories" (*Reading*, 171)—*Our Gang* seems to seek precisely that. It a long, angry, free-verse poem about Nixon aimed at exposing the president's many hypocrisies. It is telling, perhaps, that the novel, which took him only three months to complete, began as an op-ed for the *New York Times.*[45] In contrast to the unknowingness that is at the heart of much of Roth's best work, *Our Gang* is stymied by its very knowingness and lack of innovation. Indeed, the text is so derivative—both as art and politics—that at times it amounts to little more than speaking cant to power.

   In a fanciful monologue, later published under the title "The Lost
Generation"—one that illustrates precisely the sort of comic touch *Our
Gang* is missing—a young Woody Allen offered an account of his European adventures. "I remember," he observed, "Scott and Zelda Fitzgerald came home from their wild New Year's Eve party. It was April. Scott
had just written *Great Expectations*. Gertrude Stein and I read it. We
said it was a good book but there was no need to have written it because
Charles Dickens had already written it. We laughed over it and Hemingway punched me in the mouth."[46] Roth's dubious achievement in *Our
Gang* is, perhaps, equivalent to Fitzgerald's in Allen's musings: that which
he seeks to achieve has already been done, and done better.[47] *Our Gang*
is, for example, concerned with showing how Nixon, like many politicians,
manipulates language for his own purposes.[48] This is, however, not a new
theme in either fiction or political theory: the relationship between words
and deeds was, for example, a key concern of Thucydides's *History of the
Peloponnesian War*.[49] The problem with *Our Gang* is not that it should
revisit such themes, but that it should do so in such a self-conscious and
unoriginal way. Indeed, the weight of the author's intent—signaled both
by the epigraphs that precede the text and by the literary company into
which he sought to place the novel following its publication—made the
unknowingness that he claims to prize all but impossible to achieve. Roth,
it might be argued, sought to achieve transfiguration through the justifica-
tions he offered for the novel rather than through the text itself: telling his
audience how they should have reacted to his work rather than cultivating
that reaction through his writing.
   Immediately following the publication of *Our Gang*, Roth was at
pains situate it within a satirical literary-political tradition, one with, he
argued, a considerable American pedigree (*Reading*, 37–38). In addition to the epigraphs from Jonathan Swift and George Orwell, Roth also
identified H. L. Mencken, *The Satyricon*, the Marx Brothers, the Three
Stooges, Laurel and Hardy, and Abbott and Costello as among the fore-
bears of *Our Gang*. It is, to say the least, quite a pantheon of satirical and
comedic greats, but Roth was not done. "Do you remember," he asks,
"Charlie Chaplin and Jack Oakie as Hitler and Mussolini in *The Great
Dictator?* Well, in their performances there's something, too, of the flavor
I hoped to get into the more outlandish sections of *Our Gang*" (*Reading*,
40). Although Roth is not an author burdened by false modesty, this list

is, nevertheless, somewhat unusual for him in that it seeks to *tell* rather than to *show*. The author explained the perceived value of his artistry by borrowing the authority of much more inspired and far more influential works: few would, perhaps, associate the visual poetry and balletic grace of Chaplin's Hitler-and-Mussolini scene with the rather more strained achievement of *Our Gang*. Indeed, while Roth has repeatedly suggested that literature has no overarching social purpose—"Novels," he declared in a 1984 interview with the *Paris Review*, "provide readers with something to read. At their best writers change the *way* readers read. That seems to me the only realistic expectation" (*Reading*, 147)—he seemed compelled to explain his reasons for, and purposes in, writing *Our Gang* in a way that is largely anomalous in his career.[50] That he did so suggests that he was not trying to convey his concerns to the audience in the way that he argues authors should—by asking questions—but rather by telling them what he believes to be true. In this it is possible to see how the unknowingness that he prizes is a source of both literary creativity and critical political reflection: it is no coincidence, perhaps, that his most knowing text is also his worst.[51]

In her evaluation of the novel as somewhat less than successful, the always-sympathetic Pierpont suggests that with *Our Gang* Roth "was out of his element, which was writing novels about people with sometimes over scaled but always recognizable emotions."[52] Milan Kundera's observation that novels are dead in a world of certainties may, however, offer a better explanation for Roth's failure in *Our Gang*. The very questioning that Roth claims to prize is entirely absent from the text. Indeed, even Roth's occasional ambivalence about this questioning aspect of his work—at times he hints at a belief in a more involved role for literature in the political[53]—is absent from a text that might have provided an opportunity to explore, or embody, it. Knowingness wins the day to the detriment of both literature and politics: rather than offering up an alternate reality to generate critical reflection on a problematic political figure, Roth, as author and citizen, simply seems to embody in his work a mirror image of the loathing that he finds so problematic in the president.

It is against this background that the considerable achievement of *The Plot Against America* might best be judged. It is an achievement that reveals much about both Roth's method and literature's potential to transfigure the commonplace in politically productive ways.

The Plot Against Knowingness

The rich unknowingness of Roth's 2004 novel about a fictional Charles Lindbergh presidency is immediately evidenced by the fecundity of its title. Most obviously it could refer to the right-wing scheme depicted in the text and aimed at electing Lindbergh and subverting the American values of freedom, tolerance, and equality. It could also refer to a fictional story juxtaposed with an American reality—the contrasting of the written and unwritten worlds—that is at the heart of much literature and political thought. Others, however, have seen the novel as story aimed at protesting an American polity hijacked by a quasi-fascist cabal—under the nominal control of George W. Bush—that is echoed by Roth's fictional America. So rich in ambiguity and unknowingness is the title that only the definite article remains determinable. It is an unknowingness that also pervades the text. While the Roth of *Our Gang* simply asserts, for example, what it is to be American—everything that is contra Nixon[54]—a key theme of Roth's *Plot* is the *question* of what it means to be American. Like their creator, the written-world Roths see themselves as Americans before they are Jews, while the policies of the Lindbergh administration may invert this view. The conflict engendered in the notion of American-ness by the programs with the Orwellian names "Just Folks," "Homestead," and "Good Neighbor" is embodied, most obviously, in the person of Philip's older brother Sandy, whose embrace of Lindbergh meant that he "was doing what was normal and patriotic all over America and aberrant and freakish only in his own home."[55] The question for the reader is, perhaps, whether Philip or his brother best understands the nature of the Lindbergh regime.

As Roth noted in his remarks on *Our Gang*, the aim of satire is to "dislocate the reader," to "get him to view a familiar subject in ways he may be willing or unaccustomed to" (*Reading*, 42). While genres other than satire may not *aim to* have a similar impact, it can often be their effect. There is no suggestion, of course, that *Plot* is a satire, even, perhaps, among those readers who see it as a commentary on the Bush administration.[56] Indeed, Roth identifies it as a "uchronia," a hypothetical alternate timeline that is often used for critical effect.[57] Like satire though, uchronias seek to dislocate the reader as a precursor to critical reflection. As such it is telling that a persistent theme of *Plot* is that of forced homelessness: that which forces the previously comfortable to reconsider everything that they had previously taken for granted.[58] Bess Roth, the narrator's mother, repeatedly expresses concerns that her children might "be obliged to relive her own circumscribed youth as a neighborhood outsider" (*Plot*, 9). Likewise, upon hearing the news that the Republican Party had chosen Lindbergh as their candidate for the presidency, Philip recounts how his neighbors spontane-ously converged in the streets. "Entire families known to me previously only fully dressed in daytime clothing were," he observes, "wearing pajamas and nightdresses under their bathrobes and milling around in their slippers at dawn as if driven from their homes by an earthquake" (*Plot*, 16). Such is the experience of the Jews under Lindbergh, those who, Philip observes, had hitherto "retained no allegiance, sentimental or otherwise, to those Old World countries that we had never been welcome in and that we had no intention of ever returning to" (*Plot*, 17). The narrator—as a possible stand-in for all Jews—finds "assaulted, as nothing ever had been before, that huge endowment of personal security that I had taken for granted as an Ameri-can child of American parents in an American school in an American city in an America at peace with the world" (*Plot*, 7).

Tragedy, Martin Heidegger asserted, is a state of homelessness.[59] The sense of dislocation offered by tragic theater—that which recounted sto-ries of a mythical and continually reworked and reimagined past—was the major source of critical political reflection in ancient Athens. As such, it might be argued that, just as Greek tragedy depicted such disorientation in its characters to cultivate the same in its audience as a source of democratic pedagogy,[60] Roth's narrative evasiveness and allusions to a world and history beyond the text of *The Plot Against America* might also seek to generate the same productive disorientation in his readers. Roth's uchronia offers several possible sources of ambiguity, disorientation, and potential unknowingness.

In the first instance, the narrator of *Plot* seems to be a version of a young Philip Roth. Much of what we see and hear in the text is filtered through his naivety: as such, readers cannot always be sure that they are seeing a full picture. Certainly young Philip is not always able to interrogate the stories that he is told by his parents in a way that would permit readers to see whether the things that they perceive are indeed so. There are, for example, hints in the text that Herman and Bess Roth might be overreact-ing to the threat of the Lindbergh's administration, that they are know-ing readers of the social world primed, like Delphine Roux in *The Human Stain*, to perceive bias. Recounting the press coverage of his aunt's marriage to the leader of American Jewry, young Philip recalls that the guest list "was surprisingly long and impressive, and I present it here to explain why I, for one, had to wonder if my parents and their Metropolitan friends weren't completely out of touch with reality to imagine that any harm could befall them because of a government program being administered by a luminary of the stature of Rabbi Bengelsdorf" (*Plot,* 245–46). Likewise, trading on the unwritten-world status of the *New York Times* as the newspaper of record, the written-world *New York Times* observes that the polity has been marked by anti-Lindbergh "accusations so far-fetched that even a life-long Democrat may find himself feeling unexpected sympathy for the president" (*Plot,* 240). Indeed, this is but one of two editorials from the *Times* attacking the Roths' great hero—Walter Winchell—a celebrity muckraker. The Winchell we see through the Roths' eyes is speaking truth to power; the one that we catch glimpses of from other voices in the text is a scurrilous self-promoter, prone to weaving together gossip and rumor as means to public notoriety. That Winchell is the main source of the Roth's information about the Lindbergh administration should, perhaps, give us pause as readers to wonder about the veracity of young Philip's account.

The reader's sense of uncertainty may also be cultivated by the Roths' experiences of two different police officers during their trip to Washington, D.C. In the first instance, while looking upon the majesty of the Capitol Building, the Roths are approached by a motorcycle cop. "My mother," Philip recounts, "enthralled only a moment earlier by the dwarfing majesty of the Capitol, immediately went pale, and her voice was so feeble when she tried to speak that she couldn't be heard above the traffic" (*Plot,* 58). Like Bess Roth, perhaps, the reader expects the worst, certainly given much of what has seemed to precede this interaction. When the officer actually helps the family by holding up traffic before guiding them to their hotel, those expectations are possibly revealed to be misplaced. Just as the reader is getting comfortable, however, the uncertainty returns when Bess asks her husband, "But how do you know where he's taking us?" (*Plot,* 58). It is an uncertainty compounded by the Roths' second encounter with a police officer, the one who is called when Herman objects to the Roths' eviction from their hotel. The unspoken assumption of the Roths, and, perhaps, of the reader, is that the Roths' ejection is the product of anti-Semitism backed up, in this case, by the power of the state. "This policeman knows why we were evicted," cries Herman. "He knows, the manager knows, everybody in this lobby knows" (*Plot,* 70–71). That Herman Roth is right about the reason for their eviction from the hotel seems undeniable, and yet, his use of the phrase "everybody . . . knows" might cast doubt upon the certainty of the assumption. He had previously employed the phrase in his response to Rabbi Bengelsdorf's endorsement of Lindbergh (*Plot,* 35). Given the history of that claim in the Roth canon, it may be that the reader is forced to question whether Herman Roth is a voice of reason in a wilderness of insanity, or a member of the group that Sandy calls "paranoid ghetto Jews" (*Plot,* 227).

Assuming, momentarily at least, that Herman Roth is right about the second cop, we see how the author juxtaposes two different versions of America: one in which the authority figures treat all men and women equally, and one in which they embody prejudice. Such juxtaposition is a common motif in the text. Most obviously, perhaps, there is the contrast between the ideals espoused by the text of the Gettysburg Address inscribed at the Lincoln Memorial, that which promises that "all men are created equal," and the hostile interaction with the man who calls Herman Roth "a LOUDMOUTH JEW" (*Plot,* 65).[61] In these moments the reader, like the characters, is unsure about which is the "true America," or, if indeed, there is one. Ross Posnock argues that Roth encourages his readers to challenge "the inveterate American reflex to look through artifice to the (alleged) real, as if the two are neatly separable and antithetical. Roth, in short, seeks to challenge the cherished and abiding myth of the natural."[62]

It is, nevertheless, not always clear that Roth, the author of *The Plot Against America,* is as successful at achieving his goal of unknowingness as he is in other texts.[63] Many of the difficulties here seem to arise from the way in which Roth chooses to double his narrator in this novel. As has been noted, Roth makes frequent use of the literary doppelgänger, the doubled and sometimes even tripled narrator creating a polyphonic text in which it is difficult to take at face value almost anything anybody says: a perfect recipe for unknowingness. In *Plot,* however, Roth offers a doubling of the author, but one that may paradoxically serve to bolster rather than to undercut the narrator's account. Roth makes clear that the story that is being recounted by an adult who is seeking to re-create the naivety he felt as a child. This, writes Ginevra Geraci, "is why the narrator's voice can at times become ambiguous when older Philip steps in and the reader experiences a sudden transition in perspective from the supposedly naïve boy to the more experienced adult."[64] What Geraci sees as a source of ambiguity is, however, rather more likely to be a source of narrative knowingness in that it adds authority to the text, with the adult Philip possibly verifying the insights of the child and thereby undermining some of the unknowingness that the author seeks to achieve elsewhere in the text. This may, in part, be why *Plot* has produced so many knowing readings.

Discussing the origins of *The Plot Against America,* Roth noted that in December 2000 he was reading Arthur Schlesinger's autobiography when he came across a reference to a group of isolationists who sought to run Lindbergh for president in 1940. "It made me think," he later wrote, "'What if they had?' and I wrote the question in the margin. Between writing down that question and the fully evolved book there were three years of work, but that's how the idea came to me."[65] This was, of course, prior to the inauguration of George W. Bush, and long before Bush—then something of an isolationist who argued against an expansive foreign policy in his debates with Al Gore—began the wars for which his administration will probably be remembered. It was before the Department of Homeland Security, the PATRIOT Act, covert surveillance of American citizens, and before the president famously appeared in a flight suit on the deck of the aircraft carrier the USS *Abraham Lincoln* to declare "Mission Accomplished" in Iraq. That the idea came to Roth before any of these events does not, of course, mean that they did not influence him, nor that they might not have consciously or unconsciously seeped into his text. The belief that they had and did was, nevertheless, a commonplace in the popular response to the novel.

In his review of *The Plot Against America* in the *Washington Post,* Jonathan Yardley sought to put aside "the novel's subtext, which gives every appearance of being an attack on George W. Bush and his administration," but failed to do so, arguing:

> That Roth has written *The Plot Against America* in some respects as a parable for our times seems to me inescapably and rather regrettably true. When the fictional Lindbergh flies around the country "to meet with the American people face-to-face and reassure them that every decision he made was designed solely to increase their security and guarantee their well-being," the post-9/11 rhetoric of George W. Bush is immediately called to mind, as is the image of Bush aboard the aircraft carrier when Roth describes the "young president in his famous aviator's windbreaker."[66]

Likewise, responding to a suggestion, made by Ron Rosenbaum in the *New York Observer*, that Steven Spielberg should make a movie of the novel—albeit as a response to the perceived anti-Semitism of Mel Gibson's *The Passion of the Christ*[67]—Keith Gessen agreed, arguing: "But [Spielberg] must literalize Roth's metaphors: '1940' is actually 2001; 'Lindbergh' is, of course, W.; the craven antiwar lies of the America Firsters are in fact the craven pro-war lies of the American Enterprise Institute; and 'American Jews,' believers in the American Constitution and pursuers of the American Dream whose rights and protections are slowly stripped away by a hostile government and a mostly indifferent population, are, of course, Arab-Americans."[68] Writing in the *Nation*, James Wolcott declared: "Set in the 1940s, *The Plot Against America* is nevertheless pure now, the sword-flash ferocity of *Sabbath's Theater*, *I Married a Communist* and *The Human Stain* subsiding into deep foreboding, the taunting jack-o'-lantern grin of George W. Bush haunting the back of the mind as one consumes the pages." Recognizing *Plot* as an artistic as well as a political achievement, Wolcott nevertheless subsumed the former under the latter. "Roth," he wrote, "doesn't make over-explicit the parallels between America's fall to fascism under Lindbergh and Bush's fear-based presidency. He doesn't need to. The parallels are so richly implicit, they vibrate like harp strings, dissolving the distance between then and now, fact and fiction."[69]

While a number of critics on the left were all too eager to see in *Plot* an allegory for the first Bush term, many on the right also chose to underplay the literary aspects of the novel in favor of a political reading of the text and/or the Left's response to it. The conservative commentator Diana West identified those who read the text as an allegory for post–September 2001 politics as belonging to "a Left blinded by its hatred of President Bush," who "read about a fantasy-fascist in the White House who persecutes the Jewish minority, and, instead of yelling 'Claptrap!' they call for George W. Bush's head on an electoral platter."[70] Demonstrating a combination of literary sensitivity and an acute lack of self-awareness, Stephen Schwartz of the *Weekly Standard* noted that "it was doubtless foreordained that certain reviewers would try to read into Roth's latest novel something completely absent from its pages . . . [but] [o]ne can no more link Roth's new book with the politics of the reelected president than with the corruption of President Harding, or, for that matter, the mystery of the Easter Island statues," before suggesting that "one could draw much more apt comparisons between the stagey heroics of Lindbergh and John F. Kerry's ludicrous posturing at the Democratic convention, or between the corporation-bashing legal careers of Burton K. Wheeler and John Edwards."[71] Bill Kaufman, on the other hand, writing in the *American Conservative,* offered a typically unexpected and iconoclastic take on the novel. "Philip Roth's *The Plot Against America,*" he observed, "is the novel that a neoconservative would write, if a neoconservative could write a novel." It was, he said, possibly "meant to serve as the writing sample in Roth's application for a speechwriter job in the Bush administration." For Kaufman, Roth's novel bespoke an elite-driven, warmongering, interventionist foreign policy that ignored the massive human cost of America's intervention in World War II. "Campaigning in 'the remotest rural counties,' Lindbergh wins in a landslide," writes Kaufman, "the Republicans take Congress, and the threat of peace, no conscription, and full enjoyment of the Bill of Rights darkens the Rothian sky. To young Philip's parents, America is good only insofar as it sends its sons to die in foreign lands." "Unwashed Americans," he continues, "who live in places like North Dakota or Minnesota or Montana, mean harm to the Roths; their reluctance to send their sons to transatlantic graves is presented as a particularly insidious symptom of anti-Semitism." Mixing his aesthetic with political concerns—he suggests that Roth is "mediocrity . . . at the typewriter" who writes in "sodden clichés," "*Time-Life* prose," and offers "not a felicitous sentence," "spark of wit or a single subversive thought"—Kaufman concludes: "This is a repellent novel, bigoted and libelous of the dead, dripping with hatred of rural America, of Catholics, of any Middle American who has ever dared stand against the war machine. All that is left, I suppose, is for the author to collect his Presidential Medal of Freedom."[72]

That the novel should produce such a plethora of knowing readings might suggest that *Plot* fails in the same way as *Our Gang.* Certainly there seem to be a number of readers who have come away from the text with little more than the knowing politics that they brought to it. For many of these readers there appears to have been very little disorientation or transfiguration, literary or political. For these readers, novels appear to have political messages, and reading is the process of discerning the author's views and celebrating, or condemning, them to the extent that they agree with their own political outlook. It might be argued, however, that such readings reveal more about the reader than they do about the text.[73] While it has been suggested that Roth himself might be held responsible for the knowing readings of *Our Gang*—precisely because the text offered little opportunity for anything else—his culpability for such readings of *The Plot Against America* is much less clear. Many other readers showed themselves sensitive to the ambiguities of the text, noting the ways in which it tempted the reader into the sort of conflation of worlds evidenced by politically motivated critics from both sides of the aisle, but which ultimately frustrated such readings in productive ways.

Although some wished to ascribe to Paul Berman the sort of reading outlined by James Wolcott, Berman's take on *The Plot Against America* was rather more subtle and revealing of how unknowing texts might offer their readers an opportunity for critical reflection. "Not once," writes Berman, "does Roth glance at events of the present day, not even with a sly wink. Still, after you have had a chance to inhabit his landscape for a while and overhear the arguments about war and fascism and the Jews, 'The Plot Against America' begins to rock almost violently in your lap—as if a second novel, something from our own time, had been locked inside and was banging furiously on the walls, trying to get out." As for the parallels between the written and unwritten worlds, writes Berman, "I have my opinions on these matters, and so does everyone else, and so does Philip Roth, I imagine. But Roth has kept his opinions to himself. 'The Plot Against America' is not an allegorical tract about the present age, with each scene or character corresponding to events of our own time."[74] Likewise, Michiko Kakutani, though somewhat dismissive of the book, notes unknowingness in the text that some of its more strident champions and critics seem to have missed. "'The Plot Against America'" she writes, "is a novel that can be read, in the current Bush era, as either a warning about the dangers of isolationism or a warning about the dangers of the Patriot Act and the threat to civil liberties."[75]

That different readers can take different things from the same text is, of course, no surprise. That so many readers should take so many—often diametrically opposed—readings from the same text suggests, however, that the text in question is rather more unknowing than knowing. This is, perhaps, what makes it such a fecund source of political debate and discussion, even if the former—at least—is simply the shrill exchange of previously held position statements. While there will always be knowing readers about whom an author can do little, there are others for whom the text will offer the possibility of critical reflection. Certainly, some readers might come away from the text more sensitive to state encroachment upon their civil rights in a time of emergency; others to the way in which politicians twist language to their own advantage; others still to prejudice; and some to the politics of political demagoguery. Nevertheless, it may be that if Roth has any intent at all in his texts, it is to cultivate in his readers the same sense of unknowingness that fuels his art. This unknowingness may be the most political product of all: cultivating in the reader the possibility of an attitude and ethos appropriate to democratic politics.

Plots Against Dogma

Roth, it has been argued, employs multiple devices in *The Plot Against America* to offer a narrative that he also undercuts. While this undercutting is not as thoroughgoing as in say, *The Counterlife* or *Operation Shylock*, there are sufficient moments in the text to suggest that what Philip the narrator perceives may not be what—or all that—is going on. Likewise, Roth the author juxtaposes worlds, most obviously by offering an appendix to the book that includes, among other things, "A Note to the Reader." "*The Plot Against America*," Roth observes there, "is a work of fiction. This postscript is intended as a reference for readers interested in tracking where historical fact ends and historical imagining begins" (*Plot*, 364). Indeed, he also offers "A True Chronology of the Major Figures," an account of "Other Historical Figures in the Work," and "Some Documentation." Rather like a magician explaining his trick, Roth seems keen to ensure that the reader engage in the desired juxtaposition. Neither world is, the comparison suggests, complete: certainly Roth's final account of the unwritten-world Lindbergh is somewhat truncated.[76] Additionally, Lindbergh's disappearance from the text—though possibly a little too narratively convenient—leaves readers wondering as to the president's real motives. The reader must weigh the story of an anti-Semite intent on putting his views into political practice against the story of man blackmailed by a Nazi regime holding his kidnapped son hostage. It is, however, in the very first line of the novel that the unknowingness so beneficial to democratic politics is most clearly signaled.

"Fear presides over these memories," writes the adult Philip, "a perpetual fear" (*Plot*, 1). An underexamined question is, perhaps, why it is fear "*presides* over" the memories, as opposed to, say, "permeating" them. This difference suggests that it is not the child who is afraid but rather the adult.[77] If this is indeed the case, it raises the question of why, or of what, the narrator is afraid. A number of critics—such as Paul Berman—have identified Sinclair Lewis's *It Can't Happen Here* as a forerunner to Roth's text. Roth himself alludes to the novel in Mayor La Guardia's eulogy for Walter Winchell (*Plot,* 305). In the *New York Times,* Roth asserted that the "American triumph is that . . . it didn't happen here." "Why it didn't happen," he noted, "is another book, one about how lucky we Americans are."[78] It is, perhaps, such observations that lead Bill Kauffman to declare that "*The Plot Against America* is the sort of novel a bootlicking author might write to curry favor with a totalitarian government. The author puts a fictive gloss over the officially sanctioned history. Thank God things happened as they did! The alternative to the regime was madness, chaos, murder."[79] There is, Kauffman argues, a smugness about America and its values underpinning the text. Although Roth—who, Pierpont tells us, displayed a flag from the balcony of his apartment following the 2001 attacks on New York City—has articulated what might be called a "Clintonian" version of patriotism, one in which what is wrong with America can be fixed with what is right with America,[80] Kaufman could not be more wrong about the alleged complacency of Roth's novel. Roth says of *Plot* that his point is not "that this can happen and will happen; rather, it's that at the moment when it should have happened, it did not happen."[81] This is not complacency, it is history, but *Plot* suggests that it could have been otherwise. Roth identifies what he calls "the maxim that informed the writing" of the book, one "that makes our lives as Americans as precarious as anyone else's: all the assurances are provisional, even here in a 200-year-old democracy."[82] As such, the novel is driven by the unknowingness of what Roth calls "the relentless unforeseen."

"Turned wrong way round," the adult Philip declares in *Plot,* "the relentless unforeseen was what we schoolchildren studied as 'History,' harmless history, where everything unexpected in its own time is chronicled on the page as inevitable. The terror of the unforeseen is what the science of history hides, turning a disaster into an epic" (*Plot,* 113–14). It is a claim that echoes and is echoed by recent works of democratic theory, most obviously, perhaps, Bonnie Honig's *Emergency Politics,* which draws attention to the contingency of that we take for granted. "Our moral clarity regarding identities or forms of life that were once but are no longer excluded is a product of political victories" writes Honig; "victorious political actors *created* post hoc the clarity we now credit with having spurred them on to victory ex ante."[83] "Things," Honig suggests, "could have gone another way. They may yet do so."[84] This is, perhaps, the awareness of precariousness and provisionality generated by Roth's "what if?" Indeed, it might be argued that this "what if?" is the suppressed term in in almost all political thought.

In this, the unknowingness that Roth depicts in his written world is potentially transferred to his readers in the unwritten. This not only alerts them to the possibility that while *it*—in this case, fascism, but which could be all manner of catastrophes—didn't happen here, it still could, but it also provides them with an awareness of their own contingency, one that might help them prevent or deal with such an event. "But history," as Roth notes, embracing the unknown, "has the final say."[85]

Notes

1. Philip Roth, *Shop Talk: A Writer, His Colleagues, and Their Work* (New York: Vintage, 2002), 100.

2. Philip Roth, *Reading Myself and Others* (New York: Vintage, 2001), 155; hereafter cited parenthetically as *Reading*.

3. Roth borrows the term "written and unwritten worlds" from Paul Goodman, ibid., xiii. For further discussion of this distinction, see Simon Stow, "Written and Unwritten America: Roth on Reading, Politics, and Theory," *Studies in American Jewish Literature* 24 (2003): 77–87.

4. Derek Parker Royal, "Plots Against America: Language and the Comedy of Conspiracy in Philip Roth's Early Fiction," in *Playful and Serious: Philip Roth as a Comic Writer*, ed. Ben Siegel and Jay L. Halio (Newark: University of Delaware Press, 2010), 118.

5. Philip Roth, "The Story behind *The Plot Against America*," *New York Times*, September 19, 2004, www.nytimes.com/2004/09/19/books/review/19ROTHL.html?pagewanted=all&module=Search&mabReward=relbias%3Ar%2C%7B%221%22%3A%22RI%3A5%22%7D&_r=0.

6. The term "the political" is drawn from the work of Chantal Mouffe. "'The political,'" she writes, "refers to this dimension of antagonism which can take many forms and can emerge in diverse social relations. It is a dimension that can never be eradicated. 'Politics,' on the other hand, refers to the ensemble of practices, discourses and institutions that seeks to establish a certain order and to organize human coexistence in conditions which are always potentially conflicting, since they are affected by the dimension of 'the political'" (Mouffe, *Agonistics: Thinking The World Politically* [London: Verso, 2013], 2–3).

7. See, for example, Joseph H. Lane Jr. "The Stark Regime and American

Democracy: A Political Interpretation of Robert Penn Warren's *All the King's Men*," *American Political Science Review*, 95, no. 4 (2001): 811–28.

8. See, for example, Martha C. Nussbaum, *Poetic Justice. The Literary Imagination and Public Life* (Boston: Beacon, 1995); and Richard Rorty, *Contingency, Irony, and Solidarity* (Cambridge: Cambridge University Press, 1989). For an insightful discussion of these arguments, see Joshua Landy, *How to Do Things with Fictions* (Oxford: Oxford University Press, 2014).

9. Arthur C. Danto, *The Transfiguration of the Commonplace: A Philosophy of Art* (Cambridge: Harvard University Press, 1983).

10. See, for example, William Connolly, *Pluralism* (Durham, NC: Duke University Press, 2005); and William Connolly, *A World of Becoming* (Durham, NC: Duke University Press, 2010). This is not, it should be noted, an argument for ethical criticism of the sort identified by Wayne C. Booth. Booth is concerned with the ways in which texts might be said to be good or bad. The argument here is concerned less with categorizing than with identifying how texts might work to political or theoretical effect.

11. See, for example, the excellent discussion in Ella Myers, *Worldly Ethics: Democratic Politics and Care for the World* (Durham, NC: Duke University Press, 2013).

12. Indeed, "paranoid fantasist" might serve as another name for Roth's chosen profession. That "Smitty" is only "purportedly" an author further emphasizes the point.

13. Alexander Nehamas, *The Art of Living: Socratic Reflections from Plato to Foucault* (Berkeley: University of California Press, 1998), 7.

14. The desire to reduce literary texts by denying their creativity is, perhaps, akin to the "deflationary tendency" in political theory identified by J. Peter Euben. For Euben, who borrows the term from Peter Dews, this "deflationary tendency" is evident in political theory that ignores the imaginative aspects of epic thought in favor of "thin" theories of social and political life (see Euben, *Platonic Noise* [Princeton: Princeton University Press, 2003], 33–34).

15. Daniel Sandstrom, "My Life as a Writer: Interview with Philip Roth," *New York Times*, March 2, 2014, www.nytimes.com/2014/03/16/books/review/my-life-as-a-writer.html?_r=0.

16. Philip Roth, "An Open Letter to Wikipedia," *New Yorker*, September 6, 2012, www.newyorker.com/books/page-turner/an-open-letter-to-wikipedia.

17. Derek Parker Royal, "Pastoral Dreams and National Identity in *American Pastoral* and *I Married a Communist*," in *Philip Roth: New Perspectives on an American Author*, ed. Royal (Santa Barbara, CA: Praeger, 2005), 194.

18. Claudia Roth Pierpont, *Roth Unbound. A Writer and His Books* (New York: Farrar, Straus and Giroux, 2013), 127.

19. Sandstrom, "My Life as a Writer."

20. Paul Berman, "Review: *The Plot Against America*," *New York Times*, Octo-

ber 3, 2004, www.nytimes.com/2004/10/03/books/review/03BERMAN.html? pagewanted=all&_r=1&.

21. As Claudia Franziska Brühwiler notes, Roth was keen to reiterate his non-polemical stance in press interviews following the release of *Exit Ghost*. He was not, he said, "out to make fiction into a political statement. Rather, I'm out to do what fiction and only fiction does: to portray in a sustained narrative those who did make political statements" (Brühwiler, "Political Awakenings: Political Initiation in *The Plot Against America*," *Transatlantica* 2 [2007]: 3).

22. Pierpont, *Roth Unbound*, 112.

23. John Rawls, *A Theory of Justice* (Cambridge: Belknap Press of Harvard University Press, 1971). In this, literature and the literary aspects of political thought might be thought to show us something in a weaker sense of the verb "to show"—the way a car dealer or a Realtor might "show" us other options that make us reflect critically upon our initial choices—rather than in the stronger sense more associated with knowing accounts of the author and the text in which either or both "show" us in the sense of an evidentiary proof for something believed to be true. For a further discussion of this distinction, see Simon Stow, *Republic of Readers? The Literary Turn in Political Thought and Analysis* (Albany: State University of New York Press, 2007).

24. See, for example, Karl Popper, *The Open Society and Its Enemies* (Princeton: Princeton University Press, 1994). For less knowing, and thus more compelling, readings of Plato, see Danielle Allen, *What Plato Wrote* (Malden, MA: Wiley-Blackwell, 2010); and John Seery, *Political Returns: Irony in Politics and Theory, from Plato to the Antinuclear Movement* (Boulder, CO: Westview, 1990).

25. Not least, perhaps, because he has often made it clear that he expects so little of the reading public. Roth complained to Claudia Roth Pierpont that people in New York only wish to discuss movies. Similarly, in his interview with Sandstrom in the *New York Times* he celebrates "the fact that writers really don't mean a goddamn thing to nine-tenths of the population doesn't hurt. It's inebriating" (Sandstrom, "My Life as a Writer").

26. Updike says that Roth sees "the act of writing as a means of really reshaping the world to your liking" (Mick Brown, "John Updike: Descent of Man," *Daily Telegraph*, October 26, 2008, www.telegraph.co.uk/culture/donotmigrate/3562574/John-Updike-descent-of-man.html). While J. M. Coetzee says of *The Plot Against America*, "Roth has not concocted this lengthy fantasy of an America in thrall to the Nazis simply as a literary exercise" (Coetzee, "What Philip Knew," *New York Review of Books*, November 18, 2004, www.nybooks.com/articles/archives/2004/nov/18/what-philip-knew/).

27. Certainly the long history of pronouncements by multiple different Philip Roths makes any simple statement of the author's aims and views deeply problematic.

28. As far as overreading is concerned, it is perhaps telling that knowing readings are ascribed to the least attractive characters in the text and that one of the most sympathetic characters in the text, Faunia Farley, pretends not to be able to read at all (Stow, "Written and Unwritten America," 81).

29. The critical response, or lack thereof, to *Our Gang* is nicely summarized in Till Kinzel, "Philip Roth's *Our Gang*, the Politics of Intertextuality and the Complexities of Cultural Memory," *Philip Roth Studies*, 9, no. 1 (2013): 15–25.

30. Jonathan Yardley, review, "PHILIP ROTH *Novels & Stories, 1959–1962, Library of America. 913 pp. $35. PHILIP ROTH Novels 1967–1972, Library of America. 671 pp. $35*," *Washington Post*, August 28, 2005, www.washingtonpost.com/wp-dyn/content/article/2005/08/25/AR2005082501470.html.

31. In a footnote to the interview "On *Our Gang*," Roth notes: "My remarks here grew out of a lengthy conversation I had with a Random House executive who in 1971 was uneasy about publishing *Our Gang*. He objected to the book principally on grounds of taste; he also wondered if it might not be politically counterproductive—that is, if one could imagine it having any political effect at all. Since there would doubtless be other readers who would share the publisher's point of view, I asked Alan Lelchuk . . . if he would help me extend my thoughts on the subjects or satire, Nixon, and *Our Gang*" (*Reading*, 37). Among those who were offended by *Our Gang* were Nixon and his chief of staff, H. R. Haldeman. Haldeman said of the book, it's "a ridiculous book. It's sickening"; "It's sick, you know, a perverted kind of thing," while his boss was moved to observe of Roth: "He's a horrible moral leper" (Jon Wiener, "When Nixon Asked Haldeman about Philip Roth," *L.A. Review of Books*, January 26, 2014, https://lareviewofbooks.org/essay/nixon-asked-haldeman-philip-roth).

32. Margaret Anne Daniel argues otherwise, but I can see no evidence for this claim (Daniel, "Philip Roth, MVP: *Our Gang, The Breast*, and *The Great American Novel*," in *Philip Roth: New Perspectives*, 60).

33. I am, however, not sure I can think of any.

34. The alternative to "straight" readings is suggested by Eric Naiman in his *Nabokov, Perversely* (Ithaca, NY: Cornell University Press, 2010).

35. Plato, *Gorgias*.

36. Dwight McDonald, "Our Gang," *New York Times*, November 7, 1971, www.nytimes.com/books/98/10/11/specials/roth-gang.html.

37. I was reminded of this by Amy C. Oakes, author of the highly regarded, but unfunny, *Diversionary War: Domestic Unrest and International Conflict* (Palo Alto, CA: Stanford University Press, 2012).

38. I suspect that, at the mean, or even at the median, most people don't find statistics that funny.

39. Kinzel, "Philip Roth's *Our Gang*," 23.

40. See Ted Cohen, *Jokes: Philosophical Thoughts on Joking Matters* (Chicago: University of Chicago Press, 2001).

41. I will admit to laughing, once, at the following passage. "'But Secretary Lard was seen weeping as he left Walter Reed today. Surely that suggests that President Dixon is dead.' 'Not necessarily. It could just as well mean that he's alive'" (Philip Roth, *Our Gang* [New York: Vintage, 2009], 143). Keeping track of my guffaws was not, therefore, particularly difficult.

42. Pierpont, *Roth Unbound*, 73.

43. See, for example, J. D. Bloom qtd. in Kinzel, "Philip Roth's *Our Gang*," 19; and Yardley, review of "PHILIP ROTH."

44. Pierpont, *Roth Unbound*, 72.

45. Ibid., 71. The op-ed was—equally tellingly—rejected.

46. Woody Allen, *The Illustrated Woody Allen Reader*, ed. Linda Sunshine (London: Jonathan Cape, 1993), 152–53.

47. If, as Roth suggests, satire is "the imaginative flowering of the primitive urge to knock somebody's block off," then it may be that bad satire is similarly deserving of a punch in the mouth from Ernest Hemingway (*Reading*, 46).

48. Indeed, Nixon's "Justice in the Streets" initiative finds its linguistic echo in Lindbergh's "Just Folks" program in *The Plot Against America*.

49. See, for example, James Boyd White, *When Words Lose Their Meaning, Constitutions, Reconstitutions, of Language Character and Community* (Chicago: University of Chicago Press, 1985).

50. Roth has, to be sure, given many interviews in which he discusses his works, but when pushed to ascribe a particular purpose to any given text, he always demurs. Not so with *Our Gang*.

51. Roth's willingness to blame his audience for the failure of the text further suggests a decidedly knowing self-righteousness in the author that he claims to deplore in others. "In Roth's own view," notes Till Kinzel, "the reception of his book had suffered from a particular feature of the then American cultural memory," their lack of awareness a pre–Civil War tradition of eviscerating political satire (Kinzel, "Philip Roth's *Our Gang*," 18–19). Indeed, Roth suggests that the potential audience for his novel was insufficiently primed for its appearance. "Another reason," he notes, "Americans might not realize satirical writing once flourished here is that there's hardly any around today" (*Reading*, 38).

52. Pierpont, *Roth Unbound*, 72.

53. While denying the power of literature to effect social change, Roth nevertheless identifies a number of texts that have. "Even Synge's *Playboy of the Western World*," he notes, "which just toys with the idea of parricide, has been known to cause audiences in Ireland to riot" (*Reading*, 50).

54. Roth's opinions of Nixon's un-American qualities, made manifest in *Our*

Gang, are expressed most clearly in his 1974 interview published as "Writing and the Powers That Be" (*Reading*, 11).

55. Philip Roth, *The Plot Against America* (New York: Houghton, Mifflin, Harcourt, 2004), 184; hereafter cited parenthetically.

56. Joan Acocella disagrees (see her "Philip Roth's 'The Plot Against America,'" *New Yorker*, September 20, 2004, http://www.newyorker.com/archive/2004/09/20/040920crbo_books?currentPage=all).

57. Roth, "The Story Behind."

58. Cormac McCarthy's *The Road* is, perhaps, the most compelling recent example of this literary theme.

59. Neil Curtis, "Tragedy and Politics, *Philosophy & Social Criticism*, 33, no. 7 (2007): 860–79.

60. See John J. Winkler and Froma I. Zeitlin, eds., *Nothing to with Dionysos? Athenian Drama in Its Social Context* (Princeton: Princeton University Press, 1990).

61. That the Gettysburg Address itself offers such a juxtaposition, of the promise of equality embodied in the Declaration of Independence with the failure of the Constitution to offer the same, adds further resonance to this juxtaposition (see Simon Stow, "Pericles at Gettysburg and Ground Zero: Tragedy, Patriotism, and Public Mourning," *American Political Science Review*, 101, no. 2 [2007]: 195–208).

62. See Ginevra Geraci, "The Sense of an Ending: Alternative History in Philip Roth's *The Plot Against America*," *Philip Roth Studies*, 7, no. 2 (2011): 200.

63. If this is, indeed, his goal. It does not have to be for this argument to work.

64. Geraci, "The Sense of an Ending," 200.

65. Roth, "The Story Behind."

66. Jonathan Yardley, "Homeland Insecurity," *Washington Post*, October 3, 2004, www.washingtonpost.com/wp-dyn/articles/A63751–2004Sep30.html.

67. Ron Rosenbaum, "We Married a Fascist," *New York Observer*, June 21, 2004, http://observer.com/2004/06/we-married-a-fascist/.

68. Keith Gessen, "His Jewish Problem, *New York Magazine*, September 27, 2004. http://nymag.com/nymetro/arts/books/reviews/9902/index2.html.

69. James Wolcott, "The Counter Life," *Nation*, November 4, 2004, www.thenation.com/article/counter-life?page=0,2.

70. Diana West, "The Unnerving 'Plot,'" *Townhall*, October 11, 2004, http://townhall.com/columnists/dianawest/2004/10/11/the_unnerving_plot.

71. Stephen Schwartz, "American Gothic," *Weekly Standard*, November 29, 2004, www.weeklystandard.com/Content/Protected/Articles/000/000/004/936eumjm.asp?page=3.

72. Bill Kaufman, "Heil to the Chief," *American Conservative*, September 27, 2004, www.theamericanconservative.com/articles/heil-to-the-chief/.

73. Thus, for example, the Amazon.com reviewer who declared "THE PLOT

AGAINST AMERICA actually incites the very anti-semitism it condemns,"
might be thought to have revealed more about him or herself than he or she
intended (http://amazon.com/Plot-Against-America-Philip-Roth/productreviews/
1400079497/ref=cm_cr_dp_qt_hist_one?ie=UTF8&filterBy=addOneStar&show
Viewpoints=0).

74. Berman, "Review."

75. Michiko Kakutani, "A Pro-Nazi President, a Family Feeling the Effects," *New
York Times*, September 21, 2004, www.nytimes.com/2004/09/21/books/21kaku
.html. It is, perhaps, telling that in an article that otherwise offers a fine overview
of the various responses to *The Plot Against America*, Steven G. Kellman irons out
some of the nuances in the reviews he cites. Indeed, because Kakutani notes that
Plot can be read in more than one way, Kellman suggests that she has "hedged her
bets" rather than offered a complex view of a complex text (Kellman, "It Is Happening Here: *The Plot Against America* and the Political Moment," *Philip Roth
Studies*, 4, no. 2 [2008]: 113–23).

76. There is no mention, for example, of the aviator's other families in Germany
and Switzerland, at least the first of which was known to the public prior to the
publication of *Plot*. Such details confirm, perhaps, Roth's claim that reality is constantly throwing up figures that might not be believed were they to appear in fiction ("Lindbergh Fathered 'Two Families," bbc.co.uk, November 29, 2003. http://
news.bbc.co.uk/2/hi/europe/3249472.stm; and Penelope Gree, "But Enough
About Them," *New York Times*, April 17, 2008, www.nytimes.com/2008/04/17/
garden/17lindbergh.html?pagewanted=all).

77. A now archaic meaning of "to preside," according to the *Oxford English
Dictionary*, is "to play," as in a piano or other instrument. It might not be too much
to suggest that the narrator is playing (with) his memories to produce an experience in the reader.

78. Roth, "The Story Behind."

79. Kauffman, "Heil to the Chief."

80. As is suggested by Pierpont's account of Roth's debates with Harold Pinter
(Pierpont, *Roth Unbound*, 158–59).

81. Roth, "The Story Behind."

82. Ibid.

83. Bonnie Honig, *Emergency Politics: Paradox, Law, Democracy* (Princeton:
Princeton University Press, 2009), 47.

84. Ibid., 49.

85. Roth, "The Story Behind."

4

Four Pathologies and a State of Sanity

Political Philosophy and Philip Roth on the Individual in Society

Michael G. Festl

The most important task of political philosophy is the normative evaluation of society. This evaluation means separating the aspects of a societal status quo that ought to be changed from the aspects that ought to be upheld. Political philosophy criticizes the former, that is, it depicts the reasons for altering the aspects of the status quo that are in need of revision. It does so in the hope that thanks to this criticism the public will be more prone to change these aspects. Political philosophy praises, on the other hand, the aspects of society that should be upheld, that is, it renders explicit the merits of these aspects of the status quo. It does so in the hope that thanks to this affirmation the public will be more likely to cherish and, if need be, defend these aspects. Both of these endeavors—criticism and praise—must be pursued in relation to a concrete aspect of society, not as an abstract idealization. To fulfill the task thus sketched, political philosophy relies on conceptual instruments such as typologies, categories, distinctions.

As some of these conceptual instruments are applicable to an array of normative evaluations and thus of lasting concern there is—besides the evaluation side—also a conceptual side to political philosophy. The aim of this conceptual side is the construction, the improvement, and the deconstruction of the instruments recurrently relied on in concrete evaluations. Unlike the evaluations, however, the conceptual work needs to be done in the abstract, that is, without a specific aspect of society in mind. Hence, political philosophy works on two fronts: (1) it conducts concrete normative evaluations; and (2) it deals with the instruments hereby used. This is the same in dentistry, presumably in every profession. While dentistry provides concrete help to patients in operations, it, at the same time, pursues an ongoing effort to improve the instruments used in these operations. And, to linger with the analogy a bit longer, as the instruments are means for the operations (not vice versa), in dentistry as well as in political philosophy instruments get adjusted by a trial-and-error method in light of their performance in concrete operations. This explains why the conceptual toolbox of the political philosopher as well as the dentist's office looks much different today than it did, say, a century ago.

Aside from exceptions that prove the rule, novelists do not, in my opinion, help political philosophy in its normative evaluations, that is, in concrete operations. But some novelists are worth examining when it comes to the improvement of the instruments of political philosophy. Philip Roth is one of them. His work is stimulating for the conceptual side of political philosophy because much of it revolves around the influence society exerts on individuals and on the strategies individuals assume in reaction.[1] Moreover, in his novels, this mostly takes place in the United States of America in the second half of the twentieth century, a society as demanding as it gets regarding societal expectations imposed on individuals.[2] One of the overarching themes of Roth's work, as I understand it, is about individuals, often from minority groups, and their effort to find a place in American society. Roth usually treats society's expectations as a given and devotes himself to an individual's endeavor to deal with these expectations; or, as I want to put it, Roth's novels depict individuals aiming at reconciliation to society.

But, typically, these individuals fail. They fail—in richly varied and spectacular ways—in the face of a society that repeatedly leaves the desired reconciliation out of reach. And when Roth's individuals realize the unattainability of reconciliation, this often triggers the opposite reaction in them: radical protest against this very society. At times, Roth even presents what I call pathologies of reconciliation: individual efforts to reconcile to society of such enormous proportions or radical protest elicited by the reconciliation's perceived unattainability of such enormous proportions that they render a rewarding life impossible. Roth's masterpiece in this regard is the American Trilogy (AT)—a series of loosely related books that consists of *American Pastoral* (1997), *I Married a Communist* (1998), and *The Human Stain* (2000).[3] In AT, on which I will focus, Roth depicts four types of pathologies of reconciliation of individuals to the society of the United States and also leaves some traces of what a truly successful reconciliation to this society could look like—four pathologies and a state of sanity.

Why is this of relevance to the conceptual side of political philosophy? As said in the beginning, with regard to an aspect of society that deserves preservation, political philosophy needs to outline the reasons why this is the case with the aim that the public will esteem this aspect. Public affirmation of such an aspect is—at least in properly functioning democracies—necessary. Without it, society is in danger of losing something that is, according to a normative evaluation, worthy of preservation. Take, for example, social security, and let us assume that, based on an all-considered judgment, the social security system of country x *improves* the good of country x without negative effects on other countries. In such a case, the public, at least a decisive majority, needs to be aware that this is in fact the case. Otherwise, social security—a beneficial system, according to the assumption—might be reduced, maybe even abolished by the ones who do not profit from it. This is why a public needs to be reconciled to the aspects of society that should be preserved.

Political philosophy tries to contribute to that by rendering explicit the normative arguments in favor of an aspect of society that deserves preservation. To be successful in doing so it, among other things, needs to be informed of the conditions under which individuals, as the elements of which a public is made, are capable of valuing aspects of society in the first place as well as about general impediments to individuals affirming aspects of society. Without such knowledge, the efforts of political philosophy can be futile as they might miss the true causes for a public's lack of reconciliation to positive aspects of society, causes that may need to be dealt with first in order to put the desired reconciliation into effect and, as the example with social security in country x delineates, to thereby safeguard the normative achievements a society has already accomplished. Awareness of the general reasons why gaps can emerge between what deserves affirmation from a normative point of view and what is, as a matter of fact, affirmed by the public is necessary for prevailing on this front. Analogously, a successful dentist studies, first of all, the general causes for the gaps she is expected to close as well as to prevent from reemerging in the future.

In presenting different causes behind an individual's failed reconciliation to society, including the deeper psychological reasons involved, Philip Roth's AT entails fundamentals for assessing and finally getting rid of gaps between the appreciable aspects of society and the appreciated ones. This is why this essay distills AT for insights on an individual's flawed relation to society and develops—section by section—a (preliminary) typology of pathologies of reconciliation from the substance thus garnered. Whether this typology amends the political philosopher's toolbox in a useful way is to be tested in concrete normative evaluations, not in conceptual investigations like this one.[4]

As this essay belongs to political philosophy's conceptual side, not to its evaluation side, it can refrain, as far as doing so is possible, from commenting on the content to which the individuals in Roth's AT are or are not reconciled, that is, the U.S.-American value system. This is synonymous with the assumption—nothing more than an assumption!—that this value system is, at least in major parts, worthy of affirmation by individuals. Otherwise, remaining irreconcilable would be the order of the day.

Pathology One: Merry Levov and Missing Embarkment

The first pathology of reconciliation discernible in Roth's AT finds expression in Merry Levov. Merry is the daughter of *American Pastoral*'s central character, the rich, awesome-looking, successful, and extremely kind Seymour Levov, with great veneration called "the Swede," and the Swede's wife, Dawn Levov, a former Miss New Jersey who retains her looks, a hobby cattle farmer, and who is no less kind than her husband, the two of them together building one of the American "families full of tolerance and kindly, well-intentioned liberal goodwill" (*Pastoral*, 84). Except for a stutter, Merry has always looked like the logical result of perfect parents until, at the age of sixteen, during the time of the Vietnam War, she "all at once shot up, broke out, grew stout" and became "almost overnight [. . .] a large, loping, slovenly sixteen-year-old, nearly six feet tall, nicknamed by her schoolmates Ho Chi Levov" (95). She makes the opposition to America's war in Vietnam her trademark and becomes, as her uncle puts it, "the angriest kid in America" (260). She calls Lyndon B. Johnson names whenever he turns up on television: "You f-f-fucking madman! You heartless mi-mi-mi-miserable m-monster!"; when the name of some other member of the government is mentioned it can happen that Merry, in the middle of her parent's splendid house, spits on the floor in disgust (260). Soon she falls into such a maniacal opposition to the war that she bombs the local general store and thereby inadvertently kills someone. After that, she is on the run, and, as we find out later, the manslaughter she has committed does not lead her to repent but, quite the opposite, unleashes her fury even more, delivers her "from all residual fear and compunction" so that her anti-Vietnam standpoint culminates in the deliberate killing of three more people (241).

Merry's straightforward triple homicide best signifies that she is totally beyond the bounds of the value system of the country in which she lives; she trespasses with ease "that most fundamental prohibition" (241)—thou shalt not kill. What makes her case special is that her maturing, her becoming accountable for her own deeds, coincides with her transgressions. This means she has never managed to enter the circle of America's core values; she has never been reconciled to these values in the first place. Therefore, I call her pathology of reconciliation to society a failure of initiation. Merry has not been successfully ushered into the values around which the United States is built; instead, she becomes a terrorist committed to fighting these very values.

Merry, the human being behind the terrorist, is somebody we could call a short-circuit person: from childhood on, Merry desperately clings to the latest fashion and is quick to jump to the next that comes around: "She was a perfectionist who did things passionately, lived intensely in the new interest, and then the passion was suddenly spent and everything, including the passion, got thrown into a box and she moved on" (90). Thereby, the older Merry gets, the more dogmatic the worldviews at which she throws herself. There once was her love of "astronomy and before astronomy the 4-H Club," there was "Audrey Hepburn," "there was even a Catholic phase" (89). Hence, her extremism against the Vietnam War needs to count as just one of many passions along the way, but this time she "proved that being in opposition to everything decent in honky America wasn't just so much hip graffiti emblazoned on her bedroom wall" (241). And after this phase—the homicidal one—she becomes a Jain, a member of a sect that is adamant in trying to protect all life on earth, animal as well as plant life and that, hence, necessitates starvation for the strict follower of the sect. As this passion, too—the suicidal one—is more than hip graffiti to Merry; it becomes her last.

Roth tells Merry's story from the standpoint of her father and the father's desperate search for an explanation for his daughter's disruption. The most convincing of the explanations for Merry's lack of initiation that the father mulls over is that her parents failed to acquaint their daughter with a viable adult role model.[5] It all begins with the question of religion. The mother is a Catholic, the father a Jew, and Merry is initiated into neither of the two faiths. Instead, her parents, especially her father, intentionally withhold training in either faith to make sure that none of the grandparents, who hold their religions in high esteem, are offended (360). As a result, Merry feels torn and is unable to develop a serious stance with regard to religion.

Furthermore, Dawn Levov, Merry's mother, has not proved capable of developing a wholesale personality herself. As a former beauty queen who still has the look, Dawn does not want to be identified with this distinction at all, even though this aspect of her past is vital to everyone who sees her. And neither is Seymour Levov, the father, an adult against whose example Merry assesses her own standpoint because he has the habit of indulging each of his daughter's fascinations—no matter how ludicrous these or their manifestations become—with an "outsized willingness to understand"[6] instead of making clear to her the difference between being excited and being extremist. Perhaps his *"mistake* was," as he ponders at one point, "to have tried so hard to take seriously what was in no way serious; perhaps what he should have done, instead of listening so intently, so *respectfully,* to her ignorant raving was to reach over the table and whack her across the mouth" (224).[7]

If there is anything that Merry can grasp about her parents, it is their extreme beauty. But she cannot emulate this beauty in her coming of age as she has not inherited even traces of it. Therefore she decides to rebel against that beauty by ceasing to be concerned about her looks or her demeanor at all, just as she is no longer concerned about overcoming her stutter, which has been, so Roth hints, an unconscious rebellion against her parents from the start (91). Merry is hugely successful, even manages to become the "ugliest daughter ever born of two attractive parents" (227). But, just like looking beautiful, looking shitty—even world-class shitty—is not a quality around which to build a successful identity. So her father is almost exactly right when he says about his grown-up daughter that she has "gone over the edge of the ship" (228), the ship being the value system of the United States. The only problem with the metaphor is that Merry has never boarded that ship in the first place because her parents—one of the most important links between an individual born into the world and the societal value system into which an individual is born—failed when it came to their daughter's initiation.

Pathology Two: Lester Farley and Going off the Rails

Lester Farley, the Vietnam veteran who, in *The Human Stain,* forces off the street and, as a result, kills the book's protagonist, Coleman Silk, and his lover, Lester's ex-wife Faunia Farley, suffers from another type of pathology of reconciliation to society. Before going to Vietnam, Les was just a normal American, a "boy from the Berkshires who put a lot of trust in people and had no idea how cheap life could be, [. . .] happy-go-lucky Les, [. . .] tons of friends, fast cars, all that stuff," "easygoing" and "gregarious" (*Stain,* 764, 766, 1035). He went to Vietnam because his government expected him to, simple as that (768). Being the "loyal American" that he was, he even "served his country" with a second tour—"to finish the god-damn job" (764). Thus, Les does not suffer from an unsuccessful initiation; quite the opposite, as a young guy, he felt like a part of his country, and doing military service in Vietnam was part of being a part. To risk his life for his country felt natural to a young American in sync with his country's values.

Yet, after his return from the war, Les is no longer the man he used to be, let alone the man he could have become. A relaxed fellow before the war, at ease with the world, at ease with America, after his second tour in Vietnam, "he *really* doesn't belong" anymore (765). He has fallen out of the state of being reconciled to society. He "regularly" beats his wife "black and blue," he is "restless," he is a drinker, he has a "basement full of guns," he hates the government, especially the president, Bill Clinton, "that scumbag son of a bitch" (731, 766, 770, 901, 1029). He becomes the Vietnam vet of the most nightmarish form, his inner torment reaching climax in the already mentioned double murder. The only place Les can find a little peace is in unstained nature—unstained from human presence—and he aspires to the "motto," "If man has to do with it, stay away from it" (1038).[8] With post-Vietnam Lester Farley, Roth depicts a guy as unreconciled to society as it gets. Because Les was once in harmony with the society in which he was born and raised and now is no longer reconciled to it, I call this second pathology the failure of losing touch.

There are, in its Weberian ideal-typical form,[9] two sorts of dynamic that can cause this pathology. When explaining Les and his change from being in sync with society to one of the severest cases of being out of sync, Roth focuses on the personality change Les experienced in Vietnam, his personal suffering from seeing so much suffering and violence, his post-traumatic stress disorder. The alienation Les feels when around other people (maybe with the exception of fellow veterans) finds its root in having "seen and done things so outside what these people"—that is, Americans not having fought in Vietnam—"know about" (765). Hence, Les has lost touch with society because of a transformation *he* has undergone. The things he saw fellow Americans doing in Vietnam—cutting off ears would count among the more civilized acts (764–65)—as well as what *he* got used to doing as an American soldier and thus officially in the name of his own value system, were clearly among the things this very value system had educated him never ever to do. This discrepancy, the mother of all cognitive dissonances, makes it impossible for him to reconnect to the societal value system into which he had once been successfully initiated. For Les there is no way back to where he used to be because he no longer is the guy he once was, the one in harmony with America. The dynamic behind the failure of losing touch thus described is that the individual has had experiences that drove her away from her former value system. The value system remains the same; the individual changes.

Besides this recapitulation, Roth also narrates traces into the character of Les that lead to the second sort of ideal-typical dynamic that underlies getting out of touch: a change in society to which the individual cannot adapt. This is most explicit when Roth lets Les bemoan the treatment he receives as a Vietnam veteran compared to that received by veterans of World War II (765). As opposed to World War II, which has in the United States—for very good reason—always been regarded as a just war and as part and parcel of the country's mission to make the world a better place, U.S. society has undergone a shift in its evaluation of the Vietnam War. Even during that war, a large majority of the American public stopped perceiving it—also for good reason—as a necessity from the point of view of justice and instead began to deem it a failure, even an embarrassment to America's mission to make the world a better place, maybe even as the end of pursuing this mission after all. This is why, so the interpretation could run, the country is unwilling to give the soldiers who fought this war the treatment the soldiers think they deserve and the treatment World War II veterans can take for granted.

Under the circumstances thus altered, Les is no longer capable of intermingling because his country has undergone a significant change in values that went hand in hand with how the Vietnam War was experienced, scrutinized, and investigated on the home front. Les, during that time a soldier on the ground, cannot comprehend the societal transformation that is behind the lack of appreciation he thinks he gets—and without help he never will comprehend it, let alone endorse it. Consequently, Les's reintegration into the value system of his once cherished country fails. Back from the war, Les is unable to keep track, and, finally, the norms of his country, norms to which he once firmly adhered, make him run amok. Paradoxically, from a normative perspective, this is the case *because* American society has made a step that is (at least according to a majority opinion) going in the right direction when it comes to justice. However, what Lester Farley's case underlines is that the United States should have done more to usher its Vietnam War veterans back into civilian life, that is, to help them adapt to a value system that was transformed by a war that was a failure not only on military but even more so on normative grounds.[10]

Pathology Three: Eve Frame and the Narrowing of the Frame

In *I Married a Communist*, Eve Frame brings about the social annihilation of her formerly beloved husband, the story's protagonist and celebrated radio star Ira Ringold by—in the heyday of the McCarthy era—accusing him of being a Communist spy. She is supported by the popular gossip-columnist couple Bryden Grant and Katrina Van Tassel Grant, who willingly commit themselves to her mission, even push her to go through with devastating her husband (*Communist*, 650). Among the motives for the social death warrant these three impose on Ira is an urge to do away with any traces of contamination of what they deem to be the pinnacle of the American value system.[11] This leads us to the third type of pathology.

Far from being a Communist spy directed by Russia, let alone a significant one, Ira is, as a matter of fact, a member of America's Communist Party,
which consigned him to work as a "publicity agent," as a "cheap propagandist,"
mainly through his role in a radio show (651). But in 1951–1952, the time he
gets socially slain by Eve and the Grants, it is evident that the Communist
Party does not have the power to overthrow the country's political system.[12]
More importantly, Roth describes the Ira of that time as having become a
harmless, even embarrassing figure who, with his constant, repetitive and
uncreative invectives against democracy and his rants about the United States
having turned fascist, could no longer be taken seriously.[13] His celebrity status
tamed not only the beast in him but also turned him into a travesty of the
dangerous Communist, a Don Quixote of political realities.[14] Nevertheless,
the three conspirators cannot bring themselves to spare him. Not satisfied
even after they have killed his career, they also publish a book that widely
exaggerates his importance to the Communist Party and his failures as a husband and stepfather just to make sure that he will never again gain a foothold
in the entertainment industry or in what they deem to be respected society—
they publish a book that is like "a bomb that had been thrown at him" (660).

For Eve, "a pathologically embarrassed Jew" (539) who hides her Jewish origins, the social slaying of her openly Jewish husband is not only a
welcome strike against Communism but is, most of all, her way of cleansing
herself from bearing what she perceives the stigma of being born a Jew. The
annihilation of Ira is her greatest achievement in her effort "to deodorize
life and make it palatable," an effort that is otherwise a failure in that one of
"the grandest of her projects" to do just that, namely her daughter Sylphid,
has come to hate her and tries to pay her back by "giving Mom a dose of
life's dung she'd never forget" (565).[15]

That Eve's urge to pursue perfect purity is an expression of her not
being in sync with America's value system is nicely captured in AT. In a first
step, Roth (thereby preordaining the legitimacy of the life of Coleman Silk,
the protagonist of *The Human Stain*) makes clear that Eve's covering up
of her heritage is completely legitimate, even needs to count among every
American's birthright: "You're an American who doesn't want to be your
parents' child? Fine. You don't want to be associated with Jews? Fine. You
don't want anybody to know you were born Jewish, you want to disguise
your passage into the world? You want to drop the problem and pretend
you're somebody else? Fine. You've come to the right country" (545).

But in a second step, Roth argues that the urge to become someone else turns pathological as soon as it leads to the hatred of the members of the identity one wishes to abandon. Thus, Roth continues the passage just cited with: "But you don't have to hate Jews into the bargain. You don't have to punch your way out of something by punching somebody else in the face" (545). Yet, this is exactly what Eve does with a vengeance (449). Eve's failure—and now we reach full circle with the pathology in which I am currently interested—is that she does not feel fully at ease with the part of U.S.-American society to which she wants to belong, namely the "real American Gentile aristocrat," the Eleanor Roosevelt and Nelson Rockefeller types (546–47). Feeling—due to her perceived Jewish stigma—unable to reach the desired degree of belongingness herself, she develops the need to, at least, eradicate from this part of society anybody who seems to be, in one way or another, improperly partaking in it; she attacks everyone she perceives as more on the fringes than herself. Any deviator's existence—no matter how insignificant and negligible it might have become—potentially contaminates what Eve sees as the pinnacle of America's value system and needs to be disposed of if he or she comes too close.

This turns Ira, the successful radio act who always wears his heart on his sleeves, into the perfect victim—not only is he a Jew, but, even better, he is a Jew *and* a Communist. Two birds of not belonging could be killed with one stone. On him, Eve can finally satisfy her personal craving to purify the entertainment industry of Jews, and the Grants can satisfy their craving to purify the political space of Communists. Eve's fixation on purity is mirrored in Van Tassel Grant when Roth lets us know that "impeccable" is Grant's favorite word (522). And, in this case, the whole is even more than the sum of the parts: "Eve could transform a personal prejudice [against Jews] into a political weapon by confirming for Gentile America that, . . . the Communist under every rock was, nine times out of ten, a Jew to boot" (653).[16]

Because of the urge to homogenize, to cleanse society of difference and to prevent intermingling, I want to call Eve's and the Grants' craving the pathology of purification. Although not the result of being far out of the bounds of society's value system—as was the case in the former two pathologies—their behavior is nevertheless the result of a failed reconciliation to society. Their urge to cleanse America's value system from everybody who does not have the place in society he or she is supposed to have—according to *their* definition—is an expression of a lack of reconciliation to this very value system in that it tries to realize at all cost its perceived essence. In being so unrelenting, Eve and the Grants betray that they themselves are, as a matter of fact, out of sync with an important part of America's value system: they cannot accept the tensions that are an integral element of it, its unstraightforward nature, its inner bifurcations and conflicts, its multi-dimensionality. Hence, they find no rest until the last aberration is folded away, the last Communist slain, the last loudmouth Jew muted; they find no rest until they reach what they deem to be complete order in society, total purification. Behind this failure of reconciliation there is a one-sidedness, a mere partial reconciliation to American society that wrongly plays off a per-ceived essence of this society's value system against the necessary tensions within such systems, "necessary" at least when it comes to the value systems of pluralistic democracies.

Pathology Four: The Swede's, Coleman's, and Ira's Love's Labor's Lost

Whereas the first two types of pathology stem from a lack of reconcilia-tion and the third from a mere partial reconciliation, the fourth pathol-ogy is triggered by what I call overreconciliation to society. It is the main protagonists of the three books who suffer from it: Seymour Levov, a.k.a. the Swede, *American Pastoral;* Ira Ringold, *I Married a Communist;* and Coleman Silk, *The Human Stain.* They react to America's especially highly demanding value system—"especially highly demanding" when it comes to what counts as individual achievement—by mobilizing instead of shrinking. They pursue their individual realization of the American dream, of what the American value system depicts as possible roles for the successful man, with full force. Born as potential outsiders, all three uncompromisingly strive to turn themselves into what the value system of their home country deems worthy of pursuing. They are after the American pastoral with a vengeance.

There is, first and most straightforward of all, the Swede. The char-acter-shaping event of his life is the early stardom he acquires in his Jew-ish neighborhood as the local hero of the school's baseball, football, *and* basketball team. Beyond that, he is admired for his astonishingly good and extravagant looks, which earn him his nickname. As a result, "everywhere he looked, people were in love with him" (8). But the Swede does not, say, turn this adulation into self-adulation; instead, he reacts precisely in the way society expects its heroes to react: aware that "[a]ll the pleasures of his younger years were American pleasures," aware that "everything that gave meaning to his accomplishments had been American" (*Pastoral*, 199), he develops a "golden gift for responsibility" toward his family, toward his fellow citizens, toward his country (9). This responsibility manifests itself in an endeavor to live the even-beating-the-textbook American life, a "heroically idealistic maneuver," a "strategic, strange spiritual desire to be a bulwark of duty and ethical obligation" (76). He strives to become "superordinary Swede" (82).

Born in 1927, the Swede, needless to say, joins the marines as early as possible in order to do his part in World War II (17). Afterward, he forsakes the life of a professional athlete and, on his father's request, takes over—with tremendous success—the family's glove business. Following the father's wishes, however, ends for the Swede where the beating-the-textbook American life begins so that, when push comes to shove, his allegiance to country prevails over his allegiance to father. Hence, although not fitting into his father's imagination of a Jewish life, the Swede falls in love and marries the kind of girl America presumably expects its heroes to have: a beauty queen, a "shiksa. Dawn Dwyer. He'd done it" (18). Although it does not fit his father's imagination of a practical house in a prosperous Jewish neighborhood, he buys an all-American house, a castle-like brick structure dating back to the eighteenth century, all the way to America's beginnings, surrounded by vast lands on as frontier-like a place as it gets when you need to commute to Newark on a daily basis (290).[17] Last but not least, he dreams the dream of the happy father with the sweet little daughter playing in the garden on the swing he made for her.

And it all works out great, with the Swede "liv[ing] in America the way he lived inside his own skin" (199). But then it doesn't: sweet little, short-circuit Merry—we have already gotten to know her—bombs the local general store and thereby destroys his American pastoral. In order to preserve the notion that he is still intact, and with that, society's expectation that "this mythic character the Swede had no limits" (69), he needs to supplement his "golden gift for responsibility" (9) by reactivating one more quality that he has acquired as a young sports hero but that could lay dormant since his having quit sports: "bearing burdens and taking shit," what he had to do back then since the opposing teams always concentrated their energies on stopping him (67). This reawakened quality even enables him to frequent the local general store to drink his coffee and read his mail—although it is the successor to the very store that had fallen prey to his daughter's rage (163)—just to pretend that nothing can happen that disturbs the Swede's oneness with America. And then his marriage breaks down after he finds out that his wife, Dawn—because she is unable to deal with what has become of her daughter as well as with her husband's seemingly sanguine reaction—has fled into an affair with William Orcutt, his acquaintance and in many ways his antithesis. But the Swede, more than less, prevails. As Roth relates in hindsight, he remarries and begets three sons, all of them great guys: He "had got up off the ground and he'd done it—a second marriage, a second shot at a unified life controlled by good sense and the classic restraint, once again convention shaping everything, large and small, and serving as barrier against the improbabilities" (77).

All the Swede ever longed for was a life fully filled out by America, a life not disturbed by anything chaotic, by anything in need of reconciliation to America: his purpose was "to avoid anything disjointed, anything special, anything improper, anything difficult to assess or understand" (77)—such as being Jewish *and* American at the same time, Jewish-American, such a hyphenation was too cumbersome a thing for the Swede to endure. So the role model to the role model, the Swede's Swede, so to say, is Johnny Appleseed, the Disney character, not the historical figure, because Johnny Appleseed "[w]asn't a Jew, wasn't an Irish Catholic, wasn't Protestant Christian—nope, Johnny Appleseed was just a happy American. Big. Ruddy. Happy. No brains probably, but didn't need 'em" (295). Everything Johnny Appleseed has ever done, in the Swede's imagination, just came naturally to him—without the need to think—stemming from his oneness with America, which is why the Swede enriches the tale of Johnny by saying, when Merry, still the sweet girl, asks him who told Johnny to scatter apple seeds all over the country: "Nobody told him, sweetheart. You don't have to tell Johnny Appleseed to plant trees. He just takes it on himself" (296).[18]

But the total harmony, the American pastoral that Johnny Appleseed embodies is not all there is to America, this is what Roth wants to tell us as we already saw in the previous section. And just as Eve Frame's daughter makes sure her mother gets a "dose of life's dung," the Swede's daughter guarantees her father gets a truck full of it. She ensures that he also partakes in "the fury, the violence, and the desperation of the counterpastoral—

[. . .] the indigenous American berserk" (82), or, as the Swede's brother summarizes the Swede's misery:

> You wanted Miss America? Well, you've got her, with a vengeance—she's your daughter! You wanted to be a real American jock, a real American marine, a real American hotshot with a beautiful Gentile babe on your arm? You longed to belong like everybody else to the United States of America? Well, you do now, big boy, thanks to your daughter. The reality of this place is right up in your kisser now. With the help of your daughter you're as deep in the shit as a man can get, the real American crazy shit. (259)

America as the pastoral is, according to Roth, a false or, at best, truncated concept of what this country has ever stood for.[19] But right or wrong—my country! my identity! my pipe dream! is what the heroes of the American Trilogy hurl back in defiance. The next in line is Coleman Brutus Silk, the protagonist of *The Human Stain*. In his case the desire to fully belong to the country even assumes the form of an intentional destruction of any identity on the fringes of or even opposed to his utopia of America. Coleman is of African American descent, but his light skin color invites him to cover this up, an invitation he willingly accepts. He lives—at least since having joined the navy as a young man (*Stain*, 826)—by a don't-ask-don't-tell policy; people merely assume he is a Jew of Middle Eastern descent without forcing him to elaborate too much on this. Interestingly, the thrill Coleman gets from the elements of self-invention such a life entails induces Coleman to go along with this passive lie at least as much as does the increased proximity a Jew, as opposed to an African American, had in those days to the conventional American dream (804).[20] At the same time, even this thrill of breaking free from his African American upbringing is a manifestation of Coleman's overreconciliation to his country. In experiencing this thrill, so Roth remarks, Coleman mirrors America's nativity and the challenges it involved: "To become a new being. To bifurcate. The drama that underlies America's story, the high drama that is upping and leaving" (1021).

No matter how you turn and twist the matter, Coleman's story is the story of a young man magically drawn to the American dream in its mainstream form. Even more, he is one of its embodiments, and this secures his place in the American Trilogy. Consequently, after Coleman's non-African-

American identity is firmly established, he "never again lived outside the protection of the walled city that is convention," at least not openly (1015). He became, as his brother in the novel puts it, "more white than the whites," making a career in "[a]s white a college as there was in New England," teaching "[a]s white a subject as there was in the curriculum," namely classics (1015). Needless to say, Coleman's life is a success story through and through. He almost single-handedly overhauls the college he works for and turns it into a decent institution for higher education. He is married to a good-looking and intellectually concerned wife. He preserves his young boxer's body as far as this is possible in old age. He, in short, is an epitome of America's dream-men, all the way down to the exact number of children American Perfect presumably ought to have—four—although every new child's birth presents a threat to the perpetuation of his passive lie (all his kids inherit a light skin color, though). His life is simply great—almost to the very end, until America's insistence on politically correct speech is abused by vengeful colleagues of his to label him, of all people, a racist, until his light skin eclipses his over-the-top life.

In forging his future, Coleman not merely embraces Michael Jackson's "I'm not going to spend my life being a color"[21] but uncompromisingly breaks away from his upbringing as a black. The totally exaggerated way in which he cuts himself loose—"totally exaggerated" if it were only about covering up his lie—is a manifestation of the overreconciliation in which I am interested. The strictness with which Coleman draws the identity line finds expression in three acts. First and foremost, he breaks with his mother, although she has always provided him with "conscientious kindness and care," giving him "just about anything he wanted" (792). Showing no mercy, her son Coleman Brutus tells her that for the sake of him no longer being identified as black they can see each other no more and confirms that she will never get to know her grandchildren, a heartbreaking scene that Roth captures with the following words: "There was no explanation that could begin to address the outrage of what he was doing to her" (833).[22] Second, Coleman could easily have told his truly Jewish wife "that he had been born and raised in a colored family and identified himself as a Negro nearly all his life" (825). She would have kept that secret if he had wished so, even more, thanks to her rebellious character, she would have appreciated having a husband with such a secret (825). Still, he does not tell her and prefers to lie to his own wife about the origins of his—and by then also

her—last name. Third, when posing as a young Jewish boxer and fighting a
rather untalented black guy, Coleman is advised by an important promoter
to only knock his opponent out in a later round so that the spectators get
"their money's worth" (812). Of course, he does not play along, and after the
fight, cornered by the promoter over why he could not have let the fight go
on a bit longer, retorts: "'Because I don't carry no nigger'" (813).

The trinity of Coleman's obliteration of his past identity—the atrocious
act with the mother, the blasé one with the wife, the sordid one with the
promoter—betrays, I suppose, a similar urge to the one the Swede feels
when he makes Johnny Appleseed, American raw and simple, his role
model. The Swede gave his all to reach and then to sustain his truly American identity, which for him meant keeping anything remotely chaotic at bay.
In principle, Coleman does the same—avoiding complications, living a life
as little hyphenated as possible—but even goes a step further in that he
eliminates any identity he perceives to be beyond the bounds of the inner
circle of Americandom. Becoming American through and through requires
Coleman to fully break with his mother, whereas for the Swede it merely
entailed disobeying his father once in a while.

What sets Ira Ringold, the protagonist of *I Married a Communist*,
apart from the Swede and Coleman is that he starts out with a devotion
to an identity that is not only far from the center of America's value system
but opposed to it, namely Communism, and whereas the Swede embodies America's success in business, and Coleman, America's success in the
sciences, Ira stands for the success of the American entertainment industry and, in that, for the industry with the highest lure, back in the 1940s
and 1950s, when the story of Ira unfolds, as well as today. It is precisely
this lure—the pinnacle of everything that is alluring about America—that
seals Ira's doom. Having gone through a rough childhood (early death of his
mother, a loser for a father, a Jew growing up in an Italian neighborhood,
etc.), ending up with no education proper, Ira is easily won for the Communist cause by the "Big Sweeping Ideas" (*Communist*, 456) on the imminent
proletarian revolution his self-proclaimed mentor O'Day confronts him
with. Needing him as a "publicity agent" (651), the Communist Party, so
Roth hints (441, 446), succeeds in maneuvering Ira into the position of a
celebrated national radio star.

But soon enough Ira meets and marries Eve Frame, a big-time celebrity with a giant townhouse in Greenwich Village, an insatiable urge to

clean up, as we saw in the previous section, and no Communist credentials whatsoever. Eve, in the beginning, gives Ira the time of his life: he is physically attracted to her, he shows her off, he partakes in her wealth, he walks through the doors she opens. Carried by Eve, he swiftly makes the transformation to "someone of enhanced importance," with all the "invigorating" effects such a transformation involves (456). Thereby, Ira gets enmeshed in what he came to fight, and life is no longer exclusively devoted to the world revolution and to dwelling in a "proletarian shack in the backwoods" but is also about "mating with a beautiful actress and acquiring a young mistress and fiddling with an aging whore and longing for a family and struggling with a stepchild and inhabiting an imposing house in the show-business city" (617–18). Over time Ira's Communist mission falls prey to him being in the middle of all that is valuable according to America's bourgeoisie so that he "jettisons his working-class Jewish past in order to enjoy the high life of a showbusiness star."[23]

In this somewhat twisted manner, Ira's story is also the story of someone so drawn to the American dream once he is gently touched by it that the identities that lurk outside the dream's script need to back up. Akin, at least in principle, to the Swede's abandonment of his Jewish script whenever it contradicts his concept of the beating-the-textbook American life and to Coleman's desire to completely wipe off his black origins, Ira cannot stick to his once chosen identity as a Communist, an identity that is itself served with an attractive narrative.[24] Therefore, only after the intrigue already mentioned has stripped him of his celebrity life is he capable of repenting his slippery slope into America's heart and soul: "All his ranting Ira now directed at himself. [. . .] Everything to the side of the main thing, all the peripheral stuff of existence that Comrade O'Day has warned him against. Home. Marriage. Family. Mistresses. Adultery. All the bourgeois shit!" (660).

I want to call the pathology from which the three protagonists of AT suffer the pathology of complete fixation. All three overdo the effort to reconcile to society in that they try to achieve total conformity with what they deem the pinnacle of America, conformity so strong that everything not fully fitting in needs to retreat or, in Ira's case, can no longer be upheld. Although—or is it: because?—the Swede, Coleman, and Ira were, by birth, prone to be outsiders, they shape their identity exclusively along the lines of their respective utopian vision of a harmonious America, performing "Gatsbyesque experiments in American identity."[25] Ultimately, though, they fail. With a little twist of the Swede's complaint, all three have reason to bemoan their destiny: "[W]hat is wrong with [our] life! What on earth is less reprehensible than [our] life?" (*Pastoral*, 395). Well, possibly, you tried too hard to feel worthy of America's love, so hard that America was unable to bear you in the long run—your love labor had, therefore, been doomed from the start. And thus it happened that three of her most devoted wooers got brutally rejected by America's lack of virginity: lured in, spit out, and spat on.[26]

A State of Sanity: William Orcutt and the (Un-)Bearable Lightness of Being American

Clearly, Roth's interest in AT is with the cases in which the reconciliation of an individual to society fails. Nevertheless, Roth also hints at what a true reconciliation, a successful one, could look like when he offers the concept of the "real American Gentile aristocrat" (*Communist*, 546), the one Eve Frame and her conspirators were so eager to keep clean. Roth mentions Eleanor Roosevelt and Nelson Rockefeller as prime examples of such aristocrats, people who do not suffer from any pathology of reconciliation but are in a state of sanity when it comes to their relation to society. Unlike the three protagonists of AT, these two do not suffer from any sort of maniacal clinging to society. They have no urge to belong because they can take belonging for granted. Furthermore, they are able to live with the fact that, in modern times, societal value systems are not monolithic, something Eve was unable to do. Referring to the times of Roosevelt and Rockefeller, Roth develops the latter point by ascertaining that you could, as "an intelligent, sophisticated aristocrat [. . .], unlike everyone else, [. . .] force yourself to overcome, or to appear to overcome, the contemptuous reaction to difference"—"not to be able to engage Jews easily, with good-spirited ease, would [have] morally compromise[d] a true aristocrat" of that time (546–47). "Jews"—or, as I may add, any other minority group not strong enough to significantly alter society's value system—"aren't a problem for these people. Why should they be?" (547). The true aristocrat of the Roosevelt-Rockefeller bent curbs her resentment and is able to force herself to reconcile with the fact that truly democratic societies are not cast of one piece.

More light, and especially more recent light, is shed on the concept of the "real American Gentile aristocrat" by the character William Orcutt III, the already mentioned lover of the Swede's wife, Dawn Levov. Heir to a couple of generations of aristocrats' practice, Bill does not need to force himself to accept the fact of difference. His generation takes difference for granted, or so I assume from Roth's silence on the issue when it comes to Bill. This effortless tolerance does not prevent him, however, from feeling superior to the Swede and the Swede's wife, Dawn, simply for the reason that he, Bill, is a Protestant, but the Swede "only" a Jew and Dawn "only" of Irish-Catholic descent (*Pastoral*, 282). But, to belong to the ranks of America's Gentile aristocracy it is not sufficient to have the right denomination. This must be supplemented by the appropriate ancestry, in Bill's case the family patriarch who fought with George Washington, the forebear who got promoted by Andrew Jackson, the grandfather who graduated with Woodrow Wilson from Princeton—"Orcutt could spin out ancestors forever" (286). Needless to say, an Ivy League education is also part of the deal (300). Furthermore, Bill's generation carries on the aristocratic conservationist tradition by focusing on the preservation of the countryside, in Bill's case protesting the construction of highways, jetports, and the like, "to keep the modern ills at bay," as he puts it (281). But by far the most visible manifestation of Bill's blue-bloodedness is his confidence, "superconfident Orcutt" (312). This finds expression, inter alia, in his outfit, "raspberry-colored linen pants and, hanging clear of the pants, a loose-fitting Hawaiian shirt decorated with a colorful array of tropical flora," an outfit that says: "I am William Orcutt III and I can wear what other people around here wouldn't dare to wear" (312–13).

But Bill's recurring exhibitions of the latest very bad abstract works he has painted might betray a dark side. To publicly display that he partakes in such an un-WASPian activity bespeaks, so Roth, "a secret and long-standing desire" "to be *out* of tune" (302). But rather than really betraying a dark side, I think it is better to regard Bill's persistent but always controlled urge to be otherwise as the slight flaw that is necessary to round out the concept of the "real American Gentile aristocrat," just as in classical Greek architecture a temple is only taken to be of perfect proportions if its symmetry is every now and then interrupted by slight curvatures, so slight that they remain invisible to the naked eye but not so slight that they could elude the mechanic's level.

Equipped with this perfecting flaw, Bill can take for granted that he gets whatever he wants, even Dawn, the beautiful wife of a demigod like the Swede. In doing so and opposed to Eve Frame, who needs to beat down any social climbers who get in the vicinity of her social standing, Bill simply fucks, literally, the social climber Dawn—Dawn "the laughable lace-curtain Irish, a girl who'd somehow got down the knack of aping her betters so as now to come ludicrously barging into his privileged backyard" via being married to a Jew who was able to buy himself into a part of the country that is usually fully controlled by Bill and his likes (282). Bill's cunning taken-for-grantedness, combined with his preservationism, prompts Roth to provide the following denouement of this character who bears life so lightly and whose thriving is yet so unbearable to the reader: "The humane environmentalist and the calculating predator, protecting what he has by birthright and taking surreptitiously what he doesn't have. The civilized savagery of William Orcutt" (357). That precisely an individual like Bill is completely reconciled to contemporary American society—feels in it as sound as a bell, roams it effortlessly like a fish at the top of the food chain—can be taken as an indication that there is something not quite right with this society. Thus I understand Philip Roth.

Notes

1. In a study on political initiation, Claudia Franziska Brühwiler has recently demonstrated Roth's fecundity for political studies and related disciplines, such as political philosophy (see Brühwiler, *Political Initiation in the Novels of Philip Roth* [New York: Bloomsbury, 2013]).

2. The expectations imposed on individuals in the United States are high *because* the individual has a lot of freedom when it comes to the content of her life—what she wants to believe, whom she wants to marry, what profession she wants to enter, etc. This freedom, though—and this is behind the seeming paradox that more freedom leads to more societal pressure—comes with the expectation that one should make something out of that freedom, become an achiever in whatever it might be an individual commits herself to. *Grand Expectations* is therefore the fitting title of James T. Patterson's authoritative book on the United States between 1945 and 1974. Patterson traces the surge in expectations, imposed on the individual as well as on the country, at that time back to a new rights-consciousness that emerged as a result of economic prosperity (see Patterson, *Grand Expectations. The United States, 1945–1974* [New York: Oxford University Press, 1996], chap. 19).

3. I quote AT from the Library of America edition: Philip Roth, *American*

Pastoral, in *The American Trilogy,* ed. Ross Miller (New York: Library of America, 2011), 1–395; Philip Roth, *I Married a Communist,* ibid., 397–699; Philip Roth, *The Human Stain,* ibid., 701–1038; hereafter cited parenthetically. That AT is Roth's masterpiece when it comes to individual reactions to society's expectations is the starting point of David Brauner's essay on the trilogy (see Brauner, *Philip Roth* [Manchester: Palgrave, 2007], 148).

4. The well-known criticism that it is a fallacy to look at literature when developing political philosophy because literature cannot (and mostly does not) claim to tell the truth is, therefore, not applicable to the methodology employed here. (See, on this debate, Simon Stow, *Republic of Readers? The Literary Turn in Political Thought and Analysis* [Albany: State University of New York Press, 2007].) I search literature for clues with which to develop the instruments of political philosophy, but then these instruments need to stand on their own: literature is their midwife, not their guardian. Anyway, the idea that philosophy must not be permeated by literature gathers real momentum only under the assumption that there is a gulf separating literature from philosophy because the latter deals with eternal truths or something similar (it is no coincidence that this idea goes back to Plato), a conviction to which the understanding of political philosophy I offer here is not committed.

5. Brühwiler, *Political Initiation,* 106.

6. Till Kinzel, *Die Tragödie und Komödie des amerikanischen Lebens: Eine Studie zu Zuckermans Amerika in Philip Roths Amerika-Trilogie* (Heidelberg: Winter, 2006), 131, my translation.

7. The "helpless parent" is, as Brühwiler demonstrates, a characteristic part of contemporary novels about adolescents on the path to becoming terrorists (*Political Initiation,* 99).

8. For Les's longing for unstained nature as a manifestation of a misguided urge to purify—one of the leitmotifs of AT—see Kinzel, *Tragödie und Komödie,* chap. 4, sec. 12, as well as the next section of this essay.

9. Max Weber, "Objectivity in Social Sciences and Social Policy," in *The Methodology of the Social Sciences,* ed. and trans. A. Shils and H. A. Finch (New York: Free Press, 1949), 90.

10. With Les's character, Roth also ponders whether, even worse, the efforts that are actually being made to reacclimatize Vietnam veterans actually might exacerbate their sense of alienation. For Les the celebrations on Veterans Day make it even worse. Being cheered while marching in the parade makes him feeling as if he is being mocked: "*Now* he was supposed to be in some two-bit parade and march around while a band played and everyone waved the flag? *Now* it was going to make everybody feel good for a minute to be recognizing their Vietnam veterans? How come they spit on him when he came home if they were so eager to see him out there now?" (*Stain,* 933). On Veterans Day, people like Les "are more

disgusted with their compatriots, their country, and their government than on any other day of the year," so Roth ascertains (993), thus touching on what I think is a vital point when it comes to any sort of societal appreciation of individual action: idealistic veneration, such as a Day of Honor, can add value but only if it rests on a solid material foundation, such as a decent pension.

11. Revenge in Eve's case and a political promotion in the Grants' case are other motives that account for what they do.

12. That Communism will not gain a foothold in American politics is already clear after the 1948 presidential election in which the Progressives' candidate, Henry Wallace, is lambasted because of his failure to draw a distinct line between his campaign and Communism (see Patterson, *Grand Expectations*, 157).

13. Ira's diminishment is illustrated in the book by the contempt Nathan Zuckerman, the book's narrator and back then an adolescent, comes to feel for him. Starting as a completely devoted admirer of Ira, Zuckerman can, by that time, no longer endure Ira's endless rants; once having felt greatly honored when Ira spent time with him, he, by that time, is happy to get away from him (*Communist*, 574–76, 599–600, 622).

14. Cervantes's Don Quixote is, by the way, also an interesting case when it comes to pathologies of reconciliation. He, and this is partly also true for Ira, has lost not only attunement to a particular value system but, more basically, to his times as such. He is even out of the realm of what could be called the background of agreements regarding the specifics of a time that competing value systems agree on (e.g., that we live in a globalized world)—the agreed-upon facts behind disagreements on how to react in light of these facts from a normative perspective. Therefore, when it comes to reconciliation, a Don Quixote is unable to connect to any value system as he even lacks attunement to the shared facts to which different value systems answer.

15. Eve's urge to purify her daughter is obviously already behind the name she picks for her; Sylphid is based on Paracelsus's "Sylphs," spirits of the air that do not take up "room in this world whatsoever" (*Communist*, 625) and therefore do not produce dirt.

16. Roth speaks of the "latent anti-Semitism" of the "Cold War paranoia" (*Communist*, 653).

17. Glaser makes the importance of this house—"the emblem of the Swede's American dream realized"—palpable by connecting it to Freud's elaborations on the double meaning of the German word "heimlich" ("uncanny" and "homey") (see Jennifer Glaser, "America's Haunted House: The Racial and National Uncanny in American Pastoral," in *Philip Roth. American Pastoral, The Human Stain, The Plot Against America*, ed. Debra Shostak [London: Continuum, 2011], 44–59, quote on 54).

18. For the central meaning of Johnny Appleseed to the Swede, see Kinzel, *Tragödie und Komödie*, 132–33.

19. That, according to Roth, the United States has always also been a chaotic place full of injustice is Aimee Pozorski's main point, which even prompts her to make the case that the country suffers from a trauma that needs to be traced back to the fratricide that was part of the American Revolution (see Pozorski, *Roth and Trauma: The Problem of History in the Later Works (1995–2010)* [London: Continuum, 2011], 12).

20. It is hard to say whether it is rather the opportunity issue or the self-invention issue that convinces Coleman to go for the lie. Parrish stresses the opportunity issue and traces Coleman's later rage back to the lack of opportunities Coleman had as a young black man. Morley, however, is on the side of self-invention (see Tim Parrish, "Becoming Black: Zuckerman's Bifurcating Self in *The Human Stain*," in *Philip Roth: New Perspectives on an American Author*, ed. Derek Parker Royal [Westport, CT: Praeger, 2005], 209–23, esp. 213–14; and Catherine Morley, "Possessed by the Past: History, Nostalgia, and Language in The Human Stain," in *Philip Roth: American Pastoral, The Human Stain, The Plot Against America*, ed. Debra Shostak [London: Continuum, 2011], 80–92, esp. 81–82).

21. Michael Jackson, "Black or White," from the CD *Dangerous*, produced by Michael Jackson and Bill Bottrell, Epic Records, 1991.

22. He "commits a virtual matricide" (Brühwiler, *Political Initiation*, 87).

23. Brauner, *Philip Roth*, 150.

24. Derek Parker Royal makes the case that Ira and the Swede have a lot in common, especially their yearning for—though in somewhat different versions—an American pastoral (see Royal, "Pastoral Dreams and National Identity in *American Pastoral* and *I Married a Communist*," in *Philip Roth: New Perspectives on an American Author*, ed. Royal [Westport, CT: Praeger, 2005], 185–207, here 191). Brauner is enlightening when it comes to the quest for the American pastoral as the bracket that holds Ira, the Swede, and Coleman together (*Philip Roth*, 150–51).

25. Michael Kimmage, *In History's Grip. Philip Roth's Newark Trilogy* (Stanford, CA: Stanford University Press, 2012), 13.

26. Brühwiler spots a common pattern here by pointing out that Coleman shares his bad ending with "all the other Rothian figures who created an identity beyond ethnic, religious, or cultural constraints" (*Political Initiation*, 88).

5

Three Voices or One?

Philip Roth and Zionism

Louis Gordon

Over the course of his long career, Philip Roth has displayed considerable and, at times, serious skepticism toward Zionism and Israel in his fiction and nonfiction.[1] Yet while many scholars have studied Roth's two novels that deal extensively with Zionism and Israel, the *Counterlife* (1986) and *Operation Shylock* (1993), such works rarely consider Roth's early nonfictional writings and his later comments on these topics, which offer unique insights into Roth's thinking on the idea of a Jewish state.[2] Indeed, when read alongside the aforementioned novels, the nonfictional writings and other comments actually elucidate the themes encompassed by the fictional works. At the same time, many scholars have noted the varying voices that emanate throughout his oeuvre. In particular, Maureen Whitebrook has argued that the literary techniques in *Operation Shylock,* such as unreliable narration, misjudgments, and narrative gaps, confirm that "identity is not set."[3] She explains that the "confusion as to the identity of the Roth persona—author, narrator, character, or all three—is compounded by the narrative idea of doubling."[4]

Although it is clear from the texts themselves that multiple voices exist among the various characters in Roth's writings about Zionism and Israel, there also is a common, politically progressive perspective that is shared by Philip Roth the author, Philip Roth the character, and Nathan Zuckerman, the fictional alter ego of Philip Roth in *The Counterlife* and *Operation Shylock*. While there is a variety of views about Zionism and Israel expressed among the assortment of characters in Roth's writing, the viewpoints of these three figures are very similar in content. I am not claiming that these three figures are the same person or possess the same perspectives about everything, but, on the issues of Zionism and Israel, their views are very close to one another in spite of the confusion of their identities.

Classic political Zionism called for the return of the diaspora Jewish population to Palestine and the reestablishment of sovereignty over the ancient Jewish homeland. The movement was comprised of four main factions: (1) Labor Zionists, who combined Socialism and Zionism; (2) Religious Zionists, who sought to reestablish a Jewish state in accordance with religious principles; (3) Revisionist Zionists, who propounded a "maximalist" ideology that sought to establish a Jewish state on both sides of the Jordan River; and (4) General Zionists, who subscribed to the principles established by Theodor Herzl, the founder of Zionism, but who were neither socialist nor maximalist. Another strain, "Cultural Zionism," sought to emphasize Jewish national culture over political ideas.[5]

For purposes of this essay, which seeks to place Roth's ideas in a political context, it is most helpful to view Zionism as articulated by the platforms of the political parties that were seated after the 1988 Israeli elections. The wide range of parties represented in the Israeli Knesset after the election serves as a good barometer of the varying approaches to Zionism and Israel, as they existed during the years between the publication of the *Counterlife* and *Operation Shylock*.[6] In this essay, I will argue that the three voices of Roth—Roth the author, Roth the character, and Nathan Zuckerman— share the same political views with the Israeli Civil Rights and Peace Movement, which was founded in 1973 by Shulamit Aloni, who had just seceded from the Labor Alignment.

In the first section, I examine Roth's views about Zionism and Israel in several works: his essay "New Jewish Stereotypes" (1961); his nonfictional comments in *The Facts* (1988) and *Patrimony* (1991); comments from the Roth's friend and fellow writer Bernard Avishai; Roth's participation in a 1988 advertisement sponsored by *Tikkun* magazine; and Roth's comments on the book cover of Anthony Julius's *Trials of the Diaspora* (2010).[7] In the second section, I analyze Nathan Zuckerman's comments on Zionism in *The Counterlife,* paying particular attention to Zuckerman's remarks about the late Israeli prime minister Menachem Begin. In the third section, I discuss the character Philip Roth's views about Zionism in *Operation Shylock;* and in the fourth and final section, I offer my conclusions about the political views of Roth the author, the character Nathan Zuckerman, and of the character Philip Roth: their views are indeed overall very similar, although some subtle nuances exist among them.

Philip Roth, the Author, on Zionism

Roth's essay "New Jewish Stereotypes" was originally published in 1961 in *American Judaism,* the Reform Movement's magazine, and later reprinted in the first collection of writing that questioned the Zionist movement, *Zionism Reconsidered* (1970).[8] In this essay Roth attacked Leon Uris's claim that Jews had actually been fighters, citing the example of the students in his workshops as more representative than those of Uris, who had served in the U.S. Marine Corps and whose father had been in the Jewish Legion. Roth also quoted from an exchange in *Time* magazine between a former captain of the ship *Exodus* and Uris, to show that the latter's depiction of the creation of Israel was inaccurate:

> Certainly, it is unsafe to indict a man on the basis of what *Time* quotes him as having said; it may even be *Time*'s pleasure to titillate its readers with still another Jewish stereotype, the Fagan, the Shylock who will sell anything, for a price. There was a time when this image was very helpful to certain Gentiles as a tool in dealing with the Jew. Now, however, there is another ways of dealing with him—there is the image that Mr. Uris has sold, the image millions have read about and other millions have seen flickering on the screen, the image which is able to make the Jew and Jewishness acceptable and appealing and even attractive.[9]

Roth implied that such work was a sellout because it allowed the American nation to assuage its conscience about thinking about the murder of 6 million Jews, "in all its raw, senseless unavenged, and unavengeable horror."[10] He explained that now that the scales appeared to have been balanced, "there cannot but help be a sigh of relief," writing: "At long last the Jew is no longer the spectator of the violence of our age, nor is he the victim of that violence; now he is a participant. Fine then, welcome aboard. A man with a gun and a hand grenade, a man who kills for his God-given rights (in this case as the song tells us, his land) cannot sit so easily in judgment or in horror, of another man when he kills for *his* God-given rights, as he chooses to define them."[11]

In contrast to Uris's discovery that the Jew as a fighter filled him and many others with pride, Roth wrote that it filled the hero of Eli Wiesel's *Dawn* (1961) with "less satisfying and buoyant emotions."[12] Roth concluded the essay by noting that he could not help but believe that there was "a higher moral purpose for the Jewish writer and the Jewish people, than the improvement of public relations."[13]

Looking back at the essay, we see that Roth's comparison of Wiesel with Uris was inaccurate and that Roth conflated the plot of the novel with Otto Preminger's film adaptation from 1960. Still it is important to note that Roth's early views on Zionism were (1) thoroughly secular, (2) skeptical about the success of Zionism as a corrective to the injustices that had historically been perpetrated against the Jewish people, and (3) committed to the view that the Jewish people should take on a "morally just" position. It is also notable that Roth chose to publish the essay in the pro–Zionist Reform Movement's journal and did not come out directly against Zionism as a breakoff of the movement, as the American Council for Judaism did in 1942. This puts his view on Zionism somewhere on the far left of the political spectrum but not so far that he had rejected it in toto.

In *The Facts,* Roth offers some context for the origin of his feelings on the topic of a Jewish state:

Not only did growing up Jewish in Newark in the thirties and forties, Hebrew School and all, feel like a perfectly legitimate way of growing up American but, what's more, growing up Jewish as I did and growing up American seemed to me indistinguishable. Remember that in those days there was not a new Jewish country, a "homeland," to foster the range of attachments—the pride, the love, the anxiety, the chauvinism, the philanthropy, the chagrin, the shame—that have, for many American Jews now over forty, complicated anew the issue of Jewish self-definition.[14]

Roth's views of Israel are further illuminated by the reminiscences of his friend Bernard Avishai. In his book *Promiscuous* (2012), Avishai notes that during a 1988 luncheon he had arranged between Roth and then future Israeli prime minister Ehud Olmert, Roth expressed an impassioned concern reflecting a left-of-center critique as to how, in light of the violence, Israel could retain the territories populated by so many Arabs.[15] These views are later confirmed when Roth, along with Woody Allen, Arthur Miller, Betty Friedan, and other prominent American Jewish intellectuals, signed an advertisement in the *New York Times* that denounced the policies of Prime Minister Shamir as "immoral, contrary to what is best in our Jewish tradition and destructive to the best interests of Israel and American Jewry."[16] The advertisement called on Yitzhak Shamir to begin negotiations with the Palestine Liberation Organization and not to rule out the possibility that such negotiations could lead to the creation of a Palestinian state. It was sponsored by the Committee for Judaism and Social Justice, a national group organized by the U.S. bimonthly *Tikkun* magazine, which described itself as a liberal progressive alternative to the American Israel Public Affairs Committee (AIPAC).[17]

Again, we see from Roth's comments in the late 1980s, as reported by Avishai and reflected in the *New York Times* advertisement, that his views represent a politically progressive point of view. They are similar to the ideology promoted by the Civil Rights and Peace Movement in Israel. The allusion to morality in the advertisement is consistent with Roth's earlier writing, and the fact that Roth was willing to sign a statement is compatible with the earlier observation that he did not take an anti-Zionist but rather a politically progressive positon.

Along these lines, it is also helpful to consider Anthony Julius's *Trials of the Diaspora*, which recounts the history of anti-Semitism in England, including the new secular anti-Zionism of the British Left.[18] The massive history also begins with an epigraph from Roth's *Operation Shylock*, "In the modern world, the Jew has perpetually been on trial; still today the Jew is on trial in the person of the Israel and this modern trial of the Jew, this trial which never ends, begins with the trial of Shylock," which could be viewed as just a quote from a fictional character. However, *Trials of the Diaspora* also includes a ringing endorsement by Roth, the author, who calls it an "essential history" which is fortunate to have been written by a man with the "moral discernment of Anthony Julius," indicating the author

Roth's approval for Julius's interpretation of *Shylock* and a comment that is again compatible with a progressive view of Zionism.

Nathan Zuckerman on Zionism

The character Nathan Zuckerman has appeared in a number of Roth novels from *My Life as a Man* (1974) to *Exit Ghost* (2007). However, it is in *The Counterlife* where he actually speaks extensively about Zionism. Set in the form of alternative episodes, the novel examines the relationship between Nathan Zuckerman and his brother Henry, a New Jersey dentist. Nowhere else in his writing does Roth more accurately depict both sides of the argument about Israel and Zionism, than in this novel.

Roth begins the novel with the chapter "Basel," the city that was the site of the first Zionist Congress in 1897 as well as the hometown of Henry's Swiss mistress, Maria. Henry is so enamored with Maria that he would rather risk his life in surgery than live with impotence. Unfortunately for him, the surgery is not successful, and he has supposedly died. But the novel takes a different turn in the second chapter, where Nathan Zuckerman has gone to discover what has happened to his brother, who has survived the operation and moved to Israel to live the life of an Israeli settler.

Zuckerman's first meeting in Israel is with his friend Shuki, a fairly typical left-of-center secular Israeli whose brother was killed and mutilated during the Yom Kippur War.[19] Zuckerman speaks sympathetically of Shuki's brand of Zionism, which required one to take upon himself "rather than leaving to others, responsibility for one's survival as a Jew, this was their brand of Zionism. And it worked" (*Counterlife*, 53). However, Zuckerman later recounts the time when he had argued with Shuki's late father that they would be more secure in the United States than they ever could be in Israel (*Counterlife*, 54). Zuckerman also notes in another episode that "I never had enough Hebrew, Yiddish, or anti-Semitism to make me a Zionist when I was young" (*Counterlife*, 101). Israel was never at the center of his thoughts and therefore he never felt a need to return to his "homeland" (*Counterlife*, 101). In these episodes, Zuckerman's views about Zionism and Israel are similar to those of Roth the author, who expressed in *The Facts* that he had grown up without "a new Jewish state" and the consequent attachments that had complicated the issue of Jewish identification.[20]

But, in another episode, Zuckerman expresses some views that are not similar to those of Roth the author. When settlement leader Lippman's wife begins to chant traditional Sabbath songs, Zuckerman observes: "Singing in the Sabbath, Ronit looked as content with her lot as any woman could be, her eyes shining with love for a life free of Jewish cringing, deference, diplomacy, apprehension, alienation, self-pity, self-satire, self-mistrust, depression, clowning, bitterness, nervousness, inwardness, hypocriticalness, hypertouchiness, social anxiety, social assimilation—a way of life absolved, in short, of all the Jewish 'abnormalities,' the peculiarities of self-division whose traces remained imprinted in just about every engaging Jew I knew" (*Counterlife*, 120).

The description is somewhat surprising in the middle of the narrative and is actually one of the most positive depictions of a female Jewish character that Roth has ever created. More astounding is that Zuckerman remains silent when Lippman goes on about the need to stop the Arabs from throwing stones at Jews (*Counterlife*, 121–22). When Lippman posits that "the Arab can remain here and I can remain here and together we can live in harmony. He can have any experience he likes, live here however he chooses and have everything he desires—except for the experience of statehood," Zuckerman says nothing (*Counterlife*, 129).

His response comes later in the chapter "Aloft," when Zuckerman states that, although he would never criticize a Jew who chooses to go to Israel because he was in danger, he does not believe that Henry was faced with any such situation in America (*Counterlife*, 146). Thus, Zuckerman criticizes his brother not for political reasons but instead for psychological ones: Henry's adoption of a politically extreme interpretation of Zionism strikes Zuckerman as strange, as Henry had never before expressed any interest in Hebrew culture. If Henry had lived a cultural but not politically extreme version of Zionism, Zuckerman would accept his brother's new ideology without a problem (*Counterlife*, 149).

But Zuckerman knows that he cannot do anything to help his brother. The military zealotry of Henry's settlement with "the settlers' fanatic pursuit of God-promised deliverance was a Jewish Moby Dick with Lippman a Zionist Ahab" (*Counterlife*, 264). It would appear that Zuckerman's acceptance of a cultural form of Zionism, reminiscent of that espoused by the early Zionist theorist Asher Ginsburg, who is better known as *Ahad Ha'am* (or "One of the People"), would seem to put him in the box of progressive Zionism. Zuckerman is not against Zionism per se; he is opposed to its politically extreme forms.

Finally, Zuckerman reflects on Israeli prime minister Menachem Begin, which demonstrates his understanding of the value in varying types of Zionism:

> Not even Ben-Gurion's fortitude, Golda's pride and Dayan's valor taken all together could have provided him with that profound sense of personal vindication that so many of his generation have found in an Israeli Prime Minister who could pass, from his appearance, for the owner of a downtown clothing store. Even Begin's English is right, sounding more like the speech of their own impoverished immigrant parents than what emanates, say, from Abba Eban, cunning Jewish central casting's spokesman to the gentile world. After all, who better than the Jew caricatured by generation upon generation of pitiless enemies, the Jew ridiculed and despised for his funny accent and his ugly looks and his alien ways, to make it perfectly clear to everyone that what matters now isn't what goyim think but what Jews do? (*Counterlife*, 57)

The passage is remarkably similar to one that appears in Yaakov Jacob's article "Menachem Begin: A Tragedy for the Jews" (1982) in response to Marie Syrkin, who had written a scathing attack on the Israeli prime minister in 1982 in the *New Republic*. Analyzing Sykrin's assault on Begin's coalition of "economic reactionaries, orthodox dogmatists, and Greater-Israel zealots," Jacobs described the source of his own infatuation with Begin as well as "the hatred he inspired among goyim, secular Zionists and sophisticated Jews," noting:

> Critics speak of Life imitating art. . . . Menachem Begin is a caricature of the despised Jew come to life, and thumbing his hooked-nose at his oppressors. There was a time when every anti-Semitic joke began with the words: "There was this little Jew . . ."
>
> Diminutive in stature, bald-headed, hook-nosed, with professorial spectacles and vocabulary, he springs live from the pages of Nazi propaganda. He is grubby: audaciously annexing the Golan Heights, thus denying the poor Syrians forever of the privilege of logging shells down on the Jews sitting in the valley. . . . And that is why Menachem Begin engendered more wrath among the nations than for example, an Abba Eban with his Oxford accent, or the late Moshe Dayan with his swagger and stylish eye-patch.[21]

Zuckerman's discussion of Begin, while perhaps surprising for a character with such progressive views, is at somewhat of a variance from Roth, the author, who in his early writings was not so sophisticated in distinguishing among the different versions of Zionist thought.

Philip Roth in *Operation Shylock*

Not long after the publication of *Counterlife*, Roth returned to the subject of Israel in *Operation Shylock*, which takes the idea of multiple identities beyond Roth's previous work in the forms of a "fake" and "real" Philip Roth. The novel begins with the "real" Roth being advised that an imposter named Philip Roth is in Jerusalem speaking about a new solution to the Jewish problem called Diasporism, a return of the Ashkenazi Israeli Jews to Europe. Many critics discussing *Operation Shylock* have noted the significance of one fact at the book's beginning: Roth's discussion of the use of the drug halcion that sent him into a mental tailspin. For purposes of this essay, however, what seems to be overlooked is the person who helped Roth escape the effect of the drug. Though *Operation Shylock* refers to Bernard Avishai by name, and Claire Bloom's memoir depicts his role in Roth's recovery in more detail, neither author acknowledges the Zionist angle in Roth's recovery. Yet the presence of Avishai is a metaphor for those forces of progressive Zionism that, under the surface, animate *Operation Shylock* and ultimately result in what I consider the character Philip Roth's confession.

But to get to that confession we must follow the "real" Roth of the novel seeking to discourage the "fake" on a journey through Israel circa the late 1980s to visit the Demjanuk trial as well as the trial of his Palestinian friend's nephew in the West Bank. The characters more often than not speak not like Arabs or Israelis, but more like an American Jew, in setting forth the various arguments pro and con over Israel and the Jewish people, and they sometimes seemingly function as apologetics for the author Roth's views on the Jews. For instance, in an early scene, Aharon Appelfeld tells Roth that he was "a Jew par excellence" years before he came along, and the fact that Roth continues to struggle so to deny it is for him the "ultimate proof" (54).

In a similar way George Ziad, the "real" Roth's Palestinian friend from graduate school, rants on not about Palestinian politics, or the Palestinian intellectual opposition to Zionism that extends from George Antonius to

Edward Said, but rather about Jewish intellectual life in a way that sounds distinctly un-Palestinian and completely Roth.[22] Ziad dismisses Israeli culture when compared to the American Jewish one, stating: "What have they created like you Jews out in the world? Absolutely nothing. Nothing but a state founded on force and the will to dominate. If you want to talk about culture, there is absolutely no comparison. Dismal painting and sculpture, no musical composition, and a very minor literature—that is what all their arrogance has produced. Compare this to the American Jewish culture and it is pitiable, it is laughable."[23]

Later in the tirade to Ziad's wife, we see that Philip Roth, the character, does not take his own words seriously, noting before the dialogue: "If this is the way George wants to play it, then this is that way we shall go. I am not writing this then. They are. I don't even exist" (*Counterlife*, 155). After his Diasporist tirade, the Philip Roth character states, "my sympathies were entirely with George's wife. I didn't know which was more insufferable to her, the force with which I presented my Diasporist blah-blah or the thoughtfulness with which George sat here taking it in" (*Counterlife*, 158).

But what is more telling of the character Philip Roth's sentiments occurs a bit later in the novel, during his return to Jerusalem by taxi from the West Bank, where he is intensely questioned by the Arab driver, in the following dialogue:

> "Are you a Zionist?"
> "Tell me," I replied as agreeably as I could, "what you mean by a
>   Zionist and I'll tell you if I'm a Zionist.
> "Are you a Zionist?' he repeated flatly.
> "Look," I snapped back, thinking, why don't you just say no? "What
>   business is that of yours? Drive, please. This is the road to
>   Jerusalem, is it not?"
> "Are you a Zionist?"
> The driver then stops the car to defecate and when he returns again
>   asks Roth "Are you a Zionist?"
> "Why do you keep *asking* that? If you mean Meir Kahane, then I
>   am not a Zionist. If you mean Shimon Peres . . ." But why *was*
>   I favoring with an answer this harmless old man with bowel
>   problems, answering him seriously in a language he understood
>   only barely . . . where the hell was my sense of reality "Drive,

please," I said. "Jerusalem, Just get me to Jerusalem. And
without talking!" (*Shylock*, 165–66)

While Timothy Parrish argues that Roth refuses to state whether he is
or is not a Zionist,[24] I interpret the above dialogue as a subtle confession.
The meaning of Roth's remarks about Rabbi Meir Kahane (1923–1990),
the extremist Zionist leader who called for the expulsion of the Arabs from
Israel versus the dovish Labor Party politician, Shimon Peres, is clear from
the text. However, the "confession" becomes even clearer in light of Roth's
reference in *The Facts* to his role in fomenting the 1960s revolution,[25] along
with such radicals as Jerry Rubin and Abbie Hoffman,[26] who considered
Roth his favorite Jewish novelist.

Hoffman, like Roth, made the mistake of ascribing to Kahane more
influence in Israel than he actually possessed, noting in a letter to his wife,
Anita, that, while on the run from the authorities, he was "violently anti-
Israeli"; and if he were still politically active, he would have already gone
to Israel and debated someone like Kahane in Jerusalem or "whatever
place was correct."[27] In *Shylock*, Roth similarly makes the choice for Zionists between the radical Zionist who never held more than one Knesset
seat, and the Labor leader who served as prime minister and head of the
Israeli opposition. But where Hoffman never perceived Israel as anything
but extremist, the mature Roth has shown understanding of the various
nuances of Zionist thought in his "confession."

If we understand *Shylock* as a function of Roth's "confession," then
the so-called missing chapter at the novel's end that details the character of
Roth's secret mission for the Mossad can be understood for what it really is:
a literary device in the service of his confession. Still, regardless of how we
understand *Shylock* as an overall novel, one thing is clear: the sentiments by
the character Philip Roth all fall on the progressive side on the Zionist spectrum. The combination of sympathy for Ziad's wife and tacit acceptance of
Shimon Peres, and apparent mission for the Mossad, places the character
Philip Roth in the box of the skeptical yet progressive Zionist.

Three Voices or One?

A number of scholars contend that the statements of Roth the author, Roth
the narrator, and Roth the character provide different political perspec-

tives about Zionism and Israel. Certainly in the context of fiction, Nathan Zuckerman and the character Philip Roth indeed engage in a variety of behaviors. However, when their overall views are examined, as illustrated above, we do not find great differences in the ultimate attitudes toward Zionism of Philip Roth the author, Nathan Zuckerman, the character and narrator of the *Counterlife,* and Philip Roth the narrator and character in *Operation Shylock.*

The author, as seen from his early essay "New Jewish Stereotypes," took a skeptical attitude toward Israel and Zionism as a corrective for the state of diaspora, but he never espoused an anti-Zionist perspective per se. Did Roth's views change over the years? The author, as reported by Hermione Lee, would probably refer his readers back to his fiction for an answer.[28] But Roth's subsequent views on Zionism, as confirmed by his close friend Bernard Avishai and as seen in his support for the advertisement against the policies of the conservative Shamir government, indicate a progressive political view that corresponds to perspectives in line with Avishai himself, and the political ideology espoused by *Tikkun* and the Israeli Civil Rights and Peace Movement.

Nathan Zuckerman, similarly, holds a progressive political viewpoint as he comments that Shuki's father's left-wing Zionism had worked, and later states he would not question his brother if he had chosen to live a Hebrew-speaking life in Tel Aviv. Like Roth the author, Zuckerman rejects the approach of right-wing Zionism—the author condemning the Shamir government, Zuckerman seeing the "the settlers' fanatic pursuit of God-promised deliverance" as a Jewish *Moby-Dick* with Lippman as the Zionist Ahab" (*Counterlife,* 264). Still, Zuckerman's comments on Menachem Begin, while clearly not an acceptance of the latter's political ideology, show on a certain level an understanding of the former Irgun commander's political role. Such an attitude was uncharacteristic of most left-of-center Jews in that era. This is underscored by the different approaches toward Begin taken by Nathan Zuckerman and Marie Syrkin, the daughter of the socialist Zionist leader Nachman Syrkin, and a professor of comparative literature, who years earlier had been rebuked by Roth the author, as a Zionist, for her stinging criticism of *Portnoy's Complaint.*[29] It cannot be understated how shockingly similar the sentiments expressed by Yaakov Jacobs in response to Syrkin's attack on Begin are to Zuckerman's later insights on the topic, which offer some variance from the convictions of Roth the author.

The character Philip Roth in *Operation Shylock* also holds politically progressive views, though the multiplicity of views expressed in the novel and the dual aspects of the "fake" and "real" Roth characters make it at times more difficult to detect the characters' true sentiments. While Whitebrook and Harold Bloom view the character Philip Roth's tirade to Ziad's wife as a merging of the fake and real Roths, the comments before and after the tirade indicate that the character does not really believe what he spouts. This scene can also be viewed as Roth's literary answer to the Israeli Arab writer Anton Shammas, who argued that Israel's law of return reduced Arabs to second-class citizens, and which he was fond of saying, gave "someone like Philip Roth" more rights than he had.[30] The character Roth's tirade can then be viewed as a nod to Shammas, or as even as an attempt to show that like Shammas, a Christian Arab whose acclaimed novel *Arabesques* (1988) was written in Hebrew, that he too can assimilate the "other" into his work.

Still, the fact that Roth the character's confession that the Zionism of Shimon Peres was a possibility he could accept indicates again that the character holds progressive but not anti-Zionist political views. While Peres was a member of the Israeli Labor Party, his personal views were, not surprisingly, more in line with the more dovish views espoused by the Civil Rights and Peace Movement. Further, the fact that the Philip Roth character skeptically undertakes the mission to Greece on behalf of the Mossad is symptomatic of this line of political thinking. Some of the confusion on the character's views may be resolved by looking carefully at Whitebrook's observation that novel raises "acute questions of national identity," and that Jews may be Diaspora Jews, American Jews, Israeli Jews or Zionists.[31] While this is true, by making the alternative to the other options, Zionism, Whitebrook misses the fact that there are many shades of Zionism, including a progressive vision that is shared by the author Philp Roth, the character Nathan Zuckerman, and the character Philip Roth.

Ultimately, the author Philip Roth, the character Nathan Zuckerman, and the character Philip Roth in *Operation Shylock*, all espouse left-of-center political views closely resembling those espoused by the Israeli Civil Rights and Democracy Movement, and that are clearly to the right of the Democratic Front Communist Party, the Democratic Arab Party, which pursued primarily Arab interests, and even to the right of the Progressive Movement for Peace, which included socialist Jewish and Arab candidates. While at first glance it seems arguable that the author and his characters

could be associated with the Progressive Movement for Peace, their failure
to explicitly reject Zionism makes them much closer to the views held by the
Civil Rights and Peace Movement.

Finally, it should be noted that though other political expressions are set
forth in the novels, such as the religious Zionism of Mordechai Lippmann
or the Palestine Liberation Organization attitudes of Zaid, they are not
ultimately the perspectives of either Nathan Zuckerman the character, or
Philip Roth the character. Neither Philip Roth the character or, for that
matter, even Nathan Zuckerman ever holds religious Zionist, centrist, right-
wing, nationalist, or Communist views.

This essay has looked at whether a difference can be ascertained in the
attitudes of the author Philip Roth; Nathan Zuckerman, the narrator and
character of *The Counterlife;* and Philip Roth, the character and narrator of
Operation Shylock, toward Zionism and Israel. In the first section I examine
the attitudes of Roth, the author, in his essay "New Jewish Stereotypes";
his memoir *The Facts;* the reminiscences of his friend Bernard Avishai; the
New York Times advertisement he signed criticizing the actions of the Israeli
prime minister Yitzhak Shamir; and Roth's own comments for Anthony
Julius's book *Trials of the Diaspora.* In the second section, I analyze remarks
of Nathan Zuckerman in *The Counterlife* regarding Zionism, noting his progressive views, as well as the fact that his comments on Menachem Begin
are uncharacteristic of someone with such political perspectives. In the third
section, I examine the remarks of Philip Roth the character and narrator of
Operation Shylock, and question the contention of previous scholarship that
the character actually supported the doctrine of Diasporism, and make the
case that he actually expresses a support for Zionism as espoused by the dovish Israeli political leader Shimon Peres. It would be inaccurate to state that
Philip Roth, the author; Nathan Zuckerman, the character; and Philip Roth
the character are one and the same. However, it is clear from the passages
examined above that they all espouse a progressive political view on Zionism
and, as underscored by Roth's "confession," would be in general agreement
with each other in their views toward the Jewish state.

Notes

1. Philip Roth, *Goodbye Columbus* (New York: Houghton Mifflin, 1959).
2. See Andrew Furman, "A New 'Other' Emerges in American Jewish Litera-

ture: Philip Roth's Israel Fiction," *Contemporary Literature* 36.4 (Winter 1995): 633–53; Timothy Parrish, "Imagining Jews in Philip Roth's Operation Shylock," *Contemporary Literature* 40.4 (Winter 1999): 575–602; and Hillel Halkin, "How to Read Philip Roth," *Commentary* 77.4 (February 1994): 43–48. Furman argues that *Operation Shylock* is a new current in American Jewish fiction in Roth's refusal to look toward Israel with an uncritical eye (638). Parrish argues that *Operation Shylock* contains within its pages both everything Roth ever wrote as well as all the critical attacks on his work. He further sees the tension in *Shylock* as that of an important American writer dealing with meaning of his entire body of work, and then reclaiming it as another (579, 598). Halkin, among the foremost Zionist literary critics, suggests that despite the earlier accusations of Jewish self-hatred against Roth, his passion for being Jewish continues to grow stronger.

3. Maureen Whitebrook, *Identity, Narrative and Politics* (London: Routledge, 2001), 45.

4. Ibid., 47. See also Debra Shostak, *Philip Roth—Countertexts, Counterlives* (Columbia: University of South Carolina Press, 2004), 92.

5. See, in general, Arthur Hertzberg, ed., *The Zionist Idea* (New York: Atheneum, 1971).

6. Moving from left to right on a political continuum, the following are the parties seated in 1988 Israeli Knesset elections and the number of seats they held: Democratic Front Communist Party (4); Democratic Arab Party, which was concerned with largely Arab issues (1); Progressive Movement for Peace, a socialist mixed Jewish and Arab party (1); Civil Rights and Peace Movement (5); Shinui, a liberal party that also advocated fiscal responsibility (2); Mapam, the workers' party of Israel (3); Labor Alignment (39); Agudat Israel, the ultra-orthodox party (5); Shas, Sephardi ultra-orthodox party (6); Likud (40); National Religious Party, a moderate religious party that included many settlers (5); Zomet, a secular conservative party (2); Hatechiya, a mixed religious and nonreligious party supported by many settlers (3); and, lastly, Moledet, an ultra-right-wing party (2) (see *Israel, Parliamentary Chamber: Knesset, Elections Held in 1988*, www.ipu.org/parline-e/reports/arc/2155_88.htm).

7. Anthony Julius, *Trials of the Diaspora* (New York: Oxford University Press, 2010).

8. Philip Roth, "New Jewish Stereotypes," in *Zionism Reconsidered*, ed. Michael Selzer (New York: Macmillan, 1970), 107–16.

9. Ibid., 110.

10. Ibid., 115.

11. Ibid., 115–16.

12. Ibid., 116. But the comparison was inaccurate. Wiesel's protagonist was faced with executing an innocent British sergeant on the order of the underground Irgun; Uris's depiction of the underground fighter, Dov, painted a portrait of how

someone so scarred by the Nazi persecutions had been member of the same organization. Neither the authors nor their books endorse the Irgun Tzvai Leumi's
(National Military Organization's) use of violence in its effort to help bring about
a Jewish state.

13. Ibid.

14. Philip Roth, *Novels and Other Narratives* (New York: Library Classics of
America, 2008), 403.

15. Bernard Avishai, *Promiscuous: "Portnoy's Complaint" and Our Doomed
Pursuit of Happiness* (New Haven: Yale University Press, 2012), 135.

16. Charles Hoffman, "Liberal Group Formed as 'Alternative to AIPAC': U.S.
Jewish Intellectuals Join Against Shamir Policies," *Jerusalem Post*, April 5, 1989,
http://pqasb.pqarchiver.com/jpost/doc/320924016.html?FMT=FT&pf=1.

17. Ibid. Other signatories to the statement with particular relevance to Roth
included Abbie Hoffman and Irving Howe.

18. Anthony, *Trials of the Diaspora.*

19. Philip Roth, *The Counterlife* (New York: Farrar, Straus and Giroux, 1986),
63; hereafter cited parenthetically.

20. Philip Roth, *Novels and Other Narratives* (New York: Library Classics of
America, 2008), 403.

21. Yaakov Jacobs, "Menachem Begin, A Tragedy for the Jews," *Jewish Life* 5.2
(1982): 2–4.

22. See George Antonius, *The Arab Awakening* (Beirut: Khayat's College Book
Cooperative, 1955), 386–412.

23. Philip Roth, *Operation Shylock: A Confession* (New York: Vintage International, 1994), 122; hereafter cited parenthetically.

24. Parrish, "Imagining Jews in Philip Roth's Operation Shylock," 591.

25. Roth, *The Facts* (London: Penguin, 1988), 350; hereafter cited
parenthetically.

26. Jonah Raskin, *For the Hell of It: The Life and Times of Abbie Hoffman*
(Berkeley: University of California Press, 1996).

27. Anita and Abbie Hoffman, *To America with Love: Letters from the Underground* (Los Angeles: Red Hen Press, 2000), 164–66.

28. Hermione Lee, "Essentially Indiscrete," *Independent*, September 2 1990,
12, www.lexisnexis.com.libproxy.lib.csusb.edu/lnacui2api/results/listview/delPrep
.do?cisb=22_T21274245482&risb=21_T21274245479&mode=delivery_DnldRender.

29. Philip Roth, *Reading Myself and Others* (London: Corgi, 1977), 277–79.

30. Gerald Marzorati Golub, "An Arab Voice in Israel," *New York Times*,
September 18, 1988, A54, http://search.proquest.com.libproxy.lib.csusb.edu/
docview/426939367/FF8D8820E1394D81PQ/1?accountid=10359.

31. Whitebrook, *Identity, Narrative and Politics*, 55.

6

Roth at Century's End

The Problem of Progress in The Dying Animal

Matthew Shipe

As the twentieth century approaches its end, the conviction grows that many other things are ending too. Storm warnings, portents, hints of catastrophe haunt our times. The "sense of ending," which has given shape to so much of twentieth-century literature, now pervades the popular imagination as well. The Nazi holocaust, the threat of nuclear annihilation, the depletion of natural resources, well-founded predictions of ecological disaster have fulfilled poetic prophecy, giving historical substance to the nightmare, or death wish, that avant-garde artists were the first to express.

—Christopher Lasch, *The Culture of Narcissism* (1979)

The old system that made order doesn't work anymore. All that was left was his fear and astonishment, but now concealed by nothing.

—Philip Roth, *American Pastoral* (1997)

Toward the conclusion of *The Dying Animal* (2001), David Kepesh, the now seventy-year-old cultural critic whose sexual exploits Philip Roth had previously chronicled in *The Breast* (1972) and *The Professor of Desire* (1977), watches the televised millennial celebrations as they occur around the globe. Published only months before the September 11 attacks on the World Trade Center, *The Dying Animal* unwittingly anticipates the political unrest and violence that will soon come to fruition. Overshadowed by the critical success of the American trilogy, *The Dying Animal* nonetheless offers a fascinating portrait of this liminal moment in American history. Through the course of his narrative, Kepesh attempts to ascribe meaning to America's recent history—in particular, the sexual upheaval that blossomed during the late 1960s—while also pondering a future that seems anything but certain. Indeed, the novel's millennial setting allows Roth to explore the questions that haunt the nation's immediate future, a concern that is most readily apparent in this scene, late in the novel, where Kepesh witnesses the start of the new millennium alongside Consuela Castillo, a former student and lover recently diagnosed with breast cancer. The much younger Consuela—she was twenty-four when she had first dated Kepesh in the early 1990s—has returned to his apartment that night to have him photograph her breasts before she has surgery to remove the cancer. Consuela's illness hangs over the night's proceedings as her potential early death becomes the central lens through which Kepesh views the televised celebrations. "Getting old is unimaginable to anyone but the aging, but that is no longer so for Consuela," he observes of his former partner's response to her cancer. "Time for the young is always made up of what is past, but for Consuela time is now how much future she has left, and she doesn't believe there is any. Now she measures time counting forward, counting time by the closeness of death."[1]

Beginning with Kepesh's pessimistic reading of the millennial moment, this essay will explore how *The Dying Animal* challenges the myth of progress, a faith in infinite advancement that has continually informed, to various degrees, America's understanding of itself. The notion of progress—what Christopher Lasch describes in *The True and Only Heaven: Progress and Its Critics* (1991) as the "assumption that our standard of living (in the broadest meaning of that term) will undergo a steady improvement"—remains central to Roth's fiction of this period. Throughout his late work, Roth's aging male protagonists have struggled to assess the meaning of the political and cultural changes that they have experienced during their lifetime.[2] This essay will explore how Roth's later work has articulated a complex critique of progress—a critique that can be felt in such moments as Mickey Sabbath's impulse in *Sabbath's Theater* (1995) to wrap himself up in the American flag of his childhood or the horrific dinner scene that concludes *American Pastoral* (1997). Nevertheless, my argument will largely focus on *The Dying Animal* as I examine how we might read David Kepesh's effort to measure the meaning of his past alongside the uncertainties that loom on the horizon of the new century. After establishing how we might situate this slim novel within his late career, I will consider how Roth's work reverberates in interesting ways with Lasch's critique of progress, before turning back to *The Dying Animal* to consider how it imagines the nation's recent past and unsure future. At first glance, *The Dying Animal* might seem like an odd starting point for considering Roth's politics or sense of history. Among aficionados of his long career, the novel is perhaps most remembered for introducing the short, elliptical form that Roth would employ throughout his late work. In many ways, *The Dying Animal* can be read as the precursor to such late novels as *Everyman* (2006), *Exit Ghost* (2007), and *The Humbling* (2009), all relatively brief books that offer harrowing portraits of the toll that age takes on the physical body. Indeed, *The Dying Animal* remains unflinching in its portrait of the consequences of illness on the human body, and the novel, in many ways, stands as Roth's most moving meditation on aging and desire. "Can you imagine old age?" Kepesh asks early in the novel. "Of course you can't. I didn't. I couldn't. I had no idea what it was like. Not even a false image—no image. And nobody wants anything else" (*Dying*, 35). Kepesh's bewilderment over his advancing age echoes throughout Roth's subsequent novels as his aging male protagonists struggle with the increasingly grim realities of age and disease.

Beyond anticipating the terrain that preoccupies so much of Roth's late fiction, *The Dying Animal* is a work that looks back, not only to the earlier Kepesh books but also to the run of great novels that Roth produced during the 1990s—a sequence of ambitious narratives that culminated with *Sabbath's Theater* and the American trilogy. In these works, Roth returned to his American terrain—after brief sojourns in England and Israel in *The Counterlife* (1986) and *Operation Shylock* (1993)—to reconsider the political and cultural narratives that had shaped the United States' trajectory after the Second World War. "When I look back now, I see that *Sabbath's Theater* is the real turning back to American stuff. Mickey Sabbath's is such an American voice," Roth noted in an interview with Charles McGrath conducted shortly after the publication of *The Human Stain*. "And after him, if not out of him, came the American trilogy. And I see from what I'm writing right now that even if I try, I can't steer clear of our common history creeping thematically into my work. This is a result of growing older, I suppose. You don't have a historical perspective for a long time. A historical perspective requires time. Then, alas, time passes, you've got one and you're stuck with it."[3]

Roth's sense of having achieved a "historical perspective" can, in many ways, be viewed as the defining feature of his post–*Sabbath's Theater* fiction, as his later novels have illuminated the competing narratives and myths that have been integral to how the postwar United States has imagined itself. In revisiting the nation's postwar trajectory, the American trilogy does not ascribe a singular meaning to that history, but instead it engages in what Linda Hutcheon has defined as historiographic metafiction, as the series exposes the myths and beliefs that have shaped how America's post-1945 experience has been narrated.[4] In his reading of *American Pastoral,* Samuel Cohen observes: "Roth seems to see that demythologizing, novelistic or otherwise, is not a value-free activity; that is, it works from its own ideals, its own vision of perfection, and it can tear down more than it intends. What he explores in *American Pastoral* is that idea, again, that tearing things down and starting over itself partakes of the myth that such a thing is possible, that a new, innocent work can be made."[5] As Cohen suggests, the American trilogy and the historical novels that followed it seem less interested in articulating a stable meaning to America's post-1945 experience but instead demonstrate how "the American Dream and the rebellion against it, are built on the same myth."[6] Consequently, Roth's late novels have frequently fixated on the unintended consequences that have accrued as the American Century came to a close. Indeed, a pronounced sense of ambivalence toward the changes that have transformed American culture during Roth's lifetime can be felt throughout much of his later novels. That is not to say that Roth's politics have become more conservative as his career progressed; he has maintained an affinity for the Democratic Party, and he was an especially vocal critic of President George W. Bush, whom he described in an essay that appeared alongside the publication of *The Plot Against America* (2004) as "a man unfit to run a hardware store let alone a nation like this one, and who has merely reaffirmed for me the maxim that informed the writing of all these books and that makes our lives as Americans as precarious as anyone else's: all the assurances are provisional, even here in a 200-year-old democracy."[7]

No Future? The Millennial Moment in *The Dying Animal*

What distinguishes *The Dying Animal* from much of Roth's later fiction can be felt in David Kepesh's troubled, and at times highly pessimistic, vision of the nation's future. Death haunts this novel as Roth pointedly deflates the optimism that permeated the millennial moment. The novel, in the end, offers a rather limited reading of America's future, seemingly denying the utopian hope that has traditionally informed the nation's sense of itself. In his study of American culture during what he terms the long 1990s, the time period between the fall of the Berlin Wall and the September 11 attacks, Philip Wegner observes how that decade in retrospect "feels like a moment of 'terrifying monsters,' of haunting by a living dead past, and of the 'compulsion to repeat.' . . . Yet, it is also experienced as a moment of 'sublime beauty,' of openness and instability, of experimentation and opportunity, of conflict and insecurity—a place, in other words, wherein history might move in a number of very different directions."[8] The binaries that Wegner identifies offer a useful critical framework through which we might approach *The Dying Animal*, a book that is fixated on both the recent past and the uncertainty that awaits the United States in the new century.

For beyond looking back to the historical questions that haunted Nathan Zuckerman throughout the American trilogy, *The Dying Animal* anticipates the thesis that informs Roth's novels in the new century, an argument that the narrator Philip Roth pronounces in *The Plot Against America*: "Turned wrong way around, the relentless unforeseen was what we schoolchildren studied as 'History,' harmless history, where everything unexpected in its own time is chronicled on the page as inevitable. The terror of the unforeseen is what the science of history hides, turning a disaster into an epic."[9] It's the same argument that he proposes toward the conclusion of his (purportedly) final novel, *Nemesis* (2010): "Sometimes you're lucky and sometimes you're not. Any biography is chance, and, beginning at conception, chance—the tyranny of contingency—is everything."[10] Indeed, Roth's late work has repeatedly insisted on how our future remains highly tenuous. Consequently, the portrait of American life that emerges in his fiction of this century has been strikingly pessimistic, a darkening tone that should not be surprising considering how the consequences of the War on Terror and the 2008 economic collapse have hung over the opening years of this new century. This pessimism is perhaps most fully on display in *Exit Ghost,* as Nathan Zuckerman returns to Manhattan after years of living in seclusion in a house in the Berkshires. "After 9/11 I pulled the plug on the contradictions," Zuckerman acknowledges early in that novel:

> Otherwise, I told myself, you'll be the exemplary letter-to-the-editor madman, the village grouch, manifesting the syndrome in all its seething ridiculousness: ranting and raving while you read the paper, and at night, on the phone with friends, roaring indignantly about the pernicious profitability for which a wounded nation's authentic patriotism was about to be exploited by an imbecilic king, and in a republic, a king in a free country with all the slogans of freedom with which American children are raised. The despising without remission that constitutes being a conscientious citizen in the reign of George W. Bush was not for one who had developed a strong interest in surviving as reasonably serene—so I began to annihilate the abiding wish to *find out.*[11]

The overriding sense that our personal or national futures are anything but guaranteed has been the central tenet of Roth's later novels, an absence of assurance that I argue comes to the forefront in *The Dying Animal.* In her recent overview of his life and career, *Roth Unbound: A Writer and His Books* (2013), Claudia Roth Pierpont suggests how *The Dying Animal* can be viewed as "a coda to the American trilogy in the way that *The Prague Orgy* was a coda to the earlier Zuckerman books, but it's a more ambitious work, pungent and tough—an after-dinner digestif made of bitter herbs."[12] In his reading of the book, Mark Shechner reaches a similar conclusion: "*The Dying Animal* is a book about love and death, matters that Roth knows in the plasm of his cells. There is honest grief here, deep and lasting grief, and Roth composed this compact and meaningful little envoy to love with the fullness of his being and the pathos of his advancing age and kept it short so as not to diffuse its poignancy."[13]

Both Pierpont and Shechner's descriptions of *The Dying Animal* are useful, suggesting how this seemingly minor novel has also been viewed as one of Roth's most unsettling works. Indeed, the novel remains the most sexually explicit of Roth's later works, with Kepesh unabashedly anguishing over the details of his sexual life with Consuela and the details of her body, particularly her breasts: "The most gorgeous breasts I have ever seen . . .

The type with the nipple like a saucer. Not the nipple like an udder but the big pale rosy-brown nipple that is so very stirring" (*Dying*, 28).[14] Perhaps not surprisingly, the bulk of criticism that the novel has received has aimed to unravel the novel's complex and, at times, uncomfortable sexual politics, with many reviewers citing *The Dying Animal* as exhibit A when condemning Roth's treatment of his female characters.[15] In her review of the novel for the *New Republic*, Zoe Heller quipped that "Roth's prose reads like a feminist satire on the chauvinist male gaze," a conclusion that neatly sums up much of the negative criticism the book has generated.[16] While more recent scholarship has attempted to redeem (or at least complicate) the novel's sexual politics, such readings have largely downplayed the historical and political questions that animate Kepesh's recollection of his sexual past.[17] This is not to claim that questions of gender and sexuality are not important to *The Dying Animal*—critics have been correct to see the book as one of Roth's more blunt representations of male sexual desire—but I would like to broaden how this slim and troubling book has been discussed by considering how it meaningfully revisits the political and cultural questions that Roth has pursued throughout his lengthy career.

Set on the edge of the new century, *The Dying Animal* memorializes America's recent past while also remaining fixated on the uncertainties that haunt the nation's immediate future, a concern that is most readily apparent in Kepesh's skewering of the millennial celebrations. Indeed, Kepesh's critique of the evening's festivities remains the most remarkable moment of this slim novel: the rant not only offers a poignant and ironic coda to the twentieth century, but it is also characteristic of the substantial political and historical questions that have informed Roth's later fiction as he has assessed the nature and consequences of the changes that have transformed America culture during the postwar era. "We watched the New Year coming in around the world, the mass hysteria of no significance that was the millennial New Year's Eve celebration," Kepesh remarks while the evening's overproduced celebrations unfold and the predicted catastrophe of Y2K never materializes (*Dying*, 144). "Brilliance flaring across the times zones," Kepesh continues,

> and none ignited by bin Laden. Light whirling over nighttime London more spectacular than anything since the splendors of colored smoke billowed up from the Blitz. And the Eiffel Tower shooting fire,

a facsimile flame-throwing weapon such as Wernher von Braun might have designed for Hitler's annihilating arsenal—the historical missile of missiles, the rocket of rockets, the bomb of bombs, with ancient Paris the launching pad and the whole of humanity the target. All evening long, on networks everywhere, the mockery of the Armageddon that we'd been awaiting in our backyard shelters since August 6, 1945. (*Dying*, 144)

That Kepesh would compare the exploding fireworks to the violence of the Second World War seems wholly appropriate. Now in his seventies, he appears fixated on historicizing his own experience. It is perhaps not surprising, then, that he would evoke the two historical traumas that shaped his childhood (World War II) and young adulthood (the Cold War) when describing this moment of global celebration—an event, in the end, more memorable for the catastrophe that didn't occur. As Aimee Pozorski observes in her astute reading of the novel, "Y2K seemed to serve as the replacement for a disaster that had not come [during the Cold War], offering the US an opportunity to predict the disaster in advance and to know what was happening when it happened. The Y2K problem and the rhetoric of the Armageddon appeared to revive that chance. Yet, it never came, as if history were mocking any human desire to confront disaster head on."[18] Perhaps more notable from our current vantage point is Kepesh's mentioning of Osama bin Laden, a reference that, much like the image of the World Trade Center captured on the cover of Don DeLillo's *Underworld* (1997), would seem eerily to anticipate the imminent catastrophe.

Beyond the ways in which this passage would now seem to foreshadow the attacks on the World Trade Center, it also paints a highly pessimistic outlook on America's future. "Watching this hyped-up production of staged pandemonium, I have a sense of the monied world eagerly entering the prosperous dark ages," Kepesh remarks of the celebratory images being televised: "A night of human happiness to usher in barbarism.com. To welcome appropriately the shit and the kitsch of the new millennium. A night not to remember but to forget" (*Dying*, 145–46). With this critique of the millennial moment in mind, I would like to suggest how *The Dying Animal* challenges the myth of progress that has been central to the dominant political narratives that have informed American history. . . . After briefly sketching out how we might understand Roth's relationship to the critique of progress that Christopher Lasch articulates in *The True and Only Heaven,* I will return to *The Dying Animal* to consider how the novel fruitfully complicates Roth's earlier fiction, in particular *American Pastoral,* while also anticipating the rather bleak view of American life that emerges in his twenty-first-century novels.[19]

Roth and the Critique of Progress

Although Lasch and Roth might at first appear to be odd bedfellows—the former's *The Culture of Narcissism* (1979) renounces the sexual freedom that so many of Roth's protagonists have striven to secure—I would contend that the critique of progress that Lasch espouses in *The True and Only Heaven* offers a useful lens through which we may view the historical argument that Roth makes in *The Dying Animal.*[20] Considering Lasch's career, Louis Menand notes how Lasch "began to see not only liberalism, but the whole march of 'progress' itself as a creeping tyranny of centralized social and political control. Though liberalism was the ascendant political theory of this historical process, even many of the adversaries of liberalism, Lasch concluded, shared its optimism and its passion for transforming people's lives."[21] Published two years after Francis Fukuyama's oft-cited essay "The End of History?" (1989), *The True and Only Heaven* punctures the sense of triumphant that underscores Fukuyama's argument that the end of the Cold War should be read a sign that our global future was on an inherent upswing. That said, Lasch's argument centers less on the implications of the end of the Cold War but instead on deflating the notion that our economic and social conditions are destined to improve indefinitely. "Once we recognize the profound difference between the Christian view of history, prophetic or millenarian, and the modern conception of progress, we can understand what is so original about the latter," Lasch argues in *The True and Only Heaven:*

> not the promise of a secular utopia that would bring history to a happy ending but the promise of steady improvement with no foreseeable ending at all. The expectation of indefinite, open-ended improvement, even more than the insistence that improvement can only come through human effort provides the solution to the puzzle that is otherwise so baffling—the resilience of progressive ideology in the face of

discouraging events that have shattered the illusion of utopia. The idea of progress never rested mainly on the promise of an ideal society—not at least in its Anglo-American version. Historians have exaggerated the utopian component in progressive ideology. The modern conception of history is utopian only in its assumption that history has no foreseeable conclusion.[22]

As Menand points out, for Lasch "if we continue to believe, as the religion of progress encourages us to believe, that somehow everyone in the world can be given the standard of living of a middle-class American, the planet will be used up long before we arrive at that dubious utopia."[23] The skepticism that informs Lasch's reading of the United States' post-1945 trajectory can be felt throughout much of Philip Roth's fiction, from the critiques of commercial culture that are expressed in *Goodbye, Columbus* (1959) and *Letting Go* (1962) to the more complex reading of the postwar nation that he pursues throughout his later fiction.[24] Although this critique of progress surfaces in moments such as Mickey Sabbath's impulse to wrap himself up in the American flag of his childhood in *Sabbath's Theater* or the horrific dinner scene that concludes *American Pastoral,* I would contend that it is most fully articulated in *The Dying Animal* as David Kepesh's struggles to measure the meaning of his past alongside the uncertainties looming on the horizon of the new century. This is not to say that *The Dying Animal* advances the thesis that informs *The True and Only Heaven*—Roth would seem to have little interest in advocating for the populist agenda that is at the heart of Lasch's critique—but both books challenge the triumphant narrative that the United States attempted to project at the end of the Cold War, and both question how we should comprehend the nation's post-1960s trajectory.[25]

In a self-interview, collected in *Reading Myself and Others* (1975), that that he conducted after the publication of his baseball farce *The Great American* (1973), Roth memorably identified the 1960s as "the demythologizing decade," a label that begins to suggest how central the upheaval of that period was to his fictive project and his shifting sense of himself as an American novelist.[26] "I mean by this," Roth continues in the essay,

> that much that had been considered in my brief lifetime to be disgraceful and disgusting forced itself on the national consciousness, loath-

some or not; what was assumed to be beyond reproach became the target of blasphemous assault; what was imagined to be indestructible, impermeable, in the very nature of American things, yielded and collapsed overnight. The shock to the system was enormous—not least for those like myself who belonged to what may of have been the most propagandized generation of young people in American history, our childhoods dominated by World War II, our high school and college years by the worst of the Cold War years—Berlin, Korea, Joe McCarthy; also the first generation to bear the full brunt of the mass media and advertising. . . . The generation known in its college years as "silent" was in actuality straightjacketed, at its most dismal bound by the sort of pieties, fantasies, and values that one might expect to hear articulated today only by a genuine oddball like Tricia Nixon. (*Reading*, 87–88)

This sense of dissolution was one shared by many of Roth's literary contemporaries—it can be felt in Joan Didion's *Slouching toward Bethlehem* (1968), Norman Mailer's *The Armies of the Night* (1968), Saul Bellow's *Mr. Sammler's Planet* (1970), and John Updike's *Rabbit Redux* (1971) to name but a few of the books that capture the "assault" that Roth diagnoses here. Moreover, the mixture of exhilaration and confusion that Roth expresses in *Reading Myself and Others* begins to suggest the era's importance to his subsequent fiction, as his characters have attempted to identify the forces that propelled the upheaval and the ultimate consequences those revolutions had on American culture. The ambivalence that has frequently characterized Roth's assessment of that period can perhaps be most keenly felt in the horrific dinner that brings *American Pastoral* to its abrupt and haunting conclusion. Set during the summer of the Watergate hearings, Nathan Zuckerman casts the dinner party as a stage on which we can witness the full force of that era's tumult. The party concludes with a drunken Jessie Orcutt stabbing Seymour "Swede" Levov's elderly father with a fork, nearly blinding him, after he had attempted to feed her pie and milk in attempt to reason with her that she needs to stop drinking. More troubling than the violence, however, is the laughter that it produces within Marcia Umanoff, an academic who earlier in the evening had mocked the Swede's father over his outrage toward the pornographic film *Deep Throat* (1972). "Marcia sank into Jessie's empty chair, in front of the brimming glass of milk, and with her face in her hands, she began to laugh at their obtuseness to the flimsiness of the whole contraption," Roth writes in the novel's closing passages, "to laugh and laugh and laugh at them all, pillars of a society that, much to her delight, was going rapidly under—to laugh and to relish, as some people, historically, always seem to do, how far the rampant disorder had spread, enjoying enormously the assailability, the frailty, the enfeeblement of supposedly robust things."[27]

The inscrutability of this conclusion—to what extent are we to condemn Marcia's laughing?—remains central to how Roth asks us to reconsider the legacy of the late 1960s in the novel. Considering this unsettling ending, one that some critics have used to position *American Pastoral* as Roth's conservative retraction of the 1960s, Patrick Hayes points out how "the cognitive distress this final passage arouses lies in the way the reader is not only disgusted by Marcia's cruel laughter, but is also seduced into a delight in her mockery."[28] I would largely concur with this reading but would also emphasize the sense of "flimsiness" that Zuckerman highlights at the conclusion of his historical narrative. What Zuckerman leaves readers with, I would argue, is not so much a value judgment on the nature (or the consequences) of the forces that transformed American culture in the late 1960s, but a harrowing reminder of how easily the facade of American progress and infallibility crumbed at this time. We both condemn and cackle alongside Marcia—the appalling comedy of the novel's conclusion suggests that the disorder of the 1960s is not so much an anomaly within U.S. history as it is our natural condition, always on the verge of puncturing our sense of progress and order.

Revisiting the Revolution

In many ways, *The Dying Animal* serves as a forceful corrective to readers who had mistaken *American Pastoral* to be Roth's apology for *Portnoy's Complaint* (1969) and, more broadly, the excesses of the 1960s.[29] Indeed, the questions with which Roth concludes *American Pastoral* ("And what is wrong with their life? What are on earth is less reprehensible than the life of the Levovs?") echo throughout *The Dying Animal*. Pulled by a growing awareness of his impending mortality, David Kepesh reconsiders his past, in particular his decision to embrace the sexual liberation that became viable at the end of the 1960s (*Pastoral*, 423). Recounting his sexual education, one shaped by the strictures of the early Cold War years, Kepesh explains

how his experience was shaped by the limitations that defined his generation's approach to sex, limitations that collapsed with the advent of the Pill
and the onslaught of the Sexual Revolution:

> One wasn't an enfranchised man in the sexual realm while I was grow-
> ing up. One was a second-story man. One was a thief in the sexual
> realm. You "copped" a feel. You stole sex. You cajoled, you begged,
> you flattered, you insisted—all sex had to be struggled for, against the
> values if not the will of the girl. The set of rules was that you had to
> impose your will on her. That's how she was taught to maintain the
> spectacle of her virtue. That an ordinary girl should surrender, with-
> out endless importuning, to break the code and commit the sex act
> would have confused me. Because no one of either sex had any sense
> of erotic birthright. Unknown. She might, if she fell for you, agree to
> a hand job—which meant essentially using your hand with hers as an
> insert—but that someone would consent to anything without the ritual
> of psychological besiegement, of unremitting, monomaniacal tenacity
> and exhortation, well, that was unthinkable. (*Dying*, 66)

The conditions that Kepesh describes largely correspond to the portrait
that Elaine Tyler May paints in her landmark study *Homeward Bound:
American Families during the Cold War* (1988): "Vast numbers of American women and men during the early years of the cold war—more than
ever before or since—got married, moved to the suburbs, and had babies.
If they felt frustrated with their lot, the women were more likely to turn to
tranquilizers, and the men to *Playboy* magazine, for escape. But few were
willing to give up the rewards of conforming for the risks of resisting the
domestic path."[30] Like so many of Roth's male protagonists—one thinks
of the young Marcus Messner in *Indignation* (2008), who as a college
sophomore in 1951 appears utterly bewildered when he receives a blowjob from his college girlfriend—Kepesh remains deeply informed by the
sexual strictures that he experienced as an adolescent and young adult.[31]
He views his subsequent sexual history—his decision to embark on a series
of commitment-free affairs—as a response to the crumbling of the rules
that had governed his adolescent actions, the forces that persuaded him
to marry young and start a family. "There I was, still in the prime of life
and the country entering into this extraordinary time," Kepesh says of his

reaction to the Sexual Revolution. "Am I or am I not a candidate for this wild, sloppy, raucous repudiation, this wholesale wrecking of the inhibitive past? Can I master the discipline of freedom as opposed to the recklessness of freedom? How does one turn freedom into a system?" (*Dying*, 64). As he looks back on those years, Kepesh seems both attracted to and appalled by the "sloppiness" that they embodied; nevertheless, the questions that he poses here have pervaded Roth's fiction as his male protagonists have struggled to balance the appeal of freedom with the desire to maintain an orderly existence.

Despite the revolutionary rhetoric that Kepesh employs here, his continued delight in the havoc those years initiated, his narrative as whole seems much more ambivalent about the ultimate nature of the changes that the 1960s wrought. Like so much of Roth's fiction, *The Dying Animal* insists on the costs that are irretrievably intertwined with pursuit of such sexual freedom, the consequences that would seem to be the by-product of casting away familial and marital bonds. Kepesh's chief critic comes in the form of his only son, Kenny, who has never forgiven his father for leaving his mother to enlist in the Sexual Revolution. "But the *sixties?* The explosion of childishness, that vulgar, mindless, collective regression, and that explains everything and excuses it all," Kenny informs his father midway through the novel. "Can't you come up with a better alibi? Seducing defenseless students, pursuing one's sexual interests at the expense of everyone else— that's so very necessary, isn't it?" (*Dying*, 90). While he remains flummoxed by his son's objections, Kepesh nevertheless endeavors to illustrate how the Sexual Revolution was not an aberration in American history but instead can be traced back to its Puritan past, with the figure of Thomas Morton and the infamous trading post at Merry Mount, a place, that as Kepesh reminds us, was memorialized in Nathaniel Hawthorne's "The May-Pole of Merry Mount" (1837). "You have to wait three hundred years before the voice of Thomas Morton turns up in America again, unexpurgated, as Henry Miller," Kepesh notes toward the end of his history lesson. "The clash between Plymouth and Merry Mount, between rule and misrule— the colonial harbinger of the national upheaval three hundred and thirty- odd years later when Morton's America was born at last, miscegenation and all" (*Dying*, 61).

This brief mentioning of the Hawthorne tale—Kepesh cites the story's most famous line that "Jollity and gloom were contending for an Empire"—

is worth considering more fully, suggesting Kepesh's desire to locate the origins of the cultural revolutions of the late 1960s within the nation's founding (*Dying*, 58–59). As Robert Milder notes, within "The May-Pole of Merry Mount" Hawthorne traces how a "communal neurosis—hostile to pleasure, to the senses, and to art—has been implanted in New England life at the very outset, so that the archetypal growth of the soul is forced to occur within culture-specific conditions deeply inhospitable to it."[32] Kepesh would seem to find in Hawthorne's story and the actual history of the Merry Mount a precedent for the sexual freedom that became feasible during the late 1960s and whose consequences were at the center of the culture wars that were waged during the 1990s. Not surprisingly, Kepesh delights in recording the hedonistic details of the infamous trading post, details that Hawthorne politely obscured in his allegory: "Men drinking, selling arms to the Indians, palling around with the Indians. Cavorting with the enemy. Copulating with Indian women, whose custom was to assume the doggie position and to be taken from behind" (*Dying*, 58). In particular, Kepesh celebrates the figure of Morton: "He's a kind of forest creature out of *As You Like It,* a wild demon out of *A Midsummer Night's Dream.* Shakespeare is Morton's contemporary, born only eleven or so years before Morton. Shakespeare is Morton's rock-and-roll. The Plymouth Puritans busted him, then the Salem Puritans busted him—put him in the stocks, fined him, imprisoned him" (*Dying*, 59). In Morton, Kepesh locates both a forefather for the sexual exhibition that would resurface as the 1960s unfurled but also a model of sorts for how he would like to imagine himself, a self-image that fails to conceal the anguish that is at the heart of his narrative.

This lecture on Morton and Merry Mount, however, is in service of Kepesh's larger argument concerning his reading of the Sexual Revolution and how we should contextualize the political and social revolutions of the late 1960s. It is an argument deeply informed by his experience as a college professor who was initiated into the tumult by a small coterie of female students (led by Janie Wyatt and Carolyn Lyons) who proudly labeled themselves the "Gutter Girls." "Well, these girls resembled nothing I'd ever known, and not because they were swathed in gypsy rags and barefoot," Kepesh recalls. "They detested innocence. They couldn't bear supervision. They weren't afraid of being conspicuous and they weren't afraid of being clandestine. They and their adherents may well have been, historically, the first wave of American girls fully implicated in their own desire" (*Dying*,

50–51). With their sexual bravado and hippie costumes, the "Gutter Girls" recall the figure of Rita Cohen in *American Pastoral*. A young revolutionary who is an associate of Swede Levov's missing daughter, Rita emerges as a sexual terrorist ("Smell this. Smell the inside of brand-new pussy," she instructs the Swede at one point) whose violent attempt to seduce the Swede—under the guise that she will finally reveal his missing daughter's whereabouts—leaves him utterly destabilized (*Pastoral*, 146). "Her dark child's eyes. Full of excitement and fun," Roth writes of Rita's sexual performance. "Full of audacity. Full of unreasonableness. Full of oddness. Full of Rita. And only half of it was performance. To agitate. To infuriate. To arouse. She was in an altered state. The imp of upheaval. The genie of disaster" (*Pastoral*, 146).

Perhaps not surprising considering his sexual history—this is the same character who found himself transformed into an enormous female mammary gland in *The Breast*—Kepesh embraces the disorder that Swede Levov finds so terrifying in *American Pastoral*. The sexual aggression that women like Rita Cohen and the "Gutter Girls" exhibited becomes for Kepesh not a symptom of civilization's decline but instead a quality to be celebrated; from his perspective, these women should be memorialized as patriotic revolutionaries for liberating the generations of women who followed them onto American campuses—"the uninhibited everything that the Consuelas and the Mirandas nonchalantly take for granted derives from the audacity of the shameless, subversive Janie Wyatts and the amazing victory they achieved in the sixties through the force of atrocious behavior. The coarse dimension of American life previously captured in gangster films, that's what Janie hauled on campus, because that's the intensity it took to undo the upholders of the norms" (*Dying*, 53). That Kepesh would take this perspective is not all unexpected: he has been the unintended beneficiary of the revolution that the "Gutter Girls" ushered in to being. "No the sixties weren't aberrant," Kepesh asserts at the climax of his ad hoc history lesson:

> The Wyatt girl wasn't aberrant. She was a natural Mortonian in the conflict that's been ongoing from the beginning. Out in the American wilderness, order will reign. The Puritans were the agents of rule and godly virtue and right reason, and on the other side was misrule. But why is it rule and misrule? Why isn't Morton the great theologian of no-rules? Why isn't Morton seen for what he is, the founding father of

personal freedom? In the Puritan theocracy you were at liberty to do good; in Morton's Merry Mount you were at liberty—that was it.

And there were lots of Mortons. Mercantile adventurers without the ideology of holiness, people who didn't give a damn whether they were elect or not. They came over with Bradford on the Mayflower, emigrated later on other ships, but you don't hear about them at Thanksgiving, because they couldn't stand these communities of saints and believers where no deviation was allowed. Our earliest American heroes were Morton's oppressors: Endicott, Bradford, Miles Standish. Merry Mount's been expunged from the official version because it's the story not of a virtuous utopia but of a utopia of candor. Yet it's Morton whose face should be carved in Mount Rushmore. That's going to happen too, the very day they rename the dollar the wyatt. (*Dying*, 61–62)

For Kepesh, the revolutions of the late 1960s do not mark a break from history; instead he imagines them as an articulation of the nation's true counterself—a self embodied by the wildness of Merry Mount's inhabitants—that finally resurfaced after having been suppressed for centuries. Chaos and "no-rule," Kepesh argues, have been present from before the nation's founding; they are essential components in America's mythic understanding of itself. While he mischievously imagines an alternate Morton-inflected version of American history, what's most striking here is Kepesh's insistence that the United States was founded on these competing narratives of "order and no-rule," "virtue and candor." It is an argument that Roth himself begins to articulate as early as the mid-1970s, when he described the origins of *The Great American Novel*, remarking how "the fierce, oftentimes wild and pathological assault launched in the sixties against venerable American institutions and beliefs and, more to the point, the emergence of a counterhistory, or countermythology, to challenge the mythic sense of itself the country had when the decade opened with General Eisenhower, out greatest World War II hero, still presiding—it was these social phenomena that furnished me with a handle by which to take hold of baseball, of all things, and place it at the center of a novel" (*Reading*, 89).

What Kepesh recognizes in *The Dying Animal* that Roth does not fully articulate in his explanation for his baseball novel is that the countermythology that the 1960s ushered in was not without precedent, but that it has always been ingrained in how the nation has imagined itself. A longer view of American history emerges in Roth's later fiction—the product of the "historical perspective" that Roth claims as a benefit of age—and his work has been more attuned to illuminating the myths and narratives that have informed the nation's self-image. As Pozorski observes, "what's gone awry in American culture is the fantasy that its ideals and principles, so ritualistically invoked in the culture wars [of the 1990s] and after, represent the exclusive meaning of America, thus occluding its complement: that America is founded on fractious trauma."[33] Indeed, Kepesh's sense that the rebellion of the "Gutter Girls" and of Merry Mount are essential components of how the nation has always imagined itself reflects how Roth's characters in his later fiction have tended to process the disorder of the late 1960s, particularly the ways in which Nathan Zuckerman in *American Pastoral* imagines the chaos unleashed by the act of domestic terrorism committed by Swede Levov's daughter, Merry. In that novel, Jerry Levov violently insists to the Swede that he must recognize his daughter as the real "Miss America":

> You wanted Miss America? Well, you've got her, with a vengeance—
> she's your daughter! You wanted to be a real American jock, a real
> American marine, a real American hotshot with a beautiful gentile
> babe on your arm? You longed to belong like everybody else to the
> United States of America? Well, you do now, big boy, thanks to your
> daughter. The reality of this place is right up in your kisser now. With
> the help of your daughter you're as deep in the shit as a man can get,
> the real American crazy shit. America amok! America amuck! (*Pastoral*, 277)

This insistence that the "real American crazy shit" is every bit as real and pervasive as the myth of pastoral innocence—John Winthrop's famous and much-deployed image of America as a "shining city upon a hill"—remains a vital component of the historical argument that Roth has constructed throughout his later fiction. Considering *American Pastoral*, Samuel Cohen observes how Roth novel appears "motivated by the idea that, in his susceptibility to the myth of pastoral in its various iterations, he has in his work also misrepresented Newark and even his nation's past. Rereading himself in *American Pastoral*, through Zuckerman, Roth explores the way we always get history—like other people—wrong."[34] The process by which we always get history wrong—the ways in which the past can never be fully recovered or adequately narrated—has been the cornerstone of the historiographic argument that Roth has pursued in his later fiction, most explicitly in the American trilogy.

What Kepesh begins to do in *The Dying Animal*, however, is to consider the extent to which the revolutions of the late 1960s actually transformed the United States, as he attempts to construct a meaningful, or even coherent, narrative of America's post-1960s trajectory. "The idea of progress, contrary to the received opinion, owes its appeal not to its millennial vision of the future but to the seemingly more realistic expectation that the expansion of productive forces can continue indefinitely," Lasch argues in *The True and Only Heaven*. "The history of liberalism—which includes a great deal that passes for conservatism as well—consists of variations on this underlying theme."[35] Although Kepesh (and most likely Roth) would disagree with the critique of liberalism that Lasch advances—throughout *The True and Only Heaven*, he argues for the necessity of the communal bonds that Roth's protagonists so frequently and vehemently reject—I would claim that *The Dying Animal* expresses a similar skepticism toward the United States' prospects in the new century.[36] This skepticism can be felt in Kepesh's consideration of the ultimate consequences of the sexual revolution as the advances made by the "Gutter Girls" seem to disappear into the tableaux of history. Adrift in the shifting sexual mores of the late 1990s, Kepesh muses how the "Fall and Rise of the Condom is the sexual story of the twentieth century" (*Dying*, 68). "The condom came back," Kepesh marvels in one of the novel's more memorable rants,

> and with the condom, the return of all that got blown out in the sixties. What man can say he enjoys sex with a condom the way he does without? What's really in it for him? That's why the organs of digestion have, in our time, come to vie for supremacy as a sexual orifice. The crying need for the mucous membrane. To get rid of the condom, [homosexual men] have to have a steady partner, therefore they marry. The gays are militant: they want marriage and they want openly to join the army and be accepted. The institutions I loathed. And for the same reason: regimentation. (*Dying*, 68)

While there is plenty to object to within this passage, particularly Kepesh's skewed view of homosexual desire and the fight for equal rights, what I would emphasize is his sense that most of the gains seemingly won by the Sexual Revolution have been lost with the onslaught of the AIDS crisis— what had once appeared to be a clear trajectory of continually expanding sexual liberties appears at the end of the century, at least from Kepesh's rather entrenched libertine perspective, to be highly muddled. On the one hand, Kepesh's argument here would suggest that we view the 1990s as a return of sorts to the sexual repression of the Eisenhower era as the gay community fights to enlist in the very institutions that Kepesh has endeavored to escape. That said, I would argue that Kepesh's sense of history resists such a neat cyclical design; the future in *The Dying Animal* appears far too uncertain, and there is little sense that an understanding of the past can adequately prepare one for what the horizon has in store. "The loveliest fairy tale of childhood is that everything happens in order," Kepesh laments toward the end of the novel. "Your grandparents go long before your parents, and your parents go long before you. If you're lucky it can work out that way, people aging and dying in order, so that at the funeral you ease your pain by thinking that person had a long life" (*Dying*, 148–49). Kepesh realizes that such thinking is nothing more than fanciful, but the novel as a whole suggests that our simplified attempts to comprehend time's progression are confounded by the seemingly chaotic way that history appears to unfold.

Death and the New Century

Beyond the limitations of sexual freedom that have returned in the 1990s, Kepesh's critique of progress—the notion that the American experiment is somehow constantly expanding and improving—appears most pronounced in his aforementioned reading of the millennial celebrations. "Rather than the destruction of the age-old-cities, an international eruption of the superficial instead, a global outbreak of sentimentality such as even Americans hadn't witnessed before," Kepesh muses of that evening's proceedings. "From Sydney to Bethlehem to Times Square, the recirculating of clichés occurs at supersonic speeds. No bombs go off, no blood is shed—the next bang you will hear will be the boom of prosperity and the explosion of markets" (*Dying*, 145). Kepesh's reading here shifts between acknowledging, and at times mourning, the apocalypse that never materialized—the failure of history to provide a properly violent conclusion to a century of mass death and destruction—and puncturing the falsely optimistic and expansive vision of the future being projected that night, a future of exploding markets and global harmony. In this moment, Kepesh seemingly rejects the notion of progress; as he faces the reality of a new century, he can no longer maintain faith in the likelihood of a more prosperous, enlightened future, nor is he able to offer a meaningful account of his nation's postwar trajectory.

Nevertheless, the complexity of Kepesh's view of the millennial celebrations emerges most forcefully as he and Consuela, whose family was forced to leave Cuba after the fall of the Batista regime, watch the celebrations staged by Castro that night. At first, Kepesh simply records the absurdity of the gala broadcast from Havana, suggesting the garishness that characterized the evening's proceedings: "a lot of young people, ninety-six of them, ABC says—wearing silly white costumes and not so much dancing or singing as circling the stage howling into hand-held mikes. The showgirls look like leggy Latino West Village transvestites walking around in a huff. Atop their heads are overdeveloped lampshades—three feet high, according to ABC" (*Dying*, 146). More broadly, Roth's decision to bring Castro and the legacy of the Cuban Revolution into the novel calls into question how we might understand the history of the United States during the Cold War, underscoring the uncertainties that faced both nations as they entered the new millennium.[37] "Yes, this is definitely Castro saying 'Fuck you' to the twentieth century," Kepesh concludes. "Because it's the end of his adventure in history, too, of the mark he made and did not make on the course of human events" (*Dying*, 152). The carefulness of Kepesh's judgment here—his refusal to define the impact that Castro did or did not make—highlights the difficulty of evaluating the past at this moment. The Cold War may be over, but there seems to be no way of assessing the United States' post-1945 story (or Cuba's for that matter)—the meaning of the narrative remains impossible to discern. Similarly, the future for Kepesh, as seen through the lens of his age and his desire for the ailing Consuela, would seem to be anything but assured. The unnaturalness of Consuela's condition—the reality of death threatening her youthful vitality—would seem to extend to how Roth in the novel imagines the nation's troubled trajectory entering the new century.

The Dying Animal concludes shortly after Kepesh's recollection of the celebrations that night as his monologue is interrupted by a phone call from Consuela, from whom he has not heard since that New Year's Eve. This brief novel ends on a brilliantly uncertain note as the prospects of the new century are obscured by Consuela's illness and Kepesh's awareness of his own mortality. The abruptness of the conclusion—Kepesh jettisons his narrative so that he can comfort Consuela before she has her surgery—would seem to be the point, emphasizing as it does the sense of incompleteness and uncertainty that the novel depicts as hanging over the United States at the beginning of the twenty-first century. In this sense, *The Dying Animal* would seem to be the most prophetic of Roth's later work as it anticipates the violence that would define the first decade of the new century. Exploring how our lives are shaped by the whims of history would seem to be the project that has consumed Roth in his fiction of this century, and his novels beginning with *The Plot Against America* have repeatedly demonstrated the various ways that history can shatter one's existence. "It's a flexible instrument that we've inherited," Nathan Zuckerman reminds the young married couple in *Exit Ghost* who are terrified by the prospect of George W. Bush's reelection. "It's amazing how much punishment we can take" (*Exit*, 82). This is the only assurance—that we as a nation or as individuals can perhaps endure more punishment—that Roth would seem to offer in his late fiction, a lesson that begins to take shape in *The Dying Animal*.

Beyond looking ahead to the tenuous terrain that Roth will explore in his novels of this century, *The Dying Animal* presents a stark rejoinder to readers inclined to accept the triumphant narrative of progress that many Americans eagerly embraced at the end of the century as the global economy continued to expand. In reassessing his and his nation's recent past, David Kepesh offers a much more tenuous account of the cultural and political upheavals of the 1960s, his narrative suggesting the difficulty in not only recognizing the forces that triggered those revolutions but also in assessing their ultimate consequences. "Why should Castro the revolutionary care, why should anyone care, about something that gives us a sense that we're understanding something that we're not understanding?" Kepesh asks toward the end of the book. "The passage of time. We're in the swim, sinking in time, until finally we drown and go" (*Dying*, 147–48). The despair expressed within this passage is remarkable: any attempt to make sense of history or to imagine a future would seem to be impossible for Kepesh as he considers the state of the world alongside Consuela's illness and his advancing age. While Kepesh is certainly mourning his love for Consuela, for both her person and her body, he is also lamenting our inability to grasp onto a satisfactory explanation for how time progresses—both past and future here are inscrutable, and we are left to drown in time's onslaught. "But time is such a vague and elusive concept, and that is precisely the point of the text, it seems to me," Pozorski concludes of this moment. "The drowning, the sense of flailing and failing, comes in relation to time's unpredictability."[38] Like Lasch's work in *The True and Only Heaven*, which reminds us of how notions of progress have continually informed the United States' sense of itself, *The Dying Animal* exposes the myth of progress, revealing the limitations of narrative and human imagination to comprehend fully the nature of the revolutions that have transformed American culture since the end of the Second World War or to imagine what the whims of history ultimately have in store for us.

Notes

1. Philip Roth, *The Dying Animal* (Boston: Houghton Mifflin, 2001), 148; hereafter cited parenthetically as *Dying*.

2. Christopher Lasch, *The True and Only Heaven: Progress and Its Critics* (New York: Norton, 1991), 14.

3. Charles McGrath, "Zuckerman's Alter Brain," *New York Times Book Review*, May 7, 2000, www.nytimes.com/books/00/05/07/reviews/000507.07mcgrat.html.

4. In *A Poetics of Postmodernism*, Hutcheon explains that historiographic metafiction as a narrative form demonstrates a "theoretical self-awareness of history and fiction as human constructs" (Linda Hutcheon, *A Poetics of Postmodernism: History, Theory, Fiction* [London: Routledge, 1988], 5).

5. Samuel Cohen, *After the End of History: American Fiction in the 1990s* (Iowa City: University of Iowa Press, 2009), 89.

6. Ibid.

7. Philip Roth, "The Story behind *The Plot Against America*," *New York Times Book Review*, September 19, 2004, http://query.nytimes.com/gst/fullpage.html?res=9500E7DB1338F93AA2575AC0A9629C8B63.

8. Philip E. Wegner, *Life between Two Deaths, 1989–2001: U.S. Culture in the Long Nineties* (Durham: Duke University Press, 2009), 28–29.

9. Philip Roth, *The Plot Against America* (Boston: Houghton Mifflin, 2004), 113–14.

10. Philip Roth, *Nemesis* (Boston: Houghton Mifflin Harcourt, 2010), 242–43.

11. Philip Roth, *Exit Ghost* (Boston: Houghton Mifflin, 2007), 69–70; hereafter cited parenthetically as *Exit*.

12. Claudia Roth Pierpont, *Roth Unbound: A Writer and his Books* (New York: Farrar, Straus and Giroux, 2013), 261.

13. Mark Shechner, *Up Society's Ass, Copper: Rereading Philip Roth* (Madison: University of Wisconsin Press, 2003), 206.

14. Of Roth's later works only *The Humbling* (2009) revisits, with diminishing returns, the consequences of aging and sexual desire that both *Sabbath's Theater* and *The Dying Animal* chronicle more powerfully. In this later novel, Simon Axler, an aging actor who has lost the ability to perform, falls into a sexual relationship with the much younger Peegen Stapleford, a friend's daughter who has just gotten out of a long-term relationship with another woman. The book remains the last of Roth's to focus on sex—in a particularly memorable episode Axler and Peegen experiment with her green strap-on dildo which she wore like "a gunslinger"—but such moments seem less inspired when compared against Kepesh's narration in *The Dying Animal* (Philip Roth, *The Humbling* [Boston: Houghton Mifflin Harcourt, 2009], 92).

15. The exception to this trend would be Aimee Pozorski's chapter on the novel in her excellent monograph on Roth's late work. Pozorski's reading emphasizes Kepesh's viewing of the millennial celebrations, suggesting how we might identify "*The Dying Animal*—with even its title gesturing toward a non-consolatory description of humanity—a modern elegy for US culture, for the world" (Aimee Pozorski, *Roth and Trauma: The Problem of History in the Later Works [1995–2010]* [New York: Bloomsbury Academic, 2011], 118).

16. Zoe Heller, "The Ghost Rutter," review of *The Dying Animal*, *New Republic*, June 21, 2001, www.newrepublic.com/article/books-and-arts/the-ghost-rutter.

17. The spring 2012 issue of *Philip Roth Studies*, devoted to the topic of "Roth and Women," contains two articles that offer compelling readings of the sexual politics that inform *The Dying Animal* (see Velichka Ivanova, "My Own Foe from the Other Gender: [Mis] representing Women in *The Dying Animal*" and Zoë Roth, "Against Representation: "Death, Desire, and Art in Philip Roth's *The Dying Animal*").

18. Pozorski, *Roth and Trauma*, 116.

19. I would like to acknowledge Darren Surman and Kevin Stuart, whose insight helped clarify my reading of Lasch's argument in *The True and Only Heaven*.

20. In *The Culture of Narcissism*, Lasch offers a brief critique of Roth, suggesting how *Portnoy's Complaint*—along with Norman Mailer's *Advertisements for Myself*, Paul Zweig's *Three Journeys*, Norman Podhoretz's *Making It*, and Fredrick Exley's *A Fan's Notes*—"waver between hard-won personal revelation, chastened by anguish with which it was gained, and the kind of spurious confession whose only claim to the reader's attention is that it describes events of immediate interest to the author. On the verge of insight, these writers often draw back into self-parody, seeking to disarm criticism by anticipating it (Christopher Lasch, *The Culture of Narcissism: American Life in an Age of Diminishing Expectations* [New York: Norton, 1979], 18).

21. Louis Menand, "Christopher Lasch's Clash with Liberalism," in *American Studies* (New York: Farrar, Straus and Giroux, 2002), 202.

22. Lasch, *The True and Only Heaven*, 47–48.

23. Menand, *American Studies*, 208.

24. That said, much of Roth's early fiction echoes the mistrust of mass culture that Lasch identifies as one of the central failings of liberalism. Considering the stories collected in *Goodbye, Columbus*, David Gooblar observes how "Roth's individuals are each marked off from the collective by their ambivalence, self-questioning, and, often, self-contradiction—qualities that, in line with the new liberalism, are presented as in vital opposition to the idea of collective will" (David Gooblar, *The Major Phases of Philip Roth* [New York: Continuum International, 2011], 25).

25. "The populist tradition Lasch described has been transmitted through an oddly assorted sequence of thinkers," Menand notes. "These thinkers all share one attitude, of course: an antagonism to the modern liberal outlook as Lasch had described it. This may express itself in an appreciation for the 'civic virtues'—the virtues derived from personal independence, political participation, and genuinely productive labor; in an acceptance of 'fate' (one of the book's key terms) and of the idea of limits; or in an admiration for a set of characteristics that Lasch identified with lower-middle-class, or 'petty-bourgeois,' culture: moral conservatism, egalitarianism, loyalty, and the struggle against the moral temptation of resentment (that is, the capacity for forgiveness)" (Menand, *American Studies*, 210).

26. Philip Roth, "On *the Great American Novel*," in *Reading Myself and Others* (New York: Farrar, Straus and Giroux, 1975), 87; hereafter cited parenthetically as *Reading*.

27. Philip Roth, *American Pastoral*, (Boston: Houghton Mifflin, 1997), 423; hereafter cited parenthetically as *Pastoral*.

28. Patrick Hayes, *Philip Roth: Fiction and Power* (Oxford: Oxford University Press, 2014), 128.

29. This view was perhaps most notably articulated by Norman Podhoretz in an essay on Roth's career that appeared in the wake of *I Married a Communist* (1998). "Going far beyond the Zuckerman trilogy or *Patrimony* in this respect, *American Pastoral* set up a contrast between, on the one hand, the middle-class Jews who had once offered such fat targets for his poisoned arrows and, on the other, the counterculture and its academic apologists with whom in his younger days (admittedly never with a completely full heart) he had once identified and to whom he had directed his authorial winks of complicity," Podhoretz writes in the essay. "But to the delighted astonishment of some of us, and the puzzlement and disappointment of others, he now has changed sides in the distribution of his scorn and his sympathies. Here, for once, it was the ordinary Jews of his childhood who

were celebrated—for their decency, their sense of responsibility, their seriousness about their work, their patriotism—and here, for once, those who rejected and despised such virtues were shown to be either pathologically nihilistic or smug, self-righteous, and unimaginative" (Norman Podhoretz, "The Adventures of Philip Roth," *Commentary,* October 1998, www.commentarymagazine.com/article/the-adventures-of-philip-roth/).

30. Elaine Tyler May, *Homeward Bound: American Families in the Cold War Era, 20th Anniversary Edition* (New York: Basic Books, 2008), 16–17.

31. "I could not believe then—ridiculously enough, I cannot still—that what happened next was because Olivia wanted it to happen," Marcus notes in the aftermath of the blowjob as he hovers in a morphine-induced coma on the verge of dying. "This was not the way it went between a conventionally brought-up boy and a nice well-bred girl when I was alive and it was 1951 and, for the third time in just over half a century, America was at war again" (Philip Roth, *Indignation* [Boston: Houghton Mifflin, 2008], 57–58).

32. Robert Milder, *Hawthorne's Habitations: A Literary Life* (Oxford: Oxford University Press, 2013), 119.

33. Pozorski, *Roth and Trauma,* 12.

34. Cohen, *After the End of History,* 84.

35. Lasch, *The True and Only Heaven,* 39.

36. "By the time of *The True and Only Heaven,* Lasch had come to regard the belief in progress not as simply an interesting paradox in twentieth-century liberal thought, but as the dominant ideology of modern history," Louis Menand writes in his reconsideration of Lasch's career. "It is in the name of progress, he thought, that traditional sources of happiness and virtue—work, faith, the family, even an independent sense of self—are being destroyed; and he began his book with an analysis of the false values of the modern liberal outlook, proposing, for each value or attitude to be rejected, an alternative" (Menand, *American Studies,* 208–9).

37. In her reading of the novel, Pozorski usefully suggests how "in offering up Consuela as a sympathetic love interest of David Kepesh, the novel raises questions about US involvement in Cuban relations but also, more importantly, the effect of revolution on the people" (Pozorski, *Roth and Trauma,* 108).

38. Ibid., 107.

7

"Novotny's Pain"

Philip Roth on Politics and the Problem of Pain

Till Kinzel

How literature and its analysis can contribute to a deeper understanding of key features of American (or any) culture can be paradigmatically shown by examining Philip Roth's Zuckerman novels in their changing attitudes toward major events of American history and politics.[1] Roth's American trilogy comprising his novels *American Pastoral, I Married a Communist,* and *The Human Stain* offers an example of what the novelist's sharp eye can see about a culture that may escape the notice of its other members. The writer's often refracted sense of reality may offer a more convincing portrait of this reality than other forms of cultural discourse. In Roth's case, many intertextual and intermedial references in these novels build up to highlight what can be called "deep structures" of American culture. Thus, Philip Roth's novels not only offer glimpses, artfully contrived by means of Zuckerman's appropriating narrative voice, into the narrating or narrated present but also highlight the many ways in which the present is symbolically linked to the past—among others, the founding era in *American Pastoral,* 1950s McCarthyism, anticommunism and anti-anticommunism in *I Married a Communist,* and colonial Puritanism in *The Human Stain.* Roth's novels are enactments of cultural memory, and by writing themselves into the canon, the canon becomes what it always already is, the repository of cultural memory.

Not surprisingly, it is particularly these novels that have received an enormous amount of commentary. This includes a critical discussion of the political issues involved in Roth's views of America and American history from the Puritans and the founding up to the presidencies of William Jefferson Clinton and George W. Bush.[2] Instead of adding to this already formidable output, focusing on Roth's so-called minor writings can yield additional insights into the way that "the political" functions as an important framing condition of Roth's fictions. I have highlighted some of these issues in recent papers on Roth's formally odd "novel" *Our Gang*, which, at least in my view, many critics have failed to take as seriously as it deserves.[3] This is the case despite the fact that "seriousness" itself as well as its limits in connection with politics are at issue in many of Roth's fictional presentations and discussions, even if they appear to be essentially, or even frivolously, frivolous.[4]

In what follows I do not want to analyze any of Roth's acknowledged masterpieces, nor do I want to make an argument for the political significance of some of his so-called lesser works in novel form. Rather, I want to explore the connection between politics and the body, and in particular pain, as it comes to light in one of his shorter narratives, "Novotny's Pain" (1962), which may have been in part inspired by autobiographical material.[5] The fact that Roth deals very prominently with issues of (bodily) pain especially in such later major works as *The Anatomy Lesson* and *Sabbath's Theater*, not to mention *American Pastoral*, should not obscure the fact that he also has something subtle to say about them in often neglected earlier pieces.[6]

The issue of how to conceive of and contextualize pain is closely linked not only to politics narrowly understood but also to the larger frame of anthropology and even theology within which "the problem of pain" has traditionally been considered.[7] However, Roth offers a decidedly nonreligious view of pain. According to C. S. Lewis, a Christian apologist, the problem of pain is only a serious problem because there is a moral and powerful God. For such a powerful God would, if he were in fact also morally good, want to make people happy and thus eliminate their pain. But as people do suffer from pain, and therefore are not happy, God would seem to be either morally bad or neutral or not sufficiently powerful. All these options clearly involve serious problems for religious believers and for theology in general—this is the issue of theodicy. On the other hand, if there is no God, there will be no reason for pain not to exist, because there is no promise of redemption in the first place. There can then be no superior frame of reference that makes sense of the pain that human beings suffer while living in the vale of tears that is the world. Although Novotny is a Catholic,[8] religion does not influence the way he experiences pain, so the theological issues are not at all made thematic in Roth's story. On the other hand, Roth does not follow the most prominent non-Christian interpretation of pain either, the one propounded by Ernst Jünger.

For Jünger, pain acquires a positive value because it belongs to those unchangeable standards that give evidence to the significance of human beings. Pain, according to Jünger, is the strongest challenge that life provides: "Pain belongs to those keys with which one opens up not only the innermost part of man but at the same time the world."[9] For Jünger, the individual's position toward pain explains someone's identity. Mastering one's pain, a heroic undertaking, implies for Jünger complete control over one's life. Alienation from one's self, including one's body, Jünger notes, enables a kind of distancing from, as well as a defense against the attacks of, pain.[10] For Jünger, pain leads directly to the political and its corollary, the military, as the dominant military metaphors show by means of which he writes about pain. Of course, Roth takes a different track, but he also hints at a more complex connection between pain and its source, which, by means of a little interpretive stretching, can also be applied to political and social issues. For in *The Anatomy Lesson,* Roth includes the following epigraph from a medical textbook: "The chief obstacle to correct diagnosis in painful conditions is the fact that the symptom is often felt at a distance from its source."[11] This difficulty of correctly diagnosing the source of pain also applies to "Novotny's Pain," a pain that may well have its ultimate source outside the individual body, namely in the body politic.

Roth's early short story "Novotny's Pain" is of particular interest in connection with politics because Roth manages to squeeze into it a rather large number of crucial political questions, even though he offers no in-depth discussion of them. In fact, the first two paragraphs of the story present an exposition of the whole range of political issues that Roth also considers in his better-known works. The politics of pain, one might say, connects the body politic of the American republic with the body of individual citizens and more specifically the body of one such citizen called Novotny. This is not accidental, even though he is not merely an individual but also part of a larger group of "young men who suffered military life alongside him and had suffered it before him" ("Novotny's Pain," 261).

"Novotny's Pain" serves to highlight a number of points that illustrate the specific nature of the American republic around the middle of the twentieth century. Roth here may well have been influenced by the general interest of the so-called New York Intellectuals around the middle of the century, for example, in issues of alienation in connection with mass society.[12] The conflict of the allegedly autonomous individual with the conformism of mass society, encapsulated in the popular theorem of the "lonely crowd," may be regarded as a general background to Roth's early writings.[13]

Roth's story deals very explicitly with the problem of pain, as Novotny's pain is introduced in the second sentence of the story in a way that reminds the reader somewhat of Kafka's Gregor Samsa in *The Metamorphosis*: "He awoke one morning with a pain on the right side of his body, directly above the buttock" ("Novotny's Pain," 261). Whereas Samsa has inexplicably turned into a beetle, and David Kepesh, in *The Breast*, perhaps somewhat less inexplicably, into a female breast,[14] Novotny suffers from an inexplicable pain that presents him with an internal reason or necessity to grit his teeth, whereas being drafted into the army represents the external reason or necessity to grit his teeth. The internal pain points to the incommensurability of the individual's feelings, because the individual's pain cannot be subsumed to a general insight into human nature. The problem of pain, in Roth's story, can thus be compared to a similar issue presented in *American Pastoral*.[15] Here, it is the confrontation with mortality, in the context of which Zuckerman introduces references to Tolstoy's famous story "The Death of Ivan Ilyich," a story in which the famous syllogism concerning the mortality of Socrates and of all human beings is discussed.

In the context of logical conclusions, the individual's mortality is presented as an objective and impersonal insight. But it is precisely this general and impersonal insight that Ivan Ilyich feels unable to accept because it cannot capture the crucial problem, namely that it is *his own death, his* mortality that is at issue, not the abstract mortality of everyone. Whereas in *American Pastoral*, death is linked to the American body politic through the Vietnam War and its domestic consequences, particularly Merry Levov's acts of terrorism, "Novotny's Pain" offers a somewhat different scenario. Here, the setting is not the time of the Vietnam War, nor, as would easily have been possible, the Second World War, but rather the Korean War, which would also feature, if in an odd way, in one of Roth's last novels, *Indignation*.[16]

The framing of the story is thus provided by the major political conflict at the time, the competition between Western democracy and Eastern communism.[17] The political issue that confronts Novotny and his bodily pain is thus always inscribed into the larger issues of foreign policy and therefore peace and war. The foreign-policy dimension implies a definition of friend and enemy from which the individual cannot freely and actively dissent. However, even if an individual such as Novotny is in general agreement with the state's definition of the enemy ("Novotny believed in fighting for freedom" ["Novotny's Pain," 261]), there is room for less than complete acceptance of the consequences of others' political decisions. This limited form of freedom is in fact emphasized by the narrator's use of "gritting one's teeth" three times in the first paragraph of the story. Roth's narrator focalizes the story through Novotny's consciousness and his bodily reactions, particularly gritting his teeth and the ominous buttock pain that truly is almost a "pain in the ass."

Novotny also personifies a special kind of citizen who is also typical of a larger segment of the American population, for he is "of foreign extraction," although he and his family have so far not been spectacularly successful participants in the American Dream. This status of Novotny in the American republic contributes to his willingness to serve in the war as a citizen who knows his duty and his indebtedness "to this country" that is the main source of his patriotism ("Novotny's Pain," 261). Duty, though, is not, in this context, a pure and unproblematic political and moral virtue. Rather, it is the result of two different feelings or emotional states that are not in themselves morally unambiguous: namely the "sense of shame" and the "sense of necessity" ("Novotny's Pain," 261). Certain emotional states of the individual are therefore politically relevant because the politically necessary or desired behavior would only be insufficiently achieved if duty were merely a rational principle of ethics, freely assented to. A "sense of shame" can of course be instilled in persons for all kinds of reasons, including immoral ones; and a "sense of necessity" would also seem to be less than self-evident. For necessity does not exist as such but is a construction based on an analysis of a given situation; and interpretations can, of course, always be questioned. Necessity could be understood as "moral necessity," but it seems much more likely in this context to think of necessity as a transmoral form of obligation, exerted by social and political forces—such as the draft. Duty as a politically relevant virtue cannot simply rely on an individual's feeling of dutifulness but implies more. It can fully operate only when the "social context" ensures compliance with "necessity" despite gritting one's teeth.

The narrator points out the most basic political conviction of Novotny, a political conviction that is very close to the libertarian strand of American political thinking. This kind of thinking is encapsulated in the notion of negative liberty, often condensed in the phrase, "That government is best which governs least." Novotny's view is quoted as follows: "what he himself wanted most from any government was that it should let him alone to live his life" ("Novotny's Pain," 261–62). This libertarian understanding of the limits of state activity or state power, as the story's exposition makes perfectly clear, has a merely theoretical value in a state of war: Novotny is described in a way that suggests he has to suffer from certain things over which he has no control. His pain belongs to those things that "simply happened to him" ("Novotny's Pain," 261). In the decisive matters he has no choice—and this refers both to the involuntary "decisions" or reactions of his body and to the involuntary consequences of politics, as indicated by the fact that Novotny did not volunteer to fight but was drafted. The exposition of the story sets the stage for the political problem of how freedom as a political principle is connected to compulsion; or how the necessary constraints on individual freedom can serve the larger purpose of securing the political freedom of the republic at large.

The narrator explicitly refers to Novotny's patriotism but does not hesitate to immediately qualify this patriotism in a serious way by reporting Novotny's "feelings of confinement and of loss," even though he had initially even "vowed he would do whatever they told him to do, without grievance or resentment" ("Novotny's Pain," 266). This conscious rejection of resentment and grievance could be regarded as the opposite of gritting one's teeth, though it may well be another politically relevant point to note that a grievance may have more than subjective causes. A grievance that is not in some way expressed cannot be regarded as a *political* grievance but merely as a *personal* grudge.

Pain as a subjective state of mind and body poses a problem within the larger political context, here of army life. For the pain that Novotny suffers interferes with a proper fulfillment of his duties (see "Novotny's Pain," 270).

Novotny rejects "go[ing] back to duty like a man," so that he is threatened with a court-martial for disobeying orders—and that again is linked to the hierarchical structure that extends to an official interpretation of his pain. Although pain is by definition that which only the person suffering can truly evaluate, the given social context does not allow for this subjective view to be in any way authoritative: "it was for a trained doctor to decide how sick or well Novotny was" ("Novotny's Pain," 271).

Novotny's case is a troubling one, since his experience of pain in the army leads this dutiful and nonrebellious young man to reflections about what will happen to him—of all people. One can see his own surprise about his bodily reactions to what is demanded of him, since he "had never broken a law in his life" ("Novotny's Pain," 271). His alienation from the demands of society in an extreme case such as war is particularly inexplicable in view of this unqualified law-abidingness. Nevertheless, Novotny acknowledges his fear of dying as well as his hatred of the army ("Novotny's Pain," 276). This constellation indicates that Novotny's symptoms of alienation are not merely subjective feelings but rather point to an alienation that is due to structural conditions of modern society.[18]

He finds himself subjected to diagnostic attempts that wield concepts like "passive-aggressive" to explain his behavior, although this psychiatric diagnosis amounts to little more than a replacement of the word "coward" ("Novotny's Pain," 278). Novotny, it seems, will have to suffer the social consequences of his painful inability to serve his country: He will be dishonorably discharged from the army. But even here, where the contrast between the individual and the machinery of social life would seem to be most conspicuous, and most threatening, it is in fact surprising to see to what benign lengths the army goes in examining and determining the nature of Novotny's disease.

Novotny represents a visceral nonconformism as expressed by his pain. Although the pain may not have identifiable causes in purely medical and psychological terms, there is one explanation of his pain that makes sense, namely a "teleological" one. For Novotny's pain explains the far from insignificant fact of his own survival. The apparent noncausality of his pain thus becomes an expression and even a symbol of freedom. Not of freedom in the political sense but rather of personal freedom in the Hobbesian sense of bodily self-preservation (which is not a complete freedom of movement). Novotny's pain symbolizes the rational nonrationality of the body—the nonrational pain does lead to rational consequences for this particular individual. These consequences are in fundamental accord with the political anthropology of Lockean origin that would also shape the American founding; I refer to the principle of "comfortable self-preservation" or "self-interest rightly understood," a principle that is also closely linked to law-abidingness.[19] Of course, Novotny's pain has not been comfortable itself, but ironically it led Novotny to lead a much more comfortable life than, for example, Marcus Messner's in Roth's *Indignation,* whom we encounter while he is "under morphine" and who does not survive the war.[20]

In contrast to the alienated Jewish characters in his other works—just remember Alexander Portnoy's suffering under his Jewish mother—the non-Jew Novotny is in fact alienated, but his alienation is comparatively mild. The point here is that he manages to achieve in his life exactly what he set out to achieve; there is no real discrepancy between what he desires and what he gets. He manages to marry the girl he always had wanted to marry. He works on the job to which he had aspired (television cameraman in Chicago). Nobody is interested in his discharge papers, so Novotny manages to escape social stigmatization as well, quite possibly a benefit of mass society and its concomitant anonymity. And he also no longer suffers from a similar pain as in the army interlude of his life but rather from a mere "cautionary twinge whenever he bends the wrong way" ("Novotny's Pain," 280).

In fact, the story of Novotny exemplifies the limits of alienation within liberal democracy. The pain on which Novotny's army experience centered finally signals the nontragic nature of liberal democracy: The protagonist's alienation from army life and warfare, despite his theoretical acceptance of "fighting for freedom" (note the abstract nature of this slogan that makes it adaptable to a wide range of actual stances) ceases to be of any serious significance once he continues with his life plan. In the wake of World War II and before the disaster of the Vietnam War, the close link of "fighting for freedom" with American patriotism can still be taken for granted, even if the Korean War did not pose a direct threat to the American homeland. It was, however, "potentially the most dangerous war in world history."[21] This judgment finds no equivalent in Roth's story; the story itself does not even present any elaborate case for the Korean War, insofar as there is no political or ideological debate about it—which may well be the literary equivalent of the comparative public noncontroversiality of the Korean War at the time.[22] It is in line with this feature of the story that Novotny's pain serves as a nonverbal bodily sign of disagreement, and that this sign replaces any discussion of political and particularly foreign policy issues. This is surprising, since one could easily have imagined a discussion that touched on the "imperial" dimensions of American foreign policy within the Cold War framework or the fact that the United States went to war in Korea "to preserve U.S. military and diplomatic credibility in the global Cold War."[23] The arguments that representatives of the military put forth against Novotny are only low-level arguments appealing to Novotny's solidarity with those soldiers already in the field—the goodness of the cause as such is not put in question.

Novotny's alienation cannot be regarded as the kind of deep-rooted, culturally conditioned alienation that was described by some Jewish New York intellectuals such as Isaac Rosenfeld, Daniel Bell, or Irving Howe.[24] It is rather a largely nonintellectual reaction. This may well be why Novotny is not one of Roth's more memorable characters—his intellectual mediocrity implies a certain reduction of the level of complexity on which issues of politics and war can be presented and considered in this story. Thus, Debra Shostak has drawn attention to the "simple binary thinking" of Novotny; and this fact also affects the storytelling because of the dominant focalization through Novotny himself.[25]

Novotny does lead a fairly circumscribed life, symbolized by his forgoing the pleasures of bowling, of all things, but there is still love, passion—and all those troubling thoughts about the future that turn out to be nothing much of a personal problem. For these concerns, as the narrative voices makes clear at the end, are the questions everybody asks about his existence ("Novotny's Pain," 280). In the end, then, Novotny seems to have again become the unobtrusive, law-abiding citizen that he was before the Korean War in which he did not participate. All's well that ends well, one might be tempted to say, at least in this story—and merely considered from Novotny's point of view. But Roth did not stop there, of course, not the least because the march of history did not stop and went on providing ample "opportunity" for further Rothian stories of trauma, alienation, deceit, and pain after 1963, the turning-point of American postwar history.[26] The sort of American pastoral that Novotny's "quiet, ordinary sort of life" suggests will be a mere interlude in the larger trajectory of American history, which would soon lead to the upheavals and the violence of the 1960s and 1970s, both at home and abroad.

Notes

1. See Till Kinzel, *Die Tragödie und Komödie des amerikanischen Lebens: Eine Studie zu Zuckermans Amerika in Philip Roths Amerika-Trilogie* (Heidelberg: Winter, 2006) for an extended discussion; for a more overtly political stance, see Norman Podhoretz, "Philip Roth, Then and Now," in *The Norman Podhoretz Reader: A Selection of His Writings from the 1950s through the 1990s*, ed. Thomas L. Jeffers (New York: Free Press, 2004), 327–48.

2. See, for example, Velichka Ivanova, *Fiction, utopie, histoire: Essai sur Philip Roth et Milan Kundera* (Paris: L'Harmattan, 2010); Aimee Pozorski, *Roth and Trauma: The Problem of History in the Later Works (1995–2010)* (London: Continuum, 2011); Michael Kimmage, *In History's Grip: Philip Roth's Newark Trilogy* (Stanford: Stanford University Press, 2012); and Claudia Franziska Brühwiler, *Political Initiation in the Novels of Philip Roth* (New York: Bloomsbury, 2013).

3. Till Kinzel, "Philip Roth's *Our Gang*, the Politics of Intertextuality and the Complexities of Cultural Memory," *Philip Roth Studies* 9.1 (2013): 15–25; Till Kinzel, "Dialogical and Monological Madness: Philip Roth's Novel *Our Gang* as Orality Play," in *Philip Roth and World Literature: Transatlantic Perspectives and Uneasy Passages*, ed. Velichka Ivanova, 255–69 (Amherst: Cambria, 2014).

4. On Roth and seriousness, see David Gooblar, *The Major Phases of Philip Roth* (London: Continuum, 2011), 33–57.

5. See Claudia Roth Pierpont, *Roth Unbound: A Writer and His Books* (New York: Farrar, Straus and Giroux, 2013), 29.

6. See David Brauner, *Philip Roth* (Manchester: Manchester University Press, 2007), 219.

7. See C. S. Lewis, *The Problem of Pain*, in *The Complete C. S. Lewis Signature Classics*, 253–646 (New York: HarperOne, 2007); and Till Kinzel, "Der Schmerz des Menschen in der Welt: Überlegungen zu einem unvollständigen Dialog zwischen Ernst Jünger, C. S. Lewis und Josef Pieper, in *Wahrheit und Selbstüberschreitung: C. S. Lewis und Josef Pieper über den Menschen*, ed. Thomas Möllenbeck and Berthold Wald, 111–35 (Paderborn: Schöningh, 2011).

8. Philip Roth, "Novotny's Pain," in *A Philip Roth Reader*, ed. Martin Green (New York: Farrar, Straus and Giroux, 1980), 261; hereafter cited parenthetically.

9. Ernst Jünger, Über den Schmerz, in *Essays I: Betrachtungen zur Zeit*, vol. 2 of *Sämtliche Werke* (Stuttgart: Klett-Cotta, 1980), sec. 7, p. 145; my translation.

10. Ibid., 189.

11. Philip Roth, *The Anatomy Lesson* (London: Vintage, 2005), 264.

12. See Wiebke-Marie Wöltje, *"My finger on the pulse of the nation": Intellektuelle Protagonisten im Romanwerk Philip Roths* (Trier: WVT, 2006); and Oliver

Neun, *Daniel Bell und der Kreis der New York Intellectuals : Frühe amerikanische öffentliche Soziologie* (Wiesbaden: Springer VS, 2014).

13. See Gooblar, *Major Phases*, 30.

14. See Philip Roth, *The Breast* (New York: Vintage International, 1994), 637–38.

15. See Kinzel, *Tragödie und Komödie*, 116–21.

16. See Brühwiler, *Political Initiation*, 21, 26–27, 37, 40; and Philip Roth, *Indignation* (Boston: Houghton Mifflin, 2008), 103–222.

17. It would be worth looking more thoroughly at Roth in connection with communism and its images, taking into account his relationship with writers like Ivan Klíma, especially in light of microtexts such as blurbs. See, for example, Roth's comments on the back cover of Ivan Klíma, *My Crazy Century* (London: Grove, 2013), as well as the long interview printed in *Shop Talk: A Writer and His Colleagues at Work* (New York: Vintage International, 2002), 40–77.

18. See Peter V. Zima, *Entfremdung: Pathologien der postmodernen Gesellschaft* (Tübingen: Francke, 2014), 6.

19. Allan Bloom, *The Closing of the American Mind: How Higher Education Has Failed Democracy and Impoverished the Souls of Today's Students* (London: Penguin, 1988), 175–76.

20. Philip Roth, *Indignation* (Boston: Houghton Mifflin, 2008), 103–218.

21. Roy K. Flint, "Korean War," in *The Oxford Guide to American Military History,* ed. John Whiteclay Chambers II (Oxford: Oxford University Press, 1999), 369.

22. See Axel-Björn Kleppien, *Der Krieg in der amerikanischen Literatur: Untersuchung des Wandels von Beschreibung, Bewertung und Leserlenkung in der nordamerikanischen War Prose und War Poetry während des Zeitraums vom Unabhängigkeitskrieg bis zum Irakkrieg* (Frankfurt am Main: Lang, 2010), 275–76.

23. Michael Lind, *Vietnam: The Necessary War. A Reinterpretation of America's Most Disastrous Military Conflict* (New York: Touchstone, 2002), 72.

24. Neun, *Daniel Bell*, 167–78.

25. Debra Shostak, *Philip Roth—Contexts, Countertexts* (Columbia: University of South Carolina Press, 2004), 42.

26. See Josyane Savigneau, *Avec Philip Roth* (Paris: Gallimard, 2014), 45.

8

The Body Politic

Philip Roth's American Men

Yael Maurer

Philip Roth's political imagination has long centered on the Jewish male body as a site of anxiety and possible liberation. From his most controversial novel, *Portnoy's Complaint* (1969),[1] Roth's focus on the body as a site of anxiety for the male protagonist, but one that may also offer him a route to possible redemption, is very apparent. Roth explores the meeting places of the personal body and the political body of his male protagonists, examining their fears as well as their most lofty ideals. Thus, to name but one striking instance of the meeting place of the personal body and the body politic, Alex Portnoy's journey to the Holy Land marks his final attempt to redeem himself. It is here that subject positions are reversed, a place where *"we're the WASPs"* (*Portnoy*, 286, italics in original). Alex is ecstatic upon arriving in Israel: "'A Jewish country!' . . . I cannot really grasp hold of it. Alex in Wonderland" (*Portnoy*, 289). However, bodily anxieties still haunt him. His fear of venereal disease coupled with failing to perform sexually drives him to despair, and his encounter with Naomi, the Jewish "Pumpkin" who reminds him of his mother, ends up in sexual disaster. This questioning of the protagonist's manhood is thus inextricably linked to his thwarted wish to belong to a collective, to find a home in the political and the personal sense alike.

The seemingly inherent inability of Roth's protagonists to find a symbolic and literal home is a continued theme in Roth's later novels, and one that is closely linked to bodily angst. The body's failings are seen in the early piece, as in the later ones, as flaws in the protagonist's manhood, whether literally, as in Portnoy's case, or in less obvious, and more metaphorical, instances of bodily shortcomings in the later novels. Roth continues to probe the interrelatedness of the body politic and the personal body of his male protagonists and engages with the ways in which the bodily is inscribed in the fate of American Jews.

Locating the ways bodily anxieties intersect with political angst, Roth re-creates the Jewish body as a conflicted site and queries the extent to which his male protagonists fit into the collective imagination of an American republic that both embraces them and rejects them at the very same time. Roth's protagonists strive for an ideal that often eludes them. Their quest for an unachievable or a misguided ideal ultimately leads to their undoing. The personal body and the collective body politic are invested in a complex relationship where visions of the ideal body (both personal and political) are often at odds with flawed human and political bodies alike. Roth's protagonists are idealists, striving for perfection but always falling short of the mark.

This essay examines the intersections of the private and the public body in two of Roth's novels that have at their center a deluded idealist: Ira Ringold in Roth's 1998 novel *I Married a Communist*[2] and Bucky Cantor in Roth's 2010 novel *Nemesis*.[3] In both novels, the tales of Roth's deluded protagonists are transmitted to the reader indirectly. The narrators in both novels provide an account of the protagonists' lives that is filtered through their own subjective perception of past events. In both cases, the story is told in retrospect. It is this narrative and poetic effect of looking back to a no longer accessible past that gives both protagonists their nigh tragic edge, despite the narrators' damning perspective of their childhood heroes' fall from grace.

Following Debra Shostak's astute observation that "Roth's characters are nothing if not *talkers*,"[4] I suggest that we view this aspect of Roth's fiction, the construction of subjectivity via language or talk, as it meets his construction of what Shostak calls the "mythology of masculine power."[5] The disembodied nature of the confessional, seemingly at odds with Roth's insistence on the bodily, is what constitutes this mythology that Roth explores in *I Married a Communist* and *Nemesis* as he deconstructs the notion of manliness and lays it bare. A parallel demythologizing process in the public sphere is at work in both novels.

Performing the Self: Roth's Failed Idealists

Both public and private spheres are exposed and revealed to be, at least to some degree, a mere performance. The wish to make history, to become an active agent in the historical arena, ends up in glorious failure as much as the attempt to fashion a manly self, a heroic figure who combats history and comes out a winner, is doomed to fail. Both protagonists end up the victims of historical forces rather than the agents of historical change. In both novels, this failure is viewed in gendered terms: it is an elevated idea of manliness that the two protagonists fail to live up to. This inability to achieve an imagined idea of manly perfection is what causes their undoing in what amounts to an unravelling of the fiction of selfhood both work so hard to construct. As Victoria Aarons so rightly notes, the characters in Roth's later novels "imagine and, through a kind of magical thinking, attempt to recreate what might have happened, what they might have become if they lived other lives, other selves."[6]

Roth locates the failure of these grand ideals, confronted by unmerciful political and historical realities, as they are acted out on the bodies of his suffering male protagonists. The body in pain thus becomes the stage on which personal and collective dramas are played out. In both novels, whose plotlines are outlined below, the body politic is in effect almost an extension of the personal body, with both protagonists, Ira Ringold in *I Married a Communist* and Bucky Cantor in *Nemesis,* trying to live up to the fantasy of masculine prowess. However, both are undone by historical events that shape their lives but also end up destroying them.

Ira Ringold is the product of a brutalizing family who leaves high school to dig ditches and to work in the zinc mines of northern New Jersey. He joins the army after Pearl Harbor where his political worldview is shaped by Johnny O'Day, an Irish member of the Communist Party who becomes Ira's mentor. O'Day is one of many teacher figures in a novel replete with older male figures who teach the younger ones lessons in manhood. However, and in seeming contradiction to this Communist ideal, Ira becomes a celebrity, a famous radio star who uses his radio show and his public performances as Abraham Lincoln, to educate the American public. He marries a former silent-film star, Eve Frame, a Jewish woman who hides her Jewishness from the world, and whose grown-up bully of a daughter, Sylphid, is hell-bent on destroying her mother's marriage. Ira is denounced as a Communist by his wife after he has an affair with her daughter's friend. In retaliation, she ghost-writes a book about him called *I Married a Communist*. He ends his life in the very same zinc mines.

Ira's physical presence becomes thus a marker of his potential heroism. He is a "giant" among men, much like Lincoln, but like the revered president, suffers from the same bodily ailment: debilitating joint pains. The narrative situation is, in typical Roth fashion, a form of confession. Ira's story is told to the aging Nathan Zuckerman, over a period of seven nights, by Murray Ringold, Nathan's former high school teacher and Ira's brother. Murray claims that "[maybe] the antagonist who destroyed Ira was physical pain," thus locating the body in pain at the center of Roth's novel (*Communist*, 283).

In a similar vein, Bucky Cantor, the protagonist in Roth's 2010 novel *Nemesis*, is undermined by a physical flaw. Bucky is orphaned at a very young age and is raised by his grandparents. His weak eyesight prevents him from enlisting to fight in World War II, and he is therefore left behind to work as a playground director in Newark's Jewish neighborhood. It is the summer of 1944, and the polio epidemic breaks out in the city, taking a heavy toll on the neighborhood. Bucky's heroic attempts to save the children and later himself from the disease fail. He opts out of the fight, thinking he can get away from Newark to a seemingly safe haven, away from the disease and his boys. But ironically, this very place is where he contracts the disease. Although Marcia is willing to marry Bucky and to help him live with the reality of a crippled body, Bucky cannot accept her help and is left to live the rest of his life alone. The inability to see the world, both literally and figuratively, is Bucky's undoing.

Bucky's story is told to the narrator, who reveals himself only midway through the novel as Arnold Mesnikoff, "one of the Chancellor Avenue playground boys, who, in the summer of 1944 contracted polio" (*Nemesis*, 241). The narrator meets Bucky in 1971 and hears the story from Bucky: "I turned out to be the first person to whom he'd ever told the whole of the story, from beginning to end, and—as he came to confide more intimately with each passing week—without leaving very much out" (245).

The narrative structure is thus reminiscent of *I Married a Communist*. But whereas in the earlier novel, the setting and tenor of the confessional is exposed to the readers at the very beginning of the novel, in *Nemesis*, Roth retains the ambiguity regarding the source of the tale until quite late in the telling. As the narrative unfolds, the reader knows only that the unnamed narrator uses the pronoun "we" to indicate his status as one of the members of the community. But his status as a character in the novel as well as its narrator is never quite resolved, putting his reliability as narrator in question. Inbar Kaminsky claims that "the fact that the narrator is also a polio survivor complicates the issue of his impartiality as the story-teller."[7]

The ailing or imperfect body in Roth's fiction thus comes to signal the inability to achieve perfection in both the personal and political spheres. Nevertheless, Roth maintains this ideal, as he creates male protagonists who are engaged, in one way or another, on a quest for the heroic and the noble as possible antidotes to grim political and personal realities. Roth's male protagonists are faced with bodily ailments and failings and try to negotiate them in a public sphere. This representation becomes closely intertwined with the idea of the American republic as an entity that is seen as a protective force: a figure reminiscent of a benevolent father who protects his children from harm.

In Roth's oeuvre, the twin notions of fatherhood and male bonding or brotherhood are put to the test when they encounter the obstacles facing the Jewish man as he strives to reach the epitome of manhood embodied in the figure of the ultimate American Other, the Gentile, whom Roth's men want so much to emulate but are also pitted against. Thus being orphaned becomes a peril that causes both personal and political angst. Roth's doomed male protagonists are, more often than not, orphans, children who lost their parents at an early age and have to face the cruel world on their own. This amounts to a tragic fault that humanizes them while also damning them.

Bucky Cantor, the protagonist in *Nemesis*, never reaches the heroic stature he might have achieved since he was orphaned so early in life. Ira (Iron Man) Ringold in *I Married a Communist*, like Bucky, is an orphan, forced to make his way in the world by force. By the end of the novel, Murray reveals how Ira killed a man in a fit of rage when he was a teenager. This rage is later transposed into the political sphere but is clearly Ira's nemesis, as much as Bucky Cantor's naïve idealism and lack of "vision" is his undoing. As Warren Rosenberg shows, in Roth's oeuvre, "suppressed rage becomes transformed into obsessive longing"[8] Rosenberg lays bare the conflicted position of Roth's male protagonists, who are men who do not fight, but talk. However, claims Rosenberg, the underlying "anxiety that implies not a rejection of violence but a humiliation in the face of Jewish male inadequacy" is also at work [9] This mixture of shame and pride then becomes "the contemporary Jewish legacy" Roth chronicles in his novels.[10] Thus, the potential for heroism that both Ira and Bucky share is undermined by their early childhood loss as well as by what seems to be a flaw in their otherwise impressive masculine performance: Bucky's athletic prowess and grace and Ira's physical stature and impressive (though vehement) manly rhetoric that leaves such a strong impression on young Nathan.

The Men I Came From: The Romance of Manhood

Becoming a man, as Nathan Zukerman, says in *I Married a Communist*, entails finding surrogate father figures while also breaking away from them. These "parents of your adulthood" are the "men I came from" (*Communist*, 217). As Claudia Franziska Brühwiler notes, "Each father figure accompanies . . . Nathan Zuckerman through different initiatory stages, or . . . leads him toward the threshold of adolescence, until Zuckerman finds himself in the one total orphanhood 'which is manhood' (*Communist*, 217)."[11] These initiation rites are a major concern in Roth's work. Becoming a Jewish American man is a doubly fraught endeavor that is in constant risk of falling apart. This learning process is at the heart of *I Married a Communist* and *Nemesis*. The ideals of manhood, brotherhood, and fatherhood are rethought through an engagement with the body in pain or the damaged body. This idea is further complicated by the inherent and attendant fear of male bonding turning into its sinister other: homosexual relationships between men. If to learn how to be a man entails a process of personal and political maturation, the threat of the "deviant" male who provides a different kind of schooling is to be avoided at all costs.

This fear of the homosexual other is dramatized in the figure of yet another teacher in *I Married a Communist*, Leo Glucksman, who is also an "ex GI" like Ira, but unlike him, is "rosy-cheeked and a little round" (*Communist*, 217). He teaches Nathan literature at college but also wrongly assumes Nathan shares his sexual preferences. The clueless Nathan, who tells Leo of his wish to go and work with Johnny O'Day, is treated to Glucksman's outburst of frustrated rage: "You shit! You whore! Go! Get out of here! You two-faced little cocktease whore!" (*Communist,* 239). Young Nathan does not understand why Leo throws him out and why the mention of Johnny O'Day, who "looks like Montgomery Clift," should arouse such a response (*Communist,* 239). The older Nathan reflects: "Maybe he (Leo) thought I was going to undo everything," a comment that is as much about sexuality as it is about the process of learning in the novel (*Communist,* 239). Turning homosocial bonding into homosexual relations between the young student and the (older) teacher is presented as the ultimate "undoing" possible. Nowhere is this option presented as anything other than a monstrous threat to the assumed wholeness or the process of coming into being as a man. In Roth's universe, there seems to be no room for a nonheterosexual option.

However, the closest ties in both novels are between men sharing their stories and bonding in what at times borders on a homoerotic fascination with the male body in all its glory. Leo Glucksman's round body and girlish rosy cheeks become markers of his "effeminate" nature, signaling how his body, unlike Ira's and Murray's virile male bodies, does not meet the glorified ideal Nathan sets out to emulate. In *Nemesis,* Bucky's athletic prowess, admired by the narrator, one of the former playground boys who look up to Bucky as an epitome of manhood, is lost when he is crippled by polio. But the novel still celebrates, through the adoring eyes of the narrator, this past glory of the male body, positioning Bucky as a Greek god, a javelin-throwing Hercules. But Bucky is more of an Achilles than a Hercules. Despite the dramatic irony in both novels that uncover this mythology of the male body and unmask it, there is still a sense that Roth's fascination with the possibility of male grandeur that is firmly rooted in an athletic and virile body is never fully debunked.

The Wrath of History

In both *I Married a Communist* and *Nemesis,* Roth chooses a period in American history that is fraught and bespeaks a potential catastrophe. Locating the events of the narrative at times of crisis in American history, Roth looks back in anger but also with a sense of longing at his youthful self. But whereas *I Married a Communist* draws on historical accounts of the McCarthy era "witch hunt," *Nemesis* conjures up an imagined outburst of the polio epidemic in Newark in 1944. No such epidemic occurred, in fact, although the area was hit by polio in the early 1950s. Roth chooses 1944 for his novelistic purposes, as this date allows him to conflate the "War on Polio" with the war fought in Europe. I will relate more fully to Roth's manipulation of historical time below.

In Claudia Roth Pierpont's recent biography *Roth Unbound*, she records Roth's claim that *I Married a Communist* is one of his favorite novels.[12] Roth relates his fondness for Ira, who "is such an uninhibited, explosive character: a 'hothead.' He explains that there's a lot of freedom in writing a book about such a figure, a lot of open emotional space."[13] This "open emotional space" is explored in a novel that, as Pierpont so rightly points out is about "the romance of manhood."[14] However, as Pierpont comments, this description of the novel may also be Roth's defense against criticism of his novel. The Roth critic Mark Shechner, for one, denounces the book as a "headache of a novel," claiming that "the plot disappears, dragged under by the concrete shoes of fulmination.[15]

For Shechner, Roth's novel offers the reader a "cacophony of . . . voices, bearing down not only on Nathan Zuckerman but on us . . . and whatever is appealing in it can't be entangled from what is infuriating."[16] This reading does an injustice to the nuanced ways in which Roth manipulates the narrative voices in the novel, a novel that takes place in the golden age of radio and offers us, in Pierpont's terms, "[two] voices sounding in the dark . . . an ingenious scheme for a story that rests on memories of radio, and the book contains affecting tributes to the conjuring power of speech—tributes that, to judge from Roth's oeuvre, are personal and heartfelt."[17] After all, it is Nathan Zuckerman, the narrator of the tale, who comments that "listening in the black of summer's night to barely visible Murray had been something like listening to the bedroom radio when I was a kid ambitious to change the world by having all my untested convictions, masquerading as stories, broadcast nationwide" (*Communist*, 320–21).

Roth's novel of "voices in the dark" is also about the "godlikeness of having an ear," and being attuned to the stories of others (*Communist*, 321). The disembodied voices on the radio are likened to Murray's seemingly disembodied voice as the two men sit in the dark and talk to one another. However, the reality of the aging and failing bodies of both men is a constant presence. Like Scheherazade telling stories to ward off her own death, these stories in the dark are a way of trying to avoid the inevitable. This endeavor, however, is doomed to fail; Murray dies soon after telling his tale to Nathan.

Rather than a "cacophony," as Shechner would have it, we have harmony, matched only by the harmony of the night sky and the stars that Nathan ends by looking up at. The harking back to childhood memories, mediated via radio "stories," or more accurately, the radio as a vehicle for transmitting "convictions," is the key image and organizing principle of Roth's novel. If the novel is indeed about the process of becoming a man, or the romance of manhood, then the exploration of this romance is located in a historical era that the young Philip Roth knows well.

When Roth was looking for a historical period in which to locate the novel, he was at once harking back to his own youth in the late 1940s and early 1950s America but also reflecting upon the sense of personal betrayal he felt following the publication in 1996 of *Leaving a Doll's House,* his former wife Claire Bloom's searing critique of her life with Roth. This sense of personal betrayal was with him when he chose to locate his novel in the decade after the war (1946–1956), when acts of personal betrayal were rampant. Thus the novel takes the shape of a long conversation between Nathan Zuckerman and his former high school English teacher, Murray Ringold, who tells Nathan of his brother's Ira's downfall in the McCarthy era. These conversations take place on Nathan's back porch in the Berkshires in the summer of 1997. Debra Shostak tellingly describes the novel as dealing with the "wrath of history."[18] As Shostak shows, Roth describes a character who "wishes to be at the center of political upheaval—indeed wishes to *make history.*"[19]

This insistence on history as a possibly menacing force but also one that can be affected by the actions of "great men" is a repeated theme in Roth's oeuvre, perhaps most evident in his rewriting of history in his 2004 novel *The Plot Against America.* In *I Married a Communist,* Roth engages with the ways we narrate history. Shostak points out that "[the novel] . . . is virtually all talk," thus alerting us to the ways in which this "talk" is also an act of narrating a no-longer-accessible past: "*I Married a Communist* places the reader at several removes from events—we listen to Zuckerman who listens to Murray who had observed and listened to Ira and Eve."[20] This becomes Roth's "strategy to suggest not only the pastness of the past but our present helplessness to alter any of the past."[21] The very act of telling the tale then emphasizes its distance from the present moment of narration and remains a reflection on a specific historical period in American history that is loaded with both historical and political significance for Roth.

As Pierpont relates, "[the] historian Arthur Schlesinger had told Roth there were probably as many acts of betrayal perpetrated during the Revolutionary War, but that was not an ideal period for a book set in Newark."[22] Tellingly enough, however, Abraham Lincoln, the American president emulated by Ira, becomes yet another tragic hero figure in this novel. The American Civil War is seemingly a more fitting analogue to McCarthy's era, where Americans turn against each other. This association is also brought to the fore in the figure of Katrina Van Tassel Grant, the "ghost writer" of Eve Frame's damning book as well as the author of romantic historical novels that are fully ridiculed in Roth's novel. The southern belle figure is transformed into a vicious caricature of a society lady and crafty manipulator of the deluded Eve. Thus the notion of "ghost writing" so central to Roth's oeuvre in general and to this novel in particular, is given a further ironic twist. If to "make history" is to write ludicrous "bodice-ripping" historical romances, on the one hand, and the telltale story of Eve and Ira's marriage, on the other, then Roth may be commenting on his own endeavor as the writer of *I Married a Communist,* the shared title for his novel and Van Tassel's fictional book.

The location of history as a menacing force for Roth's protagonists is intertwined with their ideals of masculinity and the latter's unraveling. The aging Nathan, as Shostak points out, may be as complicit in the acts of betrayal committed in the McCarthy era as are Eve and Katrina Van Tassel, the instruments of Ira's downfall. Shostak takes this claim further to question the role of the novelist or the historian as a different kind of "informer": "[The] vengeful 'I' (in the title of Roth's novel) is also Nathan, who has, in a sense, wed the mythic Ira, felt betrayed by Ira's ideological seductions, and then retaliated by telling his secrets."[23] Thus, Nathan himself, no less than Murray or Ira, is a "historical casualty."[24] In that sense, it is the failure of trust, or the act of (literary) betrayal that links Roth's novelist alter ego to Roth himself, retaliating for his former wife's act of betrayal by writing a novel that presents a very unflattering image of a vengeful wife and a crazed daughter. The "unmanning" of the male figures, then, their bodily failures as well as their strengths, are located in the realm of the narrative wish to contain them. Looking back at the story of a seemingly great man affords the narrator the kind of melancholy pleasure that an active engagement in

life no longer seems to offer. The novel ends with a scene of a further retirement into the space of solipsistic selfhood, leaving Nathan in the quintes-
sential position of an observer rather than a doer. He is left looking at the
night sky after the last conversation with Murray, who dies soon after.

This ending signals Nathan's own impending death and his retirement
from an active role in the world. Yet the poignant notes of this ending might
also suggest a more hopeful outlook at the possibility of change and renewal.
Nathan recollects his mother's explanation that when people die, "they go
up to the sky and live on forever as gleaming stars" (*Communist*, 322). The
old Nathan lies awake thinking that "all the people with a role in Murray's
account of the Iron Man's unmaking were now no longer impaled on their
moment but dead and free of the traps set for them by their era" (*Communist*, 322). This brings him relief from the "narrative engorgement" he had
experienced (*Communist*, 322). What Nathan chooses to focus on instead
of the wrath of history is the "universe into which error does not obtrude"
(*Communist*, 323). Marveling at the "colossal spectacle of no antagonism,"
a "galaxy of fire set by no human hand" may be Nathan's ultimate retreat
from the world of men and their follies (*Communist*, 323). But this ending,
with its poetic celebration of an indifferent universe, still might offer some
comfort for a man who seems to be relinquishing his active involvement in
the affairs of men in favor of a reclusive and meditative form of peaceful
resignation. In *Nemesis,* we find a different form of resignation. Bucky Cantor seems to succumb to polio and retires from the world of virile men. But
his resignation may offer a different kind of engagement with the world, one
that is finally at peace with the God he raged against as a young man, forced
to confront the injustice in the random death of so many young men, both
victims of polio and the victims of the war raging in Europe at the time.

The Germ of Fear: Unmanning and Defeat in *Nemesis*

Roth's "solution" to the problem of Jewish American manhood is inextricably connected to overcoming the body's failings. In *Nemesis* Roth gives an
impassioned speech to Dr. Steinberg, the calm and rational Jewish doctor
who speaks out against succumbing to fear in the face of the epidemic:
"I'm against the frightening of Jewish kids. I'm against the frightening of
Jews, period. That was Europe. That's why Jews fled. This is America. Fear
unmans us. Fear degrades us" (*Nemesis,* 106). Being "here" in the safe

republic, rather than "there" in Europe where Jews are exterminated, is the only safeguard against history's menacing "plot."

The "War on Polio" becomes a parallel to the war raging in Europe at the time, a war that the novel's protagonist cannot fight due to his poor eyesight. Roth's allegory then is about the futility of all war and the ways the unimaginable or unforeseeable takes over the lives of ordinary men and women, becoming a "nemesis" over which they have no control. Roth allegorizes the Jewish condition in America by relating to what he calls in *Nemesis* "the germ of fear": it is this "disease" for which Roth seeks to find a cure in his rewriting of real and imagined events in American history.

Roth ends *Nemesis* with the word "invincible," suggesting that although none of his characters or readers is invincible, they can still become "heroes" of a different kind, fighting against the paralyzing fear that threatens to undo them. Franklin Delano Roosevelt's uplifting speech where he famously declared that "we have nothing to fear but fear itself" is echoed in the novel, showcasing Roth's commitment to the ideal of a democratic and free America as an answer to the Jewish predicament. However, like Ira Ringold, who only emulates Abraham Lincoln but never comes close to the idea embodied by the mythical president, Bucky falls short of the idea embodied in Roosevelt, himself a victim of polio. The narrator comments, reflecting on Bucky's sense of shame and failure: "He was the very antithesis of the country's greatest prototype of the polio victim, FDR, disease having led Bucky not to triumph but to defeat. The paralysis and everything that came in its wake had irreparably damaged his assurance as a virile man, and he had withdrawn completely from that whole side of life" (*Nemesis*, 246). The failure to be a "virile man," then, is presented in moral terms. Bucky fails to overcome his adversity, like FDR did, and is instead reduced to living a ghostly existence as a recluse who retires from life. In that way, he is not unlike both Ira and Nathan at the end of *I Married a Communist*.

In *Nemesis*, Roth revisits his childhood neighborhood, home of many of his novels, and a place that has become synonymous with his work. Newark, New Jersey, is where Roth locates both the terrors and the grandeur of childhood, a place where the notion of "perpetual fear" (the way Roth describes the Jewish condition in his 2004 novel *The Plot Against America*) reigns supreme. In both cases, the novels feature an unlikely neighborhood hero (Philip's father Herman Roth in *Plot* and Bucky Cantor in *Nemesis*) whose voice of reason, and unwavering belief in the good of his community, are beacons in the darkness, infected by fear and racism.

However, in *Nemesis,* the enemy from within ends up destroying the seemingly "invincible" Bucky, leaving the readers with an image of his past glory as a nearly mythological javelin thrower but also as the "invisible arrow" that carries polio with him and infects the kids he is supposed to protect, or so he believes. Arnold Mesnikoff, the narrator who meets the aging Bucky by chance, ends the novel with this poetic description of Bucky's performance, aligning him with the mythological Hercules: "The first javelin thrower was said to be Hercules, the great warrior and slayer of monsters, who, Mr. Cantor told us, was the giant son of the supreme Greek god Zeus, and the strongest man on earth" (*Nemesis,* 276).

Bucky Cantor is the orphaned son of a good-for-nothing father, making this mythological allusion doubly ironic. He is also (unlike Ira Ringold) anything but a "giant." However, this nostalgic moment of looking back at Bucky's moment of glory positions him as the ultimate hero of the playground, cheered on by his adoring fans: "All of the javelin's trajectory had originated in Mr. Cantor's supple muscles. He was the body—the feet, the legs, the buttocks, the trunk, the arms, the shoulders, even the thick stump of the bull neck—that acting in unison had powered the throw" (*Nemesis,* 279). The insistence on the magnificence of the male body as a locus of admiration borders on the homoerotic.

If we look at this section, however, following Kaminsky's suggestion that it is the narrator's "constant attempts to fit Bucky's story into the framework of Greek mythology"[25] that are at work here, then we might say that it is Bucky's own relation to his post-polio corporeality that defines his concept of himself as a man. In the last conversation with Marcia Steinberg, which he relates to Arnold, Bucky reveals his concept of himself as a polio victim: "'Then look at my leg,' he said, pulling up his pajama bottoms. 'Stop, I beg you! You think it's your body that's deformed but what's truly deformed is your mind!'" (*Nemesis,* 260). Marcia's words indicate how Bucky's symbolic "blindness" and his insistence on playing the role of a victim become his true nemesis. It is not the failure of the once glorious body but the failure of the mind that is at stake here. Bucky's nemesis is the inner doubting, self-castigating man, an orphan who cannot find a family, even when he stumbles across a seemingly perfect one.

Roth places the "War against Polio" and the "War against Nazi Germany" as two aspects of the same "nemesis" to be overcome by the protagonist. By telling the story of one young man, Roth is yet again re-creating an imagined version of a foundational time in American history, offering what he views as the moral compass in a world that has lost its moorings for one reason or another. Bucky Cantor, the young physical education teacher, the orphaned boy who wasn't drafted because of his bad eyesight, becomes the one who "sees": his voice attempts to combat the panic around him at the time the epidemic breaks out in Newark. He is the symbolic father to the kids on the playground in the long summer of the disease. His vision is one that Roth embraces, as he imagines the "heroic Jew" as an athlete, a calm and rational man, and a kind one. These traits are expressed in Bucky's impassioned speech to the worried Jewish parents at the beginning of the novel: "Look, you mustn't be eaten up with worry and you mustn't be eaten up with fear. What's important is not to infect the children with the germ of fear. We'll come through this, believe me. We'll all do our bit and stay calm, and do everything we can to protect the children, and we'll come through this together" (*Nemesis*, 38).

The notion of fear and its relationship to the "Jewish condition" is expressed in the novel via another Jewish hero: Dr. Steinberg, Marcia's father. Marcia is Bucky's girlfriend, and the fatherless Bucky goes to her father to ask him about his conduct during the epidemic. Dr. Steinberg supports Bucky's decision to keep the playground open despite the polio scare. As in *Plot Against America*, the condition of perpetual fear is linked to the "there" (Europe) from which Jews have fled, not the "America" they came to find. The belief in the power of the republic to take care of all its citizens is still strong, and the vision of America as the land that would cure Jews of their hereditary fear of persecution is still firmly believed in. Bucky questions the belief in a cruel God that takes the lives of twelve-year-old boys, like his beloved pupil Alan, who dies of polio, but he seems not to question his belief in America as the savior of the Jews.

However, as Bucky accepts Marcia Steinberg's offer to leave polio-stricken Newark for the Indian Hill summer camp where she works, the scene shifts. Roth places his protagonist, the man of ideals, in the position of a runaway, a man who gets along and saves himself rather than staying in Newark and caring for his kids. Victoria Aarons points out that by succumbing to Marcia's tempting offer, Bucky is "seduced into thinking he can walk out of one history and into a self-determined future."[26] Bucky fails to live up to a standard of Jewish manhood his grandfather insists on: "He encouraged his grandson to stand up for himself as a man and as a Jew, and to understand that one's battles were never over and that, in the relentless skirmish that living is, "when you have to pay the price, you pay it" (*Nemesis*, 25).

Bucky wants to teach his boys what his surrogate father has taught him: "toughness and determination, to be physically brave and physically fit, and never to allow themselves to be pushed around, or just because they knew how to use their brains, to be defamed as Jewish weaklings and sissies" (*Nemesis*, 28).

Here, as in *I Married a Communist*, the threat of being thought a "sissy," a potential homosexual rather than a virile heterosexual male, is at the heart of the educational journey undergone by Roth's male protagonists.

Thus, when Bucky goes "against the grain" and finds refuge in the Indian Hill Camp, a site of seeming pastoral bliss removed from the infernal Newark, his manliness is put into question. This is also the place, ironically enough, where Bucky can envision an uninterrupted sexual meeting with his fiancé, Marcia: "He could take all her clothes off, he thought, and see her completely naked. They could be alone on a dark island without their clothes on" (*Nemesis*, 87). Bucky envisions this scene as one of complete freedom from everything that weighs down on him: "He could be free of the Kopferman family. . . . And he could stop hating God, which was confusing his emotions and making him feel very strange. On their island he could be far from everything that was growing harder and harder to bear" (*Nemesis*, 87).

But as the image of this idyllic island is realized, the narrator's description of the natural scenery hints at the ways in which disease had already infiltrated this seeming haven: "All around them the island was thickly packed with clumps of trees, which weren't entirely white as they had looked to him from the waterfront, but bore black slashes encircling their bark as though they'd been scarred by a whip" (*Nemesis*, 163).

Some of the trees appear "ravaged by the weather or disease" (*Nemesis*, 163). So when, following Bucky's and Marcia's lovemaking, the ecstatic Marcia exclaims: "You're here! You didn't get it! Oh, Bucky, hold me tight, hold me as close as you can! You're safe!" the irony is doubled (*Nemesis*, 169). There is nowhere "safe," it would seem, at least not in Roth's universe.

The issue of manliness is given a further ironic twist when Bucky encounters the Indian Hill Camp funder whose "Bible" consists of camping books, modeled after the "Red Man's" mastery of nature. Bucky the city boy knows nothing about "Nature," and thus the notion of conflicting belief systems comes to the fore. Roth's biting satire is most evident here as he describes the enraptured Bucky when he first sees this seeming paradise: "This was the wide-open spaces. Here the vista was limitless and the refuge even more beautiful than the home field of the Bears" (*Nemesis*, 143). Bucky now believes he is indeed safe: "As he hefted his duffle bag strap over his shoulder, he was overtaken with the joy of beginning again, the rapturous intoxication of renewal—the bursting feeling of "I live! I live!" (*Nemesis*, 144).

Almost echoing the young Portnoy's exuberance upon arriving in the Holy Land, Bucky's enthusiasm should, and does, instantly alert us of the fall to come. As it often does in Roth's oeuvre, this kind of hyperbolic language is soon deflated and the protagonist's disillusionment follows soon after. Bucky's deluded sense of safety is brutally crushed when he falls ill and fears he had infected others as well. On the island with Marcia after he hears of the polio cases in the camp, Bucky reflects on the scenery, seeing it suddenly in a different way: "The birch trees circling them looked like a myriad of deformed silhouettes—their lovers' island haunted suddenly with the ghosts of polio victims" (*Nemesis*, 228). The pastoral becomes a gothic site. And Bucky's sense of guilt is magnified: "He was afraid to approach her because he was afraid to infect her, if he hadn't infected her already. If he hadn't infected everyone!" (*Nemesis*, 228). Bucky feels responsible for bringing the disease to Indian Hill. And although this assumption can be read as a manifestation of his guilt for abandoning his charges in Newark, the fact that Bucky himself is a carrier of the disease and falls prey to it indicates his inability to escape his tragic lot.

However, Bucky's choice to renounce Marcia's love for him and to retire from the world of virile men is juxtaposed to the narrator's decision to go on living a full life even though he too was struck by polio. This decision, as I have shown above, is also one taken by Ira Ringold and Nathan Zuckerman. Roth's protagonists seem unable to cope with the failure of their grand sense of self in favor of a less rigid engagement with the world as it is. *Nemesis*'s (somewhat unreliable) narrator describes Bucky as a man devoid of humor and a sense of irony who is "haunted by an exacerbated sense of duty" (*Nemesis*, 273). This rather unkind description of Bucky sounds nevertheless quite in keeping with his portrayal in the novel. One could say that this lack of irony is what Ira and Bucky share. Both protagonists are so caught up in their ideals of manhood that they fail to see where these ideals must make way for a more nuanced and less radical engagement with others. Both protagonists' misguided notion of what constitutes their "manhood" becomes their ultimate undoing. Both fail because they are too insistent on acting out a persona that is no longer suited to the changing times and their altered fortunes. In both novels, Roth seems to be chastising his protagonists for their blindness and lack of humor, while also presenting us with the allure of such insistence on one's "Truth" even when all else fails.

Conclusion

This elegiac tone that characterizes both novels gives them, despite the sometimes vicious satirical thrusts at both protagonists' follies, a very poignant edge. If we look back at Portnoy's travails in the Holy Land, we can see that the young Roth's presentation of the body personal and the body politic is still filtered through a vehemently comedic attitude, one that almost never allows us to feel for the protagonist's fall from idealistic grace to humiliating failure. We never really get to feel for Alex Portnoy's struggles with his failed idea of himself as a ladies' man. Alex remains, for the most part at least, a caricatured version of the good Jewish American boy who wants to conquer America by conquering its shiksas and tries to do the same thing when he encounters the Israeli version of what he mistakenly sees as a "mother figure" to save him from himself.

In the later Roth novels, however, the "romance of manhood" takes on a more serious note. Both Ira and Bucky may be almost as ridiculous as the young Portnoy at times, but their tales have more tragic proportions, making their struggles with the forces of history and their negotiation of the personal and the body politic more moving and far less humorous. The narrator accuses Bucky of being devoid of humor, but the mature Roth, while still maintaining his sharp, at times brutally comic appraisal of hu(man) nature, also succeeds in creating moving portraits of seemingly "failed" lives that are still larger than life. History's menacing forces and the personal flaws that undo his male protagonists are documented with anger and poetic clarity. Roth leaves us wondering, alongside his narrators, if we can ever make sense of the past. His failed male protagonists' search for the "romance of manhood" ends up in ruins. But the novels' mode of telling, the elegiac looking back at a no-longer-accessible past, rather than the too-urgent present of the earlier novel, demonstrates not only the force of passing years but also the menacing shadow of history as it works on the individual mind and body, undoing it rather than reviving it. At the end of both novels, the sense of loss permeates the narrative present, leaving the readers with a melancholy meditation on the ways men of ideals fare in a world in which, as Nathan Zuckerman puts it, "hydrogen alone was determining destiny" (*Communist*, 322). Human agency is lost in an indifferent cosmos.

I Married a Communist ends with the line: "The stars are indispensable" (*Communist*, 323). *Nemesis* ends with the image of the javelin-throwing Bucky: "Running with the javelin aloft, stretching his throwing arm back behind his body, bringing the throwing arm through to release the javelin high over his shoulder—and releasing it then like an explosion—he seemed to us invincible" (*Nemesis*, 280).

The earlier novel thus concludes with an image of an alien cosmos where men have no meaning. The other harks back to the image of the glorious male body but only in an elegiac note that further enhances how this "invincibility" is a mere illusion. Both novels, however, still seem to long for a time and place where a man's truth, deluded as that truth might turn out to be, still counts and where his tragic fall still amounts to a grand gesture of resignation signaling in its very futility the thwarted wish to reach a no-longer-attainable vision of heroic grandeur.

Notes

1. Philip Roth, *Portnoy's Complaint* (New York: Random House, 1969); hereafter cited parenthetically.

2. Philip Roth, *I Married a Communist* (London: Random House, 2005); hereafter cited parenthetically as *Communist*.

3. Philip Roth, *Nemesis* (London: Random House, 2011); hereafter cited parenthetically.

4. Debra Shostak, "Roth/CounterRoth: Postmodernism, The Masculine Subject, and *Sabbath's Theater*," *Arizona Quarterly* 54.3 (Autumn 1998): 119.

5. Ibid., 120.

6. Victoria Aarons, "Expelled Once Again: The Failure of the Fantasized Self in Philip Roth's *Nemesis*," *Philip Roth Studies* 9.1 (Spring 2013): 52.

7. Inbar Kaminsky, "Epidemic Judaism: Plagues and Their Evocation in Philip

Roth's *Nemesis* and Ben Marcus's *The Flame Alphabet*, *Philip Roth Studies* 10.1 (Spring 2014): 111.

8. Warren Rosenberg, *The Legacy of Rage: Jewish Masculinity, Violence and Culture* (Massachusetts: University of Massachusetts Press, 2001), 194.

9. Ibid., 1.

10. Ibid.

11. Claudia Franziska Brühwiler, *Political Initiation in the Novels of Philip Roth* (London: Bloomsbury, 2014), 42.

12. Claudia Roth Pierpont, *Roth Unbound* (New York: Farrar, Straus and Giroux, 2013), 234–35.

13. Ibid.

14. Ibid., 230.

15. Mark Shechner, "Roth's American Trilogy," in *The Cambridge Companion to Philip Roth*, ed. Timothy Parish (Cambridge: Cambridge University Press, 2007), 151.

16. Ibid.

17. Pierpont, *Roth Unbound*, 233.

18. Debra Shostak, *Philip Roth—Countertexts, Counterlives* (Columbia: University of South Carolina Press, 2004), 249.

19. Ibid., 250, italics in original.

20. Ibid., 251.

21. Ibid.

22. Pierpont, *Roth Unbound*, 229.

23. Shostak, *Philip Roth*, 257.

24. Ibid.

25. Kaminsky, "Epidemic Judaism," 111.

26. Aarons, ""Expelled Once Again," 53.

9

Philip Roth and Life as a Man

Debra Shostak

> It was the truths that made the people grotesques. . . . The moment
> one of the people took one of the truths to himself, called it his truth,
> and tried to live his life by it, he became a grotesque and the truth he
> embraced became a falsehood.
>
> —Sherwood Anderson, *Winesburg, Ohio* (1919)

Life as a Man: A Book of Grotesques

Philip Roth told Claudia Roth Pierpont that his second novel, *When She
Was Good* (1967), "might have been written by Sherwood Anderson" for
its presentation of an emotionally repressive world. He also told Pierpont
that he reread *Winesburg, Ohio* in a new edition just as he began to write
Indignation (2008), in which Roth refers directly to Anderson in the name
of the college that his protagonist, Marcus Messner, attends.[1] Roth is deeply
read, and his work betrays the influence of a host of writers.[2] One might
argue, however, that Anderson's powerful notion of the "grotesque" brackets
Roth's career, informing Roth's conception of how an idea may take hold of
a person's imagination and deform him or her to its shape. In writing "The
Book of the Grotesque," the introductory myth to his collection of stories
about an imprisoning midwestern small town, Anderson focuses on such

fin-de-siècle American "truths" concerning virginity, passion, wealth, and poverty as make grotesques of the people who cling to them.[3] A less lyrical, more clinical age might call these truths ideologies.

The truth that principally drives and contorts Roth's protagonists is what Pierpont likes to call "the romance of manliness."[4] That "romance" is highly inflected by Roth's position as an American male, born to middle-class New Jersey Jews in 1933, with the contradictory rights and responsibilities of a New Deal, liberal humanist ideological pedigree his protagonists often share. Roth's fiction has been at once nostalgic and bitterly critical about how American men of his generation have been gripped by the myths of "manliness," which as often as not transform his characters into grotesques when their ideals are tested by the dynamics of power and the conditions of self-doubt elicited within real social and sexual relations.

Insofar as Roth exhibits a politics of gender, it is not didactic, doctrinaire, systematic, or collective, or for that matter very accessible as a consistent *politics*. In this sense, Roth's views about gender are less available explicitly *as* political than, say, his views on the politics of Zionism or of the American nation-state at various moments of history, treated elsewhere in this volume. Rather, his politics of gender reside in Roth's insight into the material and psychological particularities of individuals living in twentieth-century American culture, largely middle-class, secular Jewish heterosexual men in the Northeast, and are discernible only within a representational practice consistent with a liberal humanism that looks to particular cases and refuses to generalize or persuade. Indeed, Roth's frequently dialogical narrative forms militate against presenting a coherent *position*, and no single criterion exists for what one might call, following the title of one of Roth's novels, *life as a man* in twentieth-century America. At best, his fiction bears witness to several cross-cutting ideological categories that press upon American men, which Roth channels into Peter Tarnopol's plaintive cry of disempowerment in *My Life as a Man* (1974), "I wanted to be humanish: manly, a man."[5] Three such rough categories animate Roth's imagination, each built upon oppositional terms for manliness, and each exposing the male subject's anxious desire to claim an "I" registering as legitimate within the discourses of power that construct modern masculine selfhood—a desire that frequently contorts them into grotesques.

The category for which Roth became notorious, after the publication in 1969 of *Portnoy's Complaint,* is heterosexual male sexuality. Indeed, that

novel, in all its comic agonies, exemplifies each of the discursive categories I sort out here.[6] Laying out the pervasive Western myth of male sexuality under the term of "masculinism," Arthur Brittan pithily describes a
"hydraulic model" of masculinity driven by a capitalist ethos of competition,
according to which, "A man is only a man in so far as he is capable of using
his penis as an instrument of power."[7] The model equates—and conflates—
bodily with social potency. This model of phallic masculinity poses a threat,
Roth finds, to a man like Portnoy, who at the height of his virile powers
is crushed by values that compete with his will to sexual satisfaction. The
struggle between these warring impulses causes Alexander Portnoy's psy-
choanalytic "complaint": "as a consequence of the patient's 'morality' [. . .]
neither fantasy nor act issues in genuine sexual gratification, but rather in
overriding feelings of shame and the dread of retribution, particularly in the
form of castration" (*Portnoy*, vii).

Potency, taken figuratively rather than bodily, informs the discourse of
another fundamental category of manliness for Roth. Like the category of
male sexuality, it assumes that a heteronormative ideal determines the performance of gender—how the "manly" man takes up his activities, behaviors, and gestural being in the world, demonstrating competence rather
than anxiety. George Mosse summarizes the relevant "manly virtues," origi-
nating in the late eighteenth century, as "will power, honor, and courage."[8]
Within this category, a man's greatest anxiety obtains in his fear of femi-
nization, which may find expression as homophobia. Portnoy, for example,
enraged when his mother praises him as a "little gentleman," lashes out:
"Little *fruitcake* is what you saw—and exactly what the training program
was designed to produce" (*Portnoy*, 140; italics in original). The bourgeois
image of the father as protector and provider is one figuration within this
category, constructed by the deeply rooted patriarchal values of Western
society that constitute the "training program" in the United States. "Some
time in the mid-twentieth century," Kelly Oliver writes, "fatherhood became
almost synonymous with responsibility. [. . .] As they became the breadwin-
ners, men became responsible for family finances and ultimately the family
itself, its material as well as moral and spiritual survival and growth."[9] This
figure's wretched counterimage appears in Portnoy's father, a man so devot-
edly anxious about his work that he suffers headaches and constipation;
Portnoy despairingly concludes, "How could he wield power?—he *was* the
powerless" (*Portnoy*, 43; italics in original). The conception of manhood

that conflates virility with paternal—and paternalistic—virtues inscribes this category within the sphere of an ethical masculinity, as well. Roth defines the underlying tension in terms of the struggle between instinctual satisfaction and renunciation that Freud first outlined in *Civilization and Its Discontents* (1930): how impossible it is both to do right and to fulfill one's desires.[10] "To be *bad,*" Portnoy cries, "is the real struggle: to be bad—and to enjoy it!" Portnoy is modern man, operating under the rule of "That tyrant, [his] superego" (*Portnoy,* 138, 181; italics in original).

For Roth, Freud's arguments illuminate the final discursive category, focused on an ethnically constructed Jewish manhood. Raised in a tradition that directs him more toward the book than the body, the Jewish male was also victimized by the feminizing anti-Semitic fantasies of European non-Jews. Roth epitomizes the resultant conflicts of Jewish manhood when he contrasts the "Jewboy," signifying "aggression, appetite, and marginality," with the "nice Jewish boy," marked by "repression, respectability, and social acceptance."[11] Likewise, Portnoy's battle-cry—"LET'S PUT THE ID BACK IN YID!" (139)—pinpoints the crisis for the Jew who wishes to perform a potent masculinity.

Roth returns repeatedly to Portnoy's dilemma. Too stringent a commitment to the "truths" of the masculine myth dooms his characters to become grotesque deformations of themselves rather than agents experiencing themselves as potent subjects. Indeed, Roth has devoted much of his fifty-odd-year writing career to the exploration of manliness, with all its ambiguities and wounds. In addressing the intersecting discourses of manhood suggested above, Roth affirms gender as a psychological and social construct expressed especially in performative acts and routinely a source of anxiety in those who attempt so to express themselves. His novels expose the paradoxes blurring matters of mind and body, deconstruct heteronormativity, and lay open the existential menace the body poses to the masculine subject by its failures to perform. Apparently missing from this account are the lives of women, but only apparently; Roth is alert to the consequences that the romance of manhood has for the female subject who operates within the sphere of the masculine subject as well as in her own right. He demonstrates profound insight into how, at least within the matrix of heterosexual norms, questions about life as a man and life as a woman are complementary and mutually embedded.

Since Roth addresses these matters in so many works of fiction, this essay can only suggest the horizons of his concerns with how ideological discourses of gender and sexuality deform the human subject. These concerns appear within two capacious and overlapping categories of representation, concerning "the matter of manhood, in an era when manhood is a moral achievement"; and the gendered *I* as it exists in relation to the body, specifically the pressure of sexual, material, or physical existence on masculine subjectivity and the perceptions and performances of manhood.[12] As a coda, the essay takes up the struggles of women who answer to the men who turn themselves into grotesques. Furthermore, as Roth writes novels, whose *form* is always in the foreground of and inextricable from any discernible politics, the essay keeps in view just how Roth's structures and devices of narration—from point of view to storytelling frames to figurative motifs—shape his inquiry into the life of a man. And since Roth's politics of gender inhere not in what the novels *say* but in what they *do,* my analysis follows his lead by focusing on close rather than stringently theorized readings. Finally, because critical work has explored Roth's representations of gender in his early and midcareer fiction, this essay mainly focuses on the late-career novels of the 2000s, but begins with *My Life as a Man* to establish a useful baseline of his preoccupations—not least because its title puts the central problems of gendered politics into relief.[13]

My Life as a Man: The Myth of Male Inviolability

Roth puts the difficulty of saying "I" at center stage in *My Life as a Man.* The assertion of "my life" no less than "man" is linked by a term shadowed by doubt: "as" emphasizes likeness, the sphere of the simile rather than identity; it offers itself as a weak preposition rather than a strong copula. Conspicuously absent is a form of the verb "to be." The focus on language, like the theatrical metaphor of the stage, is fundamental to Roth's reflexive conception of the novel, which enacts the problem of performing a "manly" self by way of the struggle to write a life story. Roth's neurotic, at times hysterical, protagonist Peter Tarnopol, who is, like Portnoy, under the care of a psychoanalyst, tries three times to tell his story—to give an account of his "life as a man." If Karl Marx saw history as occurring the first time as tragedy, the second time as farce, Roth goes Marx one better: the emasculated Tarnopol presents his history first as "perverse" comedy, second as "dull" melodrama (*My Life,* 117), and finally as shrill, defeated autobiography, and the novel's cruel joke is that each inadequate telling testifies to the man's failure to *be* a man.[14] Roth thus in the form of his novel enacts what has become a commonplace of postmodern ontology: that the "self" is no more than a gathering of occasional, constructed selves, textualized products of varied utterances by a subjectivity that, in its linguistic evanescence, portends that there is no one—or at least no *one*—there at all. As Patrick O'Donnell suggests, what Tarnopol senses with dread "goes beyond the idea that the 'self' is a collection of its different versions to a questioning of what, if anything, defines these as variations of some single [. . .] subject."[15] Lacking the stability of a self, where might manhood lie? If he cannot *be*, how can he be *a man?*

Tarnopol finds himself irredeemably driven by the "myth of male inviolability, of male dominance and potency" (*My Life*, 173) that shapes the discourses of mid-twentieth-century heterosexual American masculinity. After Tarnopol is tricked into marrying the troubled Maureen Johnson when she plays on his sense of guilty responsibility, his only conception of constructing his manhood is as a sexual contest: to "win" his "balls back" (322). Both characters are scripted by a 1950s culture in the United States that celebrates "Decency and Maturity, a young man's 'seriousness,'" that deems "it was only within marriage that an ordinary woman could hope to find equality and dignity," and that finds that a "young college-educated bourgeois male [. . .] who scoffed at the idea of marriage for himself [. . .] laid himself open to the charge of 'immaturity,' if not 'latent' or blatant 'homosexuality.' Or he was just plain 'selfish'" (*My Life*, 170). Tarnopol feels betrayed and emasculated by Maureen—her deceit, her irrationality, and her claims on him as first a sexual partner and then a husband. Convinced that he has been a victim not just of a mad, lying woman but also of his own higher principles, he frames his stories in terms of what his psychoanalyst judges a "narcissistic melodrama" (167). He thus fails to gain a necessary critical distance on the ideologically determined principles that cause him to feel emasculated in the first place.

The self-righteous convictions that make a grotesque of Tarnopol enable the framing of the novel in three stories: the two "Useful Fictions," offering Roth's first use of the alter-ego character Nathan Zuckerman, and "My True Story." In "Salad Days," Tarnopol first projects his idealized antithesis into a Zuckerman who goes off to college with an unchallenged "sense of superiority" and whose girlfriend perfectly embodies the male fantasy of a sexual adventurer, whispering "I want to be your whore" to him in her parents' living room (*My Life,* 11, 28, 27). Yet Tarnopol, narrating in the third person to achieve an "amused, Olympian point of view," lacks the heart or imagination to continue the story without burying it under his own biography and so aborts his telling, only to show how he came to pay "for the vanity and the ignorance [. . .] and the lewd desires [. . .] and the manly, the *magisterial* ambitions" (31; italics in original). When he turns in "Courting Disaster" to a first-person narration, he makes plain his failure to distance himself from his protagonist. The solemn account of Zuckerman's marriage to the incest victim Lydia Ketterer, whose "dwarfish," "mannish" appearance makes him "recoil" sexually (33), offers a drearily noble fictional transformation of Maureen's madness and Tarnopol's commitment to repression and responsibility. By the time he gives up this displaced telling at the end of the tale with the defeated judgment that "I squandered my manhood" (96), the "I" of Zuckerman is indistinguishable from the "I" of Tarnopol. His claim at the beginning of "My True Story" that he is "preparing to forsake the art of fiction [. . .] and embark upon an autobiographical narrative" in order to have "exorcised his obsession once and for all" (100) thus seems redundant. Tarnopol's third attempt to write himself into confident subjectivity makes clear that he already, in "Courting Disaster," forsook the art of fiction. Though Maureen has died, he falls short of "the picture of a man whose nemesis has ceased to exist" and again faces the problem of the personal pronoun in his final sentence: "This me who is me being me and none other!" (334). Who *is* he?

Roth's emphasis on the discursive construction of his protagonist's selfhood in *My Life as a Man* causes Tarnopol to remain, despite his sexual entanglements, curiously disembodied in the narrative. Except for a few key scenes, such as when, enraged, Tarnopol literally beats the shit out of Maureen to assert his masculinity (*My Life,* 283–84)—instead proving his impotence—the novel focuses almost entirely on scenes mediated by his *voice.* In the six shorter novels of the 2000s, however, Roth's reflexive attention to discourse appears to recede to the background. The comparative *realism* of these narratives engages the materiality of existence—the desires and bodily failures that, together with the "truths" that still drive his protagonists, constitute their politics of masculinity. Yet Roth's forms are essential to the critique each late novel provides of the romance of manliness that is, like Maureen, the relentless "nemesis"—the archaic term that

Roth chooses for the title both of his final novel and his last tetralogy. Roth's manipulation of voices, pronouns, and narrative framing enables his fiction to open up consistent tensions in the life of a man. In each of his late-career novels one can trace how, filtered through such formal devices, his intensified focus on the stresses of embodiment—especially within the aging or injured male body—illuminates the politics of contemporary masculinity.

The Dying Animal: Who Are "You"?

Roth at first presents David Kepesh in *The Dying Animal* (2001), though in his advanced years, in the full arrogance of his sexual powers, seducing new young women annually with his intellectual celebrity.[16] Yet *The Dying Animal* intimates that Kepesh barely suppresses the fear that his powers will dwindle to nothing: "In every calm and reasonable person," he admits near the novel's conclusion, "there is a hidden second person scared witless about death" (*Dying*, 153). Roth captures in Kepesh the astonishment and incredulity of watching oneself age; the wisdom Edna O'Brien expresses in the line Roth takes for his epigraph is out of reach for Kepesh: "The body contains the life story just as much as the brain" (ix).[17] Aging, the frailty of the body, the diminishment of capacities: all the natural processes of the dying animal make us self-divided, between the "calm and reasonable" self that knows its inevitable decline *intellectually* and the "scared witless" self that cannot at bottom grasp that knowledge, that does not *feel* old—that, paradoxically, attempts to smooth over the Cartesian split between mind and body.

Roth cues the reader to the divided self by the narrative situation that he establishes casually, almost invisibly, from the outset of the novel. The second paragraph of *The Dying Animal* begins, "Now, I'm very vulnerable to female beauty, as you know" (2). The "as you know" may seem little more than a rhetorical trick, conveying Kepesh's character through a confiding, conversational style to win over the reader by his vulnerability and deflect attention from his controversial masculinist views, wherein he treats women as objects, exploits them sexually, and commits himself to being emotionally uncommitted.[18] Kepesh fortifies his manhood according to the twin principles that sex is "the revenge on death" (69) and is always about power: "There is no sexual equality. [. . .] What it is is trading dominance, perpetual *imbalance*" (20; italics in original). Yet the address to "you" also establishes a rhetorical situation. Kepesh's seeming monologue, drawing on the convention in which a first-person voice speaks directly to the reader, is instead a one-sided dialogue, whose form Roth reveals as significant only in the novel's final pages. Kepesh's speaking only rarely draws attention to itself as overtly *dialogical,* in moments that often seem a slippage in his *self-*reference rather than an address to an *other.* If the "you" Kepesh addresses is not always a diegetic interlocutor but rather himself—the scared witless self—then his arguments for behaving callously thinly veil a dilemma about ethical masculinity that Kepesh in his narcissistic assertions of phallic manhood openly dismisses. The "distancing effect" that Peter Mathews identifies in the novel's "trope of performance and spectatorship" thus gains poignancy. Kepesh may be whistling in the dark, performing callousness so that he may watch and thereby gain manly courage from it.[19]

Roth puts shifting pronouns in Kepesh's mouth repeatedly. For example, although Kepesh recites a memory of Consuela Castillo by situating his interlocutor in the "real" space of the scene—"I was sitting where you are, at the corner of the sofa" (24)—the slippage begins as he recounts his flirtatiousness when she says she cannot be his girlfriend: "right there, of course, you start the lying" (25). The "you" here is a displaced "I," the present tense implying a past-tense action. Yet Kepesh also makes his interlocutor, or any heterosexual male auditor or reader, complicit in the deceits of heterosexual male desire that he at once exposes and excuses: a "manly" man lies to a woman to secure her sexual favors. Elsewhere, Kepesh describes Consuela's "erotic power" by comparing her to the Modigliani nude on a postcard she has sent him: "One long, undulating line, she lies there awaiting *you,* still as death" (98; italics added). "She" is not only the sensuous rendering of the artist's model but also Consuela; the simile that allies her erotic power with death summons the "you" who is the "I" of the vulnerable Kepesh. Later, explaining the tormenting jealousy he feels in anticipating how he will lose Consuela through the "wound of age" (41), Kepesh imagines a pornographic film in which both a younger man and an intimate "you" displace him as the "I" of narration: "This devastating woman is coming to meet *me.* Only it isn't *me* in the pornographic film. It's *him* who was once *me* but is no longer. [. . .] it is impossible to think in what *you* rationally construe as *your* own self-interest" (42; italics added). The shift from the first and third person, the male rivals in the sexual game, to the second person expresses Kepesh's instability, as "you" denotes a selfhood desperate to reject identification "with the person who has lost" (42). What is lost is the power attending the romance of manliness.

The most telling example, however, appears early in Kepesh's narration, when he explains that having a sexual relationship as an aging man with a young woman makes "you feel excruciatingly how old you are, but in a new way." Kepesh registers little distance between the I and the you. He then describes the "new way" in a wrenching meditation addressed explicitly to "you": "Can you imagine old age?" he begins. "Of course you can't. I didn't. I couldn't" (35). Curiously, if one imagines the addressee as Kepesh's friend, the sexually provocative contents of his confession might suggest that his friend is both male and an age-mate. If so, however, the past tense of "I didn't" rings falsely with the present tense of "you can't," making Kepesh older since he has already imagined what he couldn't when he was his auditor's age. If this seems convoluted, I mean merely to highlight the instability of the "you" whom Kepesh addresses, reinforcing that he conducts an internal dialogue among his selves. Kepesh next replaces the "you" with an impersonal "one" as he plays with the temporal conundrums of the verb "to be": "To those not yet old, being old means *you've been.* But being old also means that despite, in addition to, and in excess of your beenness, you still are. [. . .] You still are, and one is as haunted by the still-being and its fullness as by the having-already-been." When Kepesh invokes desire, he signals that he does not contemplate the end of things neutrally: asking, "should a man of seventy still be involved in the carnal aspect of the human comedy?" he answers his own question: "as far as I can tell, nothing, *nothing* is put to rest, however old a man may be" (36–37; italics in original). The further shift from "one" and "you" to "a man" is revealing—at issue for Kepesh is the possibility of retaining not only a self-hood but also one defined by masculinity.

That remains the primary question when, at the close, the interlocu-tor emerges from the shadows and the monologue at last takes the shape of a dialogue on the page, with quotation marks that appear outside the retrospective narration. Summoned to Consuela's bedside after her mas-tectomy by a phone call that jolts the narration into the diegetically "pres-ent" moment (155), Kepesh at last uncovers the novel's underlying ethical dimension. To go to her is to assume the role of manly responsibility at the expense of masculinist power, to be, in the terms mentioned earlier, the nice Jewish boy rather than the Jewboy. Yet Roth has it both ways by reversing the positions of the "I" and the "you" and closing without resolution. When

Kepesh asserts, against his earlier arguments, "I have to go. She wants me there," the other voice warns him, "'Don't go. [. . .] Because if you go, you're finished" (156). The "you" now speaks anxiously for unfettered manliness and the romance of freedom, and does have the last word; but the "I" has reaffirmed the position of ethical masculinity in its final words, "I'm going." We do not learn what Kepesh chooses; Roth's dialogical device leaves the closing suspended and indeterminate. The "you" and the "I" disagree so as to highlight the stakes: has Kepesh unified a self in ethical action, or is he forever split and paralyzed? Is he antagonist or protagonist? Is a *man* virtuous, or is he free?

He and She: *Exit Ghost* and *The Humbling*

Such teasing out of the ambiguities in Roth's play with pronouns and multiple selves does not argue that *The Dying Animal* is simply a disguised internal monologue between the anxious and confident, or moral and amoral, Kepeshes. Yet these interpretive uncertainties point up the tensions among the various discourses of masculinity and, especially, the obstacles to heterosexual male sexual performance with which Roth has his protagonists, and specifically his aging men, contend. Three of his other late novels, *Exit Ghost* (2007), *The Humbling* (2009), and *Everyman* (2006), take up the distresses of men facing the decline of their powers, and each protagonist brings into relief the particular ways in which the male body, like Delmore Schwartz's heavy bear, is always, inescapably, with him.[20] Unlike *The Dying Animal,* however, the formal focus in these novels externalizes the anguish, moving outward from the "I" and the (displaced) "you" toward the discourse of the "he" and "she," a dyad fraught with erotic tensions and temptations.

That Roth is especially tuned to discourse *as* erotic performance becomes increasingly apparent in his career beginning with *The Counterlife* (1986), when Nathan Zuckerman, in one avatar, seduces the figure of Maria through *talk. Deception* (1990) goes even further, stripping away all narration in favor of play-like dialogues, many of them male/female. Roth recycles the device of intensely erotic, seemingly staged dialogue in the Jinx Possesski/"Philip" interchanges of *Operation Shylock* (1993) and in *Sabbath's Theater* (1995), both in some erotic foreplay between Drenka and Sabbath and in the Kathy Goolsbee episode, which records an X-rated conversation between her and Sabbath via an embedded typographical device.[21]

In *Exit Ghost,* Roth makes the dialogue device more self-conscious when Zuckerman, now incontinent and literally impotent after prostate surgery, returns briefly to New York City from his reclusive life, in a doomed attempt to reenter the "Here and Now" (*Exit,* 41). His only creative activity is to invent five theatrical set-pieces between a "He" and a "She," and in these dialogues, as Matthew Shipe observes, "Zuckerman strips all the artifice away from his fiction and reduces it to its core: a male and female voice *talking.*"[22] Yet these conversations are also nothing *but* artifice; the anonymous pronouns project his barely disguised, fantasized conversations between himself and the young, attractive Jamie Logan. Zuckerman devises a verbal intercourse that replaces, in his imaginative life, the sexual intercourse of which he is no longer capable, as a stay against "the bitter helplessness of a taunted old man dying to be whole again" (67).

Roth emphasizes the devastations of age on Zuckerman's body and mind—diminished memory as well as physical humiliations—as he pursues Jamie in a final quest to perform his manhood, stimulated by her "gravitational pull on the ghost of [his] desire" (*Exit,* 66). As if acknowledging the absurdity of his pursuit, Zuckerman overtly expresses his desire for Jamie only in his fantasized playlets—ironically relegating his bodily presence to just the ghostliness he desperately wishes to reembody. Four of the five *He and She* scenes develop from cautious flirtation toward explicit, if solely *spoken,* erotic playfulness. There is no touching. The projection of the diegetically "real" characters into fabricated conversations offers a painful reminder of how they remain *dis*embodied, unconsummated, disempowered, residing solely in Zuckerman's head, and speaking only his desire and not, as far as he or the reader knows, any desire of Jamie's. In fact, she admonishes him that "You've imagined a woman who isn't me" (277)—as if, shockingly, she has secretly read the dialogues he has just as secretly composed. Whereas Zuckerman could initially view Jamie as "having the effect of rousing the virility in me again" (103), he ruefully recognizes at last that he is beaten: "Why must strength's abatement be so quick and cruel? Oh, to wish what is into what is not, other than on the page!" (273).

That Zuckerman's wishes find fruition on the page alone—that he remains effectively a disembodied ghost—is reinforced in the narrative's structuring. Roth confronts him with two doubling figures in New York who represent to him, wittingly and unwittingly, his failing manhood. Richard Kliman, Jamie's former lover and the arrogant would-be biographer of

Zuckerman's first mentor (E. I. Lonoff, introduced in *The Ghost Writer* [1979]),[23] mirrors Zuckerman's own lost youthful power; Kliman offends the older writer in his "tactless severity of vital male youth, [. . .] blind with self-confidence" (*Exit*, 48), and he exposes how both conceive masculinity as a contest when he remarks that "old men hate young men" (50). When Zuckerman angrily refuses to help Kliman with his invasive biographical project, Kliman cruelly speaks Zuckerman's repressed fear—"You're dying, old man [. . .] You smell of decay! You smell like death!"—returning him to the shame of his embodied selfhood: "All I smelled of was urine" (104). The pathos and humiliations of the aging body are also thrust in Zuckerman's face by his encounter with Amy Bellette, Lonoff's former young lover and Zuckerman's object of fantasy in *The Ghost Writer*, now laid waste in her old age by a brain tumor. Amy is clearly an enfeebled antithesis of the seductive female represented by Jamie—Roth signifies their doubling both in their rhyming names and when Zuckerman writes Jamie's phone number on the obverse of the scrap of paper on which he has written Amy's name (29)—but she also, in her illness and mental confusion, projects Zuckerman's decline. Roth underscores the parallel when Amy recounts the tender conversations she conducts "all the time" (174) with the dead Lonoff; like Zuckerman, her only remaining erotic life exists in the ghostly dimension of imagined dialogues between He and She.

Roth signals Zuckerman's defeat when he has him invent Kliman, not Zuckerman himself, to voice the He of the penultimate playlet. Zuckerman's imagination invests Kliman with sexual brutality. He boasts of his phallic power, reminding Jamie of her praise for his penis (*Exit*, 257), and dismisses her increasingly agitated attempts to repel his overtures—"You love to yield," He says (259)—until the scene ends when "she flees" (260). The display of naked power that Zuckerman gives to this image of his "nemesis" (274) admits to his own comparative weakness. It also stands in sharp contrast to the final, melancholy *He and She* fantasy in which He seems to convince Jamie to join him for a tryst, even as She diagnoses him as "a virtually inhumanly disciplined, rational person who has lost all sense of proportion and entered into a desperate story of unreasonable wishes" in an effort to "*forge* a life" (291; italics in original). She unveils the grotesque into which his longing to be other—as Tarnopol would have it, to be "manly, a man"— has turned him. That Zuckerman *imagines* her this way underscores the self-critical insight Roth gives him. In the close of the playlet, which also closes the novel, Zuckerman bolts, terrified that She might actually confront him in the flesh—"*She's on her way and he leaves. Gone for good*" (292). The final stage direction, which by its rhetorical form invokes the condition of performance, seems to make literal the clichéd laments that appear earlier in His voice: "This is *killing* me, so I'm going to leave. I'm not going to follow my inclination and try to kiss you" (143); and "You're *charming* this man *to death*" (235; italics added). Roth slyly reanimates dead metaphors that link *eros* to *thanatos:* the threat of an embodied woman heralds Zuckerman's final disappearance as a man.

When Zuckerman bemoans how he has been "buffeted by the merciless encounter between the no-longers and the not-yets," he concludes, "That was humbling enough" (279); perhaps Roth had begun to intimate his penultimate novel, *The Humbling* (2009). Indeed, the *He and She* dialogues register Zuckerman's desire to control a woman who will not submit to his control, as the key to reasserting his phallic masculinity. This desire, wedded to a more literal representation of the problem of performance, constitutes the crucial subject matter of *The Humbling*. Like Zuckerman, Simon Axler is an artist past his prime. Unlike Zuckerman, Axler, as an actor, expresses his art physically; time has deprived him of his magnificence as a man "on the grand scale who looked as if he could stand up to anything and easily fulfill all of a *man's* roles, the embodiment of invulnerable resistance" (*Humbling* 6; italics added). Dethroned by age, and finding himself unable to act—"He'd lost his magic" (1), the novel begins—Axler, like Zuckerman, turns to a much younger woman to help him find his way back into a potent performance of masculinity. Like Zuckerman, Axler undertakes his transformation by attempting to script the selfhood of his erotic object, Pegeen Mike. Roth sets up Axler's rewriting of Pegeen as especially jarring, since she has been living for years as a lesbian and he revises her radically, from her sexual practices to her haircut and clothes.

According to Axler's fantasy of "The Transformation" (Roth's title for the second of the three chapters, or acts, of the novel), he is to achieve his metamorphosis through hers; it chillingly recalls Scottie's (James Stewart's) fantasy of transforming Judy (Kim Novak) into the dead Madeline of Hitchcock's *Vertigo* (1958).[24] Axler's fantasy is, like Scottie's, equal parts tragic, absurd, and unethical. Scottie is a notoriously emasculated figure who fatally tries to "cure" his impotence by exercising his will over a woman to make his fantasy flesh. Like Scottie, Axler is deaf to his political offenses, as in his rationalization that "All he was doing was helping Pegeen to be a woman he would want instead of a woman another woman would want." Yet when he sees Pegeen awaiting her expensive haircut, "silent, sheepish, [. . .] at the edge of humiliation," he has an inkling that he has stepped over the ethical line, wondering "if he wasn't being blinded by a stupendous and desperate illusion. [. . .] Wasn't he making her pretend to be someone other than who she was?" (65). But he quickly turns the insight on its head, reading the power dynamic in reverse to salve his conscience, speculating, "if indeed it wasn't she who had taken him over completely, taken him up and taken him over" (66). After she has spurned him, Axler must accept the wisdom of the lover whom Pegeen left for him: "It's we who endow her with the power to wreck" (88). Those who already lack power cede it in the game of eros—to unleash fantasy into the world is to lose control over it. Those who especially lack power are those who define the possibility of selfhood in terms of power. Hence Roth humbles Axler, sending him to his suicide and, as he identifies with Shakespeare's Prospero, "into thin air" (6).

Hold Your Ground: *Everyman*

The delusions about power and performance under which Axler and Zuckerman operate, fostered by the contradictory discourses of masculinity to which they feel bound, also trap the anonymous protagonist of *Everyman* (herein called Everyman). Roth engages the problem of male bodily performance; like Zuckerman in *Exit Ghost*, Everyman faces the facts of illness and mortality on almost every page. Roth structures the novel as a circle, moving from Everyman's burial back through his life to his death; the form emphasizes the thematic premise of death's inescapability. Yet despite all signs to the contrary, Everyman refuses to see what is right before him. Victoria Aarons puts it succinctly: "The real adversary here is not death but the protagonist himself, who is both preoccupied with his own death and in narcissistic denial of its inevitability."[25]

Roth organizes the novel as a chronology of Everyman's illnesses, punctuated by tales of his failed relationships with the women who attend him. Everyman's narration of decline centers on two facts of his bodily selfhood—his health and his sexuality. Roth develops his protagonist's awareness of his body, its power and its failings, through the trope of *swimming*, which he frames by a metaphoric contrast between the freedom of the water and the claustrophobic facticity of the *ground*. When Everyman's daughter recalls at his graveside advice he once gave her, she establishes just what he could not do: "There's no remaking reality. [. . .] Just take it as it comes. Hold your ground and take it as it comes" (*Everyman*, 5, 78–79). The line sounds the dirge of fatalism that *Everyman* intones. Spoken at the cemetery, holding one's *"ground"* proves nothing if not ironic. All Everyman can finally hold *is* his ground—the earth of the graveyard, where he cherishes and laments the "bones in a box" (170) that are all that remain of his own parents.

Competing in the texture of Roth's narration with the command to hold one's ground, with all it implies of resignation to death, is the urge toward unfettered life in a self defined by sensual pleasure and sexual potency, evident in the numerous references to swimming. From the novel's opening, when Everyman's wife, Phoebe, expresses her shock at his death—"It's just so hard to believe. I keep thinking of him swimming in the bay" (*Everyman*, 2)—swimming stands for the potent male experiencing the joy of his body, in strength and health, oblivious to decay. In the metaphor, Roth links physical prowess with sexual potency: Everyman's "single noteworthy physical skill was swimming" (100), and Phoebe recalls their month on Martha's Vineyard, "swimming and hiking and [. . .] easygoing sex at all times of the day" (29). To Everyman, his power as a swimmer is his proof against the forces of nature and the depredations of time: "he'd always loved swimming in the surf and battling the waves" (93); he removes his watch—banishing the blatant signifier of time—only when he swims (12). The metaphor, however, drives home the irony that Everyman suppresses knowledge of his perishability. For example, his first inkling of death comes from hearing as a child about the "drowned body" of a seaman who washed up on the beach during the war (25). Even at Martha's Vineyard, he has intimations of his mortality when "the thunder of the sea [. . .] made him want to run from the menace of oblivion" (30). The symptom that sends him into emergency bypass surgery appears "when he wound up badly short of breath in the City Athletic Club swimming pool" (41). And when in old age he confesses to his daughter that "I don't go in the surf anymore [. . .] I've lost the confidence for the surf" (107), he marks his decline by retiring to the "Starfish Beach retirement village at the Jersey shore" (63), where he is reduced from the beach to the swimming pool.

That the swimming metaphor refers to Everyman's masculine sufficiency as well as to his health appears in its narrative juxtapositions. The narration of his nearly fatal peritonitis, one of whose symptoms is that "he gave up his morning swim" (34), is interrupted briefly by reference to his first divorce—his failure, that is, to fulfill the image of Mosse's "manly virtues." Indeed, having been as a child "too much the good boy," he finds that "marriage became his prison cell" (31) and manages to fail at three marriages. To represent Everyman's most humiliating moment, when in his later years he flirts with a young runner along the boardwalk, Roth's language echoes his description of the fear his protagonist developed of the surf: "lost was the pleasure of the confidence" (133).

Roth thus brings Everyman to his doggedly unanticipated death by way of this central metaphor. The narrative establishes a rapturous memory of Everyman's childhood at the beach, in rhapsodic prose that suggests a child's impression of bodily immortality: "Along with the ecstasy of a whole day of being battered silly by the sea, the taste and the smell intoxicated him so that he was driven [. . .] to tear out a chunk of himself and savor his fleshly existence" (127). The passage enables Roth to highlight the bitter ironies when, slipping under anesthetic during his final, fateful surgery, Everyman again deludes himself about the possibility of his own extinction. He thinks of the "words spoken by the bones" of his parents in the cemetery that "made him feel *buoyant* and indestructible" (181; italics added), but they are words that he could only imagine. He then drifts into the same blissful memory of swimming—"Oh, the abandon of it"—before the narrator indicates how deceived and unprepared his buoyancy has made him for precisely the knowledge he should have gleaned: "he never woke up. [. . .] He was no more, freed from being, entering into nowhere without even knowing it" (182). If the main emphasis of the allegorical name "Everyman" lies typically on *every,* on the universality of the human confrontation with death, Roth rests it equally on *man.* Everyman's delusion that he is "anything but doomed" (182) is the fantasy of a subject who has placed his faith, all appearances to the contrary, in the romance of manly strength, sexual performance, and modest virtues.

Olivia's Scar and Bucky's Javelin: *Indignation, Nemesis,* and the Desiring Body of Youth

Whereas in the four late novels addressed so far, Roth explores the threats to selfhood for men facing the exigencies of their aging bodies, he returns in both *Indignation* (2008) and *Nemesis* (2010) to the struggles of young men.²⁶ And whereas he situates these four novels in an American culture— of the 1990s to 2000s—roughly contemporaneous with their writing, the latter two return Roth to periods that seem most pungent to his historiciz-ing imagination: the 1950s in *Indignation* and the 1940s in *Nemesis.* Roth frames both narratives according to the tensions between male desire and the myths of "manly" responsibility. He thereby teases out the stresses that the masculinist myth in America places on the bodies and minds of those who, as idealistic youths, feel the most pressure to measure up. His young males are like Tarnopol, but with more subterranean, if more culturally endemic, hysteria—troubled, trapped, longing, and self-doomed. Taking up protagonists in the bloom of their youth, these two novels seem even more forthright than Roth's prior fictions in criticizing the cultural mores that deform men into grotesques.

Indignation's Marcus Messner narrates most of the novel in the first person while "Under Morphine," as the title of the long first chapter puts it, in the moments before he dies at the age of nineteen, mangled on a Korean battlefield in 1952. His shocking, if misleading, confession less than a quarter of the way through the novel, that he is narrating from beyond the grave—"even dead, as I am and have been for I don't know how long" (*Indignation,* 54)—is realized at the close of the novel, where a shift to a third-person narrator conveys "the bayonet wounds that had all but severed one leg from his torso and hacked his intestines and genitals to bits" (225). Roth plays for heavy irony in that last detail, since it is Marcus's simple desires as a young man—both to be virtuous *and* to seek pleasure, to be (again) the Jewboy and the nice Jewish boy—that send him from the safety of Winesburg College into battle. Marcus's butchered body fulfills the novel's central metaphor of *blood,* anticipated in his account of the ritual slaughter of chickens at his father's butcher shop, with the blood that he "never got used to" (36). Like the trope of the "human stain" anchoring Roth's novel of that title, blood signifies the body itself, with its desires and flaws—its humanity—and also the punishments wrought upon the body whose subject falls short of or resists performing the expectations of cul-ture. Pulled by contrary "truths," Marcus "never got used to" the reality of his bodily existence. Roth makes the image of blood starkest in the traces implied by the scarred wrist of Olivia Hutton, the young woman with whom Marcus has his only sexual encounters. The vestige of her suicide attempt,

Olivia's scar marks Marcus as much as it marks her, as the sign of internal conflict: transgressive desires subjugated by the strict regulation of social life in 1950s America. Olivia's scar serves as the novel's leitmotif, invoking the realism of social relations that Erich Auerbach famously ascribed to Odysseus's scar in Homer's epic.[27]

Marcus's self-regulation is first externalized in his fearfully protective, upright father, from whom he learns the watchwords of responsible manly behavior: "you do what you have to do" (*Indignation* 5). He is straitjacketed by his father's notion of virtue—"I wanted to do everything right" (35)—such that, after Olivia on their first date astonishes him with a blowjob, he is so terrified by both her desire and his own that he avoids her. "I was afraid of her. I was as bad as my father. I *was* my father," he thinks, but then writes to ask her forgiveness, proud of his sexual maturation, "I'm ten years older than when we met. I'm a *man*" (68; first italics in original, second italics added). His growing obsession with Olivia's scar conveys both his delusions about his manliness and his contrary inability to meet that image. He considers that "it marked, if anything, the beginning of my manhood. [. . .] the scar did it. I was transfixed. [. . .] I was in bondage to it all. To the heroism of it all" (77). Yet Marcus senses the demands the body places upon the subject's "heroism"; the scar obliterates other aspects of selfhood: "you would have thought the whole of Olivia lay in her laughter, when in fact it lay in her scar" (137). Marcus, too, is subjugated by the scar's significations when, weakened by his worried mother's claims on his loyalty and love when she has seen Olivia and her scar, he promises her that he will no longer see the young woman. Marcus's willing, if grudging, renunciation of her confirms his emasculation.

Indignation suggests that the iron fist of social coercion embedded in the patriarchal order inevitably not only trumps desire but also scars the body for its longings. In the novel's climactic panty raid, Roth unleashes the forces of youthful sexuality such that, for one carnivalesque night, Nature thwarts the Law. But the patriarchal law at once reasserts its dominance in manifold punishments. Marcus's former roommate, Elwyn, is killed in his car—that cliché of American masculinity—while trying to outrace a train at a crossing. The young men who, in drunken frenzy, their "faces smeared blue-black with ink and crimson with *blood* [. . .] masturbated into pairs of stolen panties" (205; italics added), are publicly excoriated for their Bacchic rites by the college president, who berates them for their lack of "manly courage" and "honor" (219–20). A surrogate paterfamilias, the president avows that "Human conduct *can* be regulated, and it *will* be regulated!" and that "order," "decency," and "dignity" will be restored to Winesburg— and then he expels the "uninhibited he-men" to likely death in the Korean War (223; italics in original). Marcus's own nemesis and doppelgänger, his former roommate Flusser, has masturbated all over Marcus's room, leaving everything "steeped in sperm" (194). This imp of the perverse, whom Marcus sees as a "one-man bacchanalia [who] was the revenge on me" externalizes Marcus's unlawful desires, and he literally gags, "as much from the shock as from the smells" (195), as his body registers its own self-loathing.[28] Scarred by the "rectitude tyrannizing my life" (193), Marcus can no more perform the uninhibited he-man than he can, in the end, evade the Korean bayonets that slash him to bits.

Although Roth's final novel, *Nemesis*, is not as blood-soaked as *Indignation*, it registers much the same desperation and, yes, indignation over the "constricting rectitude" (*Indignation*, 193) that governs the consciousness and conscience of mid-twentieth-century American men. Impotent in the face of the polio epidemic that takes over Newark, Bucky Cantor echoes Marcus's conception of manly virtue when he tells the grieving father of a boy who has died, "You do only the right thing, the right thing and the right thing and the right thing, going back all the way. [. . .] and then this happens. Where is the sense in life?" (*Nemesis* 47). Roth depicts Bucky's version of the masculinist ideology in paternalistic terms, according to which he believes that his expression of manly selfhood resides in both knowing and controlling experience—that a man can both do the right thing and understand the sense in life. He is therefore shamed that, despite his physical strength and athleticism, he cannot serve in the war because of his poor eyesight. And he is devastated to surmise that he has carried the polio virus from Newark to the pastoral haven of Camp Indian Hill, where he flees to join his girlfriend, Marcia, after she—and his desire for her—persuade him to do "something so out of keeping with who he really was" (137). That is, in obeying his survival instinct, he believes he has failed the "ideals of courage and sacrifice" (135) that he takes as his self-definition and that made him continue to direct a playground in Newark, ineffectual as he must be in the face of a virus.

One might read Bucky as simply heroic in his commitment to doing good were it not for the narrative frame that Roth provides, which uncovers how his heroism is a narcissistic delusion. The structure of *Nemesis* echoes that of *Indignation,* in which the final chapter shifts register and view-point to recast the narrative in an ironic light. Roth reveals only in passing that a child from the playground, Arnie Mesnikoff, who, like Bucky, con-tracted polio, narrates Bucky's story nearly three decades later (108). Arnie has no overt presence until the final chapter, when he passes judgment on his former teacher for his arrogant conception of manliness as knowledge and control. In Arnie's voice, we discern how Roth has built the critique throughout the novel. Arnie recognizes that "there's nobody less salvageable than a ruined good boy" (272), and he opens up the ways in which Bucky's short-sightedness is not only physical but psychological and moral—that his *nemesis* is not polio—or more broadly nature—but himself.[29]

As conventional ideas of manliness toll through this text, as often as they appear in *My Life as a Man,* Roth's indictment of the masculinist myth becomes increasingly scathing. The discourse emphasizes control of oneself and the world around one as well as the denial of pleasures; thinking he is safe at the camp, Bucky reflects, "the happier he felt, the more humiliat-ing it was" (173). Bucky is raised by his grandfather, who "saw to the boy's masculine development, always on the alert to eradicate any weakness [. . .] and to teach the boy that a man's every endeavor was imbued with responsi-bility" (22). As a playground teacher, Bucky hopes to teach his boy charges "never to allow themselves to be pushed around" (28). When, faced by the widening epidemic, he visits Marcia's father for a pep talk, Dr. Steinberg insists that "Fear unmans us. Fear degrades us" (106). And the ethos of Camp Indian Hill, disguised in the stereotypes of Indian lore, finds expres-sion in Ernest Thompson Seton's *Manual of the Woodcraft Indians,* from which Roth has the camp director quote: "Manhood [. . .] is the first aim of education" (146). The most insidious representation of the ideal, however, appears in Bucky's distorted notion of fatherhood, which he displaces into his conception of God. Bucky conceives the original sin in his life as his father, a thief who abandoned his mother, and his fury at the patriarch's abuse and abandonment translates into his quarrel with God for the "luna-tic cruelty" (75) of unjustly, inexplicably causing the death of innocents.

In Bucky's conception of God as "a sick fuck and an evil genius," Arnie diagnoses his "stupid hubris," discerning the fatal paradox in Bucky's think-ing.[30] As "this martyr, this maniac of the why" (265), Bucky sacrifices him-self to the belief that he must be able to explain "pointless, contingent, preposterous, and tragic" (265) events as expressions of God's rational will.

At the same time, his guilty conviction that he is responsible for others' deaths—"Who brought polio here if not me?," he thinks (224)—presumes that, though he could not know if he carried the virus, he must have had intention and choice, which is to say he must have willed it. Why else punish himself for the rest of his life for a consequence over which he had no control? Bucky's only way, in the end, to accord himself manly potency is to presume he holds the position of the God at whom he rails. Roth thus indirectly exposes the egotism of masculine power in the West that has traditionally depicted the image of godhead as male.

Once the image of physical virility and selfless action according to which Bucky has defined his selfhood are damaged by his withered arm and leg and his guilt over fleeing Newark, he considers himself "a gender blank—as in a cartridge that is blank" (247), and he rejects Marcia's love, fancying himself "no longer man enough to be a husband and a father" (258). Indeed, the letter he shows Arnie from Marcia, received before the epidemic struck, in which she has simply written "My man" 218 times (252–52), rubs salt in his wound. Bucky inhabits his self-image as a castrated man. He embraces his existential blankness, inscribed by his insistence on impossible truths, in Anderson's sense of the term. Roth's decision to conclude the novel with Arnie's memory of Bucky in the full glory of his bodily power, demonstrating to the boys at the playground before the epidemic takes hold how to throw the javelin, thus places the problem of masculine selfhood into relief. The image is absolutely moving, and absolutely false, because it can only be temporary and innocent. Arnie reinstalls the romance of manliness by describing Bucky in mythic terms—"the first javelin thrower was said to be Hercules" (276); his glowing description of Bucky's supple, powerful body before he faces the *real* inserts Bucky, and his young watchers, into "the historical saga of our ancient gender" (279). The last word of the novel is "invincible" (280), which Roth places with heavy irony against the events of the novel and the doom its title announces. Yet the close also implies Roth's deep nostalgia for some ideal that could be imagined, if never realized, an ideal of knowledge and control that would deny the realities of natural and social contingencies.

Coda: Life as a Woman—Olivia's Scar Revisited

It no doubt seems belated to mention that the ideological pressures on manly performance necessarily imply complementary pressures on the performance of female identity. Because Roth largely takes manhood as his subject, however, some readers fail to discern just how acutely he notices the conditions in which women in general, and his protagonists' beleaguered women in particular, have lived. Because his male characters, struggling to be the men that the masculinist mythology tells them to be, often perceive women as objects for their distorted purposes, Roth has been taken to task over the years as himself a misogynist rather than being understood as a writer who exposes the misogyny that the hegemonic system of gendered performances promulgates. As Pierpont points out, Roth has been harshly criticized for his representations of women by the likes of Vivian Gornick and Michiko Kakutani, for, respectively, Maureen in *My Life as a Man* and the roman à clef of his former wife Claire Bloom and her daughter in *I Married a Communist* (1998). David Gooblar also notes unfavorable reviews, including those from Julia Keller and Linda Grant, who lament in part simply that Roth does not develop his female characters with the depth he gives to his men.[31] Roth has not been silent on the matter, either, wittily parrying the accusations of misogyny within his fiction. One of the dialogues in *Deception* stages a courtroom scene charging "Philip" with "sexism, misogyny, woman abuse, slander of women, denigration of women" and so forth (113). And *The Human Stain* (2000) tweaks the self-righteous feminist politics of Delphine Roux, who tries to expose Coleman Silk for a sexual affair only to broadcast her own erotic longings to her departmental colleagues.[32]

Space allows for only the outline of a defense here. Roth in 2014 told an interviewer, "Misogyny, a hatred of women, provides my work with neither a structure, a meaning, a motive, a message, a conviction, a perspective, or a guiding principle."[33] More to the point, one can go to the books to find women characters who are objects largely insofar as the perception of them is mediated by male characters. When Roth's men objectify women in the narratives, they reveal their damage or misperceptions, not some essential feminine identity. Even in *My Life as a Man*, in which Maureen may justly be viewed as a monstrous feminine figure, Roth provides a countering image in Tarnopol's other lover, Susan McCall, to reveal the larger cultural stakes. Susan offers Maureen's antithesis, with her "sedate and mannerly masochism" and a "lifelong style of forbearance" (*My Life,* 136–37), but Tarnopol recognizes that both women respond to "deprivation" (136) and that Susan "wanted what she wanted in order to rid herself of the woman she had been"

(137). And that is the woman from whom the "myth of male inviolability" demands the performance of a "damsel in distress" (172). Indeed, Tarnopol diagnoses both women as suffering from a "social malaise" that causes "virulent strains of a virus to which only a few women among us are immune" (172). Roth shows in his disease metaphors the degree to which men and women are equally victimized by mid-twentieth-century ideologies of gender—by the stultified subject positions into which, in Louis Althusser's terms, they are interpellated, or hailed.[34] Indeed, considering how few—or perhaps none—of Roth's male characters escape the probings of his scalpel, it should be no surprise to readers that he likewise inquires scrupulously into the socially produced ailments of women characters.

Roth provides other examples, however, of women who, in their resistance to men or patriarchal expectations, belie accusations that his imagination works toward misogynist ends. If anything, they point up Roth's critical acumen with respect to how, under the spell of the romance of manliness, men may be tempted to abuse the agency of women, who nevertheless may escape them. There is Maria Freshfield in *The Counterlife,* whose erotic play with Zuckerman ends with her disavowal; she refuses to be ventriloquized for the sake of Zuckerman's writerly fabrications, even as she acknowledges the "diabolical" power he has to turn her into "just one of a series of fictive propositions" (*Counterlife,* 319). Or there is Drenka Balich in *Sabbath's Theater.* Although one could make a case that she embodies male fantasy insofar as she is receptive to numerous transgressive sexual acts, she asserts her position as a subject through both her wantonness and her malapropistic speech, which, by breaking semantic rules, shows her as entirely individualistic. Or consider Jamie Logan in *Exit Ghost,* who calls Zuckerman's bluff on his attempt to imagine of her what she is not. Or Consuela Castillo, in *The Dying Animal,* who, despite her compliant reserve, shocks Kepesh out of his position of dominance during a "ferocious" sex act by a show of her teeth, "as though she were saying, [. . .] that's what I wanted to do, and that's what I didn't do" (*Dying,* 31). Or Marcia Steinberg, who, wounded by Bucky's renunciation of her but with utterly clear sight, offers the most succinct diagnosis of his diseased egoism: "You think it's your body that's deformed, but what's truly deformed is your mind!" (*Nemesis,* 260). Roth has each of these female figures pull the narrative's normative values—and sympathies—toward her viewpoint and away from the grasp of the men who might wish to dominate them.

Among the most telling of Roth's women figures, and the one with whom this essay will conclude, is Olivia Hutton in *Indignation*. At first blush, Olivia might seem to exemplify the misogynist's disparaging fantasy of a woman: she lies about herself, and she has a reputation on campus as a "'nutcase'" for her sexual availability as "the Blowjob Queen of 1951" (*Indignation,* 123, 122). Yet Roth makes clear that she suffers under the same proscriptions against desire as do her male counterparts. Indeed, it is significant that it is *Olivia's* scar that bears the metaphoric weight of the gendered system of 1950s America in the novel, for she is as scarred, if not more so, than the men around her. The men are expected at least to *possess* desire even if they must master it. Elwyn simply calls her a "cunt" (72); Marcus observes that "the rules regulating the lives of the girls at Winesburg were of the sort my father wouldn't have minded their imposing on me" (48). Marcus himself is unable to breach the conventional ideological hold on his conceptions of femininity. Figuratively, he reinjures Olivia at the site of her scar; she discerns, despite his denials, that he thinks she's a "slut" (65). Astonished by her sexual advances, he reports, "As far as I knew, girls didn't get fired up with desire like that; they got fired up by limits, by prohibitions, by outright taboos," and the only explanation he can conjure for her uncensored expressions of desire is that her parents' divorce must have caused her "abnormality" (58–59). Marcus buys wholly into the gendered system; his is the conception of women that causes Olivia's suicide attempt, marked by her scar, and the nervous breakdown that takes her finally away from Winesburg and out of his narrative. She is punished for her appetites nearly as much as Marcus is, and with far fewer overt expressions of empathy than Marcus garners from his own narrative; even his loving, sensible mother exhibits little feeling toward Olivia beyond the fear that she might, by her desires, ruin him. It is difficult, therefore, to conclude that Roth is insensible to the traps in which women are caught, which, denying them their sexuality, effectively deny them selfhood. His representation of a character like Olivia shows all too clearly Roth's intimation that the patriarchal law is indiscriminately damaging.

This is not to say that Roth generally places the constraints on the performance of femininity at the center of his novels, since his male protagonists always demand the most narrative space and time. Close examination of his novels, however, reveals that they provide no arguments, disguised in fictional forms, for a masculinist ideology. To the contrary, they divulge the fissures in that ideology. As Roth told Daniel Sandstrom, "my focus has never been on masculine power rampant and triumphant but rather on the antithesis: masculine power impaired. [. . .] The drama issues from the assailability of vital, tenacious men [. . .] bowed by blurred moral vision, real and imaginary culpability, conflicting allegiances, urgent desires, uncontrollable longings, [. . .] self-division, betrayal," and two dozen other harms, and he concludes that "It is the social struggle of the current moment on which a number of these men find themselves impaled."[35] Identifying this social struggle has been one of Roth's primary concerns, expressed succinctly when Pierpont summons Alfred Kazin's verdict, to wit, that Roth writes about "people trying to live by unfulfillable notions of themselves."[36]

Notes

1. Claudia Roth Pierpont, *Roth Unbound: A Writer and His Books* (New York: Farrar, Straus and Giroux, 2013), 47, 297.

2. See, for example, Ross Posnock, *Philip Roth's Rude Truth: The Art of Immaturity* (Princeton, NJ: Princeton University Press, 2006); and Catherine Morley, *The Quest for Epic in Contemporary American Literature* (New York: Routledge, 2008), 35, who places Roth within a web of "transnational and transtemporal interconnections."

3. Sherwood Anderson, *Winesburg, Ohio* (New York: Viking, 1964), 24.

4. Pierpont, *Roth Unbound*, 17.

5. Philip Roth, *My Life as a Man* (New York: Vintage, 1993), 174; hereafter cited parenthetically as *My Life*.

6. Philip Roth, *Portnoy's Complaint* (New York: Fawcett Crest, 1985); hereafter cited parenthetically as *Portnoy*.

7. Arthur Brittan, *Masculinity and Power* (Oxford: Blackwell, 1989), 4, 47, 16, 47.

8. George L. Mosse, *The Image of Man: The Creation of Modern Masculinity* (New York: Oxford University Press, 1996), 3–4.

9. Kelly Oliver, *Subjectivity without Subjects: From Abject Fathers to Desiring Mothers* (Lanham, MD: Rowman and Littlefield, 1998), 3.

10. Sigmund Freud, *Civilization and Its Discontents*, trans. James Strachey (New York: Norton, 1961).

11. Philip Roth, "In Response to Those Who Have Asked Me: 'How Did You Come to Write That Book, Anyway?,'" in Philip Roth, *Reading Myself and Others* (1975; New York: Farrar, Straus and Giroux, 1985), 35. For excellent extended analysis of the modern history of Jewish masculinity and its discontents, espe-

cially the enduringly troubling figure of the emasculated Jew, see George Mosse on the "countertype," *The Image of Man,* 56–76; and Neil R. Davison, *Jewishness and Masculinity from the Modern to the Postmodern* (New York: Routledge, 2010).

The particularity of explicitly *Jewish* male experience preoccupies much of Roth's work, up to around the turn of the century. But since Roth moves that subject matter somewhat to the background of his late fiction, which will be the primary concern of this essay, his exploration of Jewish masculinity will also take a back seat in the argument. The work that has been done on Roth and Jewishness is voluminous; one might simply take as a solid starting point Alan Cooper's *Philip Roth and the Jews* (Albany: State University of New York Press, 1996); or, for focus on Jewish masculinity as such, chapters 2 and 3 of my *Philip Roth—Countertexts, Counterlives* (Columbia: University of South Carolina Press, 2004).

12. Pierpont, *Roth Unbound,* 314.

13. Despite Claudia Roth Pierpont's startling assertion at the Roth@80 conference and celebration of Roth's eightieth birthday (Newark, New Jersey, March 19, 2013) that no one had yet talked, or at least talked favorably, about Roth's depiction of women, a number of critics have done just that. To name just a few examples, one might look to the special issue "Roth & Women" published in *Philip Roth Studies* 8.1 (spring 2012), especially David Gooblar's excellent introduction (7–15); Miriam Jaffe-Foger and Aimee Pozorski, "'[A]nything but fragile and yielding': Women in Roth's Recent Tetralogy," in that special issue, 81–94; the early, even-handed consideration in Patricia Meyer Spacks, "Male Miseries," review of Philip Roth, *The Professor of Desire, Nation,* October 15, 1977, 373–76; Marshall Bruce Gentry, "Ventriloquists' Conversations: The Struggle for Gender Dialogue in E. L. Doctorow and Philip Roth," *Contemporary Literature* 34.3 (1993): 512–37; and my "Roth and Gender," in *The Cambridge Companion to Philip Roth,* ed. Timothy Parrish, 111–26 (Cambridge: Cambridge University Press, 2007).

14. Karl Marx, *18th Brumaire of Louis Bonaparte* (1852; London: Electric Book Company, 2001), 7.

15. Patrick O'Donnell, "'None Other': The Subject of Roth's *My Life as a Man,*" in *Reading Philip Roth,* ed. Asher Z. Milbauer and Donald G. Watson (New York: St. Martin's, 1988), 154.

16. Philip Roth, *The Dying Animal* (Boston: Houghton Mifflin, 2001); hereafter cited parenthetically as *Dying.*

17. Roth quotes O'Brien from an interview he conducted with her in 1984 and published in *Shop Talk: A Writer and His Colleagues and Their Work* (Boston: Houghton Mifflin, 2001), 105.

18. Roth here capitalizes on the levels of irony in Kepesh's assertion; to claim vulnerability seems at once a confession and a deflection. Velichka Ivanova teases

out these ironies in "My Own Foe from the Other Gender: (Mis)representing Women in *The Dying Animal*," *Philip Roth Studies* 8.1 (spring 2012): 31.

19. Peter Mathews, "The Pornography of Destruction: Performing Annihilation in *The Dying Animal*," *Philip Roth Studies* 3.1 (spring 2007): 45. Mathews focuses on Kepesh's theatrical act of confession, in a performance for the silent auditor to whom he is allegedly directing his speech. While arguably such a performance is self-serving for the performer, Mathews does not go so far as to eliminate the "real" auditor from the scene of narration.

20. Philip Roth, *Exit Ghost* (Boston: Houghton Mifflin, 2007), *The Humbling* (Boston: Houghton Mifflin 2009), and *Everyman* (Boston: Houghton Mifflin, 2006); hereafter cited parenthetically as, respectively, *Exit*, *Humbling*, and *Everyman*.

Delmore Schwartz, "The Heavy Bear Who Goes with Me," from 1938, takes as its epigraph "the witness of the body." Schwartz begins the poem, "The heavy bear who goes with me, / A manifold honey to smear his face," and adds that the bear "Howls in his sleep for a world of sugar," and "Trembles to think that his quivering meat / Must finally wince to nothing at all" (*The Norton Anthology of Modern Poetry*, ed. Richard Ellmann and Robert O'Clair [New York: Norton, 1973], 864–65).

21. Philip Roth, *The Counterlife* (New York: Farrar, Straus and Giroux, 1986); *Deception* (New York: Simon and Schuster, 1990); *Operation Shylock* (New York: Simon and Schuster, 1993); and *Sabbath's Theater* (Boston: Houghton Mifflin, 1995); hereafter cited parenthetically as, respectively, *Counterlife*, *Shylock*, and *Sabbath*.

22. Matthew Shipe, "*Exit Ghost* and the Politics of 'Late Style,'" *Philip Roth Studies* 5.2 (fall 2009): 189–204.

23. Philip Roth, *The Ghost Writer* (New York: Farrar, Straus and Giroux, 1979); reprinted in *Zuckerman Bound* (New York: Farrar, Straus and Giroux, 1985), 1–180.

24. *Vertigo*, dir. Alfred Hitchcock, Paramount, 1958.

25. Victoria Aarons, "'There's no remaking reality': Philip Roth's *Everyman* and the Ironies of Body and Spirit," *Xavier Review* 27.1 (spring 2007): 116–27.

26. Philip Roth, *Indignation* (Boston: Houghton Mifflin, 2008); and *Nemesis* (Boston: Houghton Mifflin, 2010); hereafter cited parenthetically as, respectively, *Indignation* and *Nemesis*.

27. Erich Auerbach, *Mimesis: The Representation of Reality in Western Literature*, trans. Willard R. Trask (1953; Princeton: Princeton University Press, 1974), 3–23. In an essay on *Indignation*, Alan Cooper footnotes Auerbach's chapter on Odysseus's scar in relation to Roth's interruptive prose style but does not make the connection to Roth's trope in the novel (Alan Cooper, "*Indignation*: The Opiates

of the Occident," in *Playful and Serious: Philip Roth as a Comic Writer*, ed. Ben Siegel and Jay L. Halio, 255–68 [Newark: University of Delaware Press, 2010]).

28. Flusser, as a closeted homosexual, represents an important, if largely unexplored, dimension of Roth's representations. In *Indignation*, he dramatizes a generalized unspeakable male desire—the taboo sperm become visible—and his homosexuality serves as a foil for Marcus's fear of emasculation, expressed as homophobia. But, as a brilliant unpublished essay by David Brauner, "Queering Philip Roth: Homosocial Discourse in the 'American Trilogy,'" demonstrates, Roth's representation of the sexual continuum is far more nuanced, the boundaries between the homosocial and the homosexual far less distinct, than has heretofore been recognized.

29. Emily Budick offers the important reminder that Nemesis is the Greek goddess of divine retribution directed specially at those, like Bucky, "who suffer from hubris or arrogance or narcissism" (Budick, "Roth's Fiction from Nemesis to *Nemesis*," *CLCWeb: Comparative Literature and Culture* 16.2 [2014]: 2).

30. Victoria Aarons astutely points out Bucky's hubris in the context of a somewhat different, but related, delusion—that, like others of Roth's protagonists, he desires to live out a counterlife to the life he has been given, especially the fear of the epidemic, in his retreat to the "false sanctuary, an Eden imaginable only in fantasy," when he retreats to Indian Hill (see "Expelled Once Again: The Failure of the Fantasized Self in Philip Roth's *Nemesis*," *Philip Roth Studies* 9.1 [spring 2013]: 53, 59.

31. Pierpont, *Roth Unbound*, 81, 237; Gooblar, "Introduction," 8–9.

32. Philip Roth, *The Human Stain* (Boston: Houghton Mifflin, 2000).

33. Philip Roth, "My Life as a Writer," interview by Daniel Sandstrom, *New York Times Sunday Book Review*, March 2, 2014.

34. Louis Althusser, *Lenin and Philosophy and Other Essays*, trans. Ben Brewster (New York: Monthly Review Press, 2001).

35. Roth, "My Life as a Writer."

36. Kazin qtd. in Pierpont, *Roth Unbound*, 34.

10

The American Berserk in *Sabbath's Theater* (1995)

Brett Ashley Kaplan

> This person had a certain fortunate, brilliant exceptional look . . . which would have made almost any observer envy him at a venture. . . . His companion . . . was a person of a quite different pattern, who, although he might have excited grave curiosity, would not, like the other, have provoked you to wish yourself, almost blindly, in his place.
>
> —Henry James, *The Portrait of a Lady* (1881)

> Concerning the factors of silence, solitude and darkness we can only say that they are actually elements in the production of the infantile anxiety from which the majority of human beings have never become quite free.
>
> —Freud, "The Uncanny" (1919)

I argue that Philip Roth's novels teach us that Jewish anxiety stems not only from fear of victimization but also from fear of perpetration. It is impossible to think about Jewish victimization without thinking about the Holocaust; and it is impossible to think about the taboo question of Jewish perpetration without thinking about Israel. I use the word "taboo" here contextually as of course it is not at all taboo in some cases—but it is in the context of a Jewish American writer's works. The history of Jewish victimization predates by a long stretch the Nazi genocide, and this dual anxiety is perhaps not only a "Jewish" concern. That perpetration and victimization can sometimes be uncomfortably close is part of what Roth explores throughout his oeuvre. Roth's texts probe Israel-Palestine and the Holocaust with varying degrees of intensity, but all his novels scrutinize perpetration and victimization through examining racism and sexism in America. The novels set in America often feature racist, ranting characters who express anti–black American or anti-Japanese sentiment; progressive figures who explicitly challenge this racism often oppose these characters. The totemic presence of people of color who seem to be randomly plunked into Roth's texts without developing as fully formed characters formally shadows these debates within the narratives about racism in America. I suggest that these characters are problematic on the one hand because they are not granted the full consciousness that many of the white characters achieve; but, on the other hand, Roth may be (intentionally or accidentally) replicating and critiquing the very structure of racial division by having these figures be so evanescently sketched. Because copious numbers of Roth's Jewish men try (but fail) to identify with some of these characters, an endlessly deferred alliance appears as a spectral presence that conjures up a shared oppression that will always be dissolved by white privilege. By placing Jewish identification with usually black characters in proximity to (often Jewish) racist ranting, Roth subtly demonstrates the danger of Jews becoming the very thing the aftershock of the Holocaust would make them despise most: racist.

Roth's main characters—almost all men—express much anxiety about the various masculinities they inhabit. They are sometimes put either literally or figuratively on trial for sexual aggression in ways that align them with perpetrators of racially based hate crime. While race, class, gender, sexual orientation, and other identitarian markers all intersect and overlap, Roth makes a parallel move in the case of gender to how he treats race. Just as overt arguments about racism figure in much of his writing, so do disputes over feminism. Although there is only one major black character (*The Human Stain's* Coleman Silk), there are abundant major female characters, almost all white, mostly not Jewish, and quite varied and complex in their portrayals. The women fluctuate widely from sexually repressed hysterical feminists, to gender-bending queer characters, to one-dimensional sexual fantasies, to multivalent, inventive figures, to stereotypical caricatures of overbearing Jewish mothers, to subtly painted and immensely strong and admirable Jewish parents. This variety of female characters coupled with anxieties over masculinity makes it impossible to generalize about what exactly goes on with gender in Roth's oeuvre. However, gender plays a central role in unpacking the exploration of perpetration and victimization that I argue is crucial to understanding Roth because he consistently challenges the victim-perpetrator expectations in situations wherein there is a power and/or generational difference between men and women. Men, in these situations, are not always the perpetrators, and women are not always the victims. In what follows I focus on *Sabbath's Theater* as a springboard to illuminate the intersecting problematics of victimization and perpetration; masculinity and femininity; racism and anti-Semitism. For if, as I argue here, Jewish anxiety is not only about the fear of being oppressed, we can begin to see how anxiety functions in terms of fears of perpetration, then perhaps we can better understand how to navigate through the mined terrain of Israel-Palestine.

Sabbath's Theater (1995) charts the decline and fall of Mickey Sabbath, a middle-aged former puppeteer living in the tiny town of Madamaska Falls (whose name, of course, underscores the fall of Sabbath and recalls Milton's *Paradise Lost,* a text about the fall from grace (among other things). Sabbath's name initially conjures the traditional Jewish time of rest, but the third meaning in the *Oxford English Dictionary* is "a midnight meeting of demons, sorcerers and witches presided over by the Devil, supposed in medieval times to have been held annually as an orgy or festival."[1] Thus the main character is marked at once as embodying a tension between a peaceful practice and rabble-rousing with the Devil. His name, then, contains both sides of a dynamic between "good and evil" as construed through a religious lens. The novel is set from 1993 to 1994 (and toggles back and forth between different time zones), so stay with me as we move through the roller-coaster ride of crazy stuff that Roth has Sabbath perform. Five years before the diegetic time of the novel, Sabbath had been disgraced by the broadcasting of recordings of sexually explicit conversations between him and one of his former students, Kathy Goolsbee (whose name resonates with the witches and demons embedded in Sabbath's name because, to my ears, it sounds like "ghoul"). While getting over the sting of the disgrace, three ghosts haunt Sabbath: his first wife, Nikki, who disappeared without trace; his brother, Morty, killed during World War II; and his mother, destroyed and never to regain herself after the death of her eldest son. Sabbath remains in a hate-filled marriage with his second wife, Roseanna, a woman whom he once fervently desired and now blatantly ignores, while he carries on a thirteen-year-long affair with Drenka, a Croatian immigrant who, with her husband, Matija, runs a hotel in the area. Drenka recounts her exploits with myriad lovers to Sabbath while he enjoys the spectacle of her middle-aged sexual flowering. After Drenka dies quite suddenly of cancer, Sabbath begins to spin: going to New York for the funeral of a suicided friend, he takes up residence with his old chum Norman and his wife, Michelle, only to abuse their adult daughter's underwear and photo and to steal illicit images of Michelle along with huge wads of cash. Finally returning, draped in his brother Morty's American flag and carrying the uncanny objects he left behind, to Madamaska Falls, Sabbath discovers Roseanna in bed with Christa (a young German woman with whom he and Drenka had carried on a threesome) and returns to Drenka's grave to piss all over it. I am not sure that I can adequately analyze the pissing and coming all over graves that Roth has Sabbath engage in so heartily. Is it just that death and sex are close for Sabbath? (The ghost of his mother does appear while he has sex with Drenka, for instance, and, conversely, he feels he can no longer be attracted to Nikki precisely because she was too attached to her mother's corpse). Is this "shocking" habit of Sabbath's Roth's way of driving home his most colorful character's "perversity?" I don't have the answer, but it is clear that the landscape of the cemetery is crucial to this text and that this very landscape offers Roth an opportunity to put victimization and perpetration into play.

When Sabbath scouts a burial plot for himself, he imagines it next to that of a grave marked "Holocaust Survivor." In stark contrast he envisions his headstone as reading: "Beloved Whoremonger, Seducer/Sodomist, Abuser of Women,/Destroyer of Morals, Ensnarer of Youth,/Uxoricide, / Suicide /1929–1994" (716).[2] Roth thus juxtaposes (quite literally) a person structurally situated as a surviving victim of the Holocaust with Sabbath poised to reside in perpetuity under his own invented memorial stone that places him in the position of perpetrator. In a similar fantasizing about his own death, at one point Sabbath concocts an obituary that launches various accusations at him including, "Mr. Sabbath did nothing for Israel" (549). Having failed to support Israel takes its place along with uxoricide in a list of wrongdoings. When Sabbath pens his will, he leaves "twenty dirty pictures

of Dr. Michelle Cowan to the State of Israel" (779), thus at once resolving
the crime of having done "nothing for Israel" and continuing the hostility
Sabbath feels toward the imagined Jewish homeland. The final scene of
the novel takes place at Drenka's grave when her enraged son, Matthew,
the state trooper, discovers Sabbath there and hauls him into the squad
car. Sabbath tells him to "Take me in so I can purge myself publicly of my
crimes and accept the punishment that's coming to me" (786) but Drenka's
son refuses, thereby denying Sabbath the exculpation from his crimes in the
form of punishment.

As is the case in these graveyard scenes, Roth sets Sabbath up structurally as a perpetrator throughout the text but simultaneously undoes this
structural positioning by clouding the parameters of victimization and perpetration. Sabbath pretends to have murdered his first wife, Nikki, claiming
to Kathy Goolsbee that he strangled Nikki during a rehearsal for *Othello*.
Sabbath alleges that because it "perpetuates the stereotype of the violent
black male" (592), Kathy would never have heard of Shakespeare's play.
"I played the stereotypical violent black male," Sabbath tells her; "In the
scene in which he murders her I did it" (592). By titling his novel as he
does, Roth stresses the importance of the theatrical in both the general
sensation of Sabbath as a character who plays all sorts of tricks and also in
the more specific scenes such as this one where theater or puppetry appear.
Roth has Sabbath playfully present himself as an embodiment of the very
kind of stereotyping that PC-consciousness deplores. Roth features Sabbath
at once identifying with a Moorish character (Othello) and with perpetration in the form of murder. Both Sabbath and *The Human Stain*'s Coleman
Silk are disgraced teachers: Sabbath because of the exposure of taped sexually detailed conversations with a student, Coleman because of a supposed
racial slur. In both cases Roth is careful to discharge the charge: Sabbath
was just a much a "victim" of Kathy as she was of him; Coleman could not
possibly have issued a racial slur because he did not know the race of the
absent students whom he terms "spooks."

Another moment when Roth reverses perpetration and victimization
occurs during the scene where Sabbath recounts his arrest, in 1956, for
fondling the breast of Helen Trumbull, an audience member at the puppet
show he regularly performed as street art on 116th and Broadway. While
Sabbath is on trial for "disorderly conduct and obscenity" (666), Helen
Trumbull bravely arrives at the courtroom to testify in his defense: "Here's

the alleged victim testifying for the perpetrator" (663). As she attempts to defend him, the prosecutors and the judge demean her by making her out to be a "whore" (664, 666) and thus discredit her testimony. Sabbath is nonetheless let off with a fine instead of jail time; the perpetrator is saved by the "traumatized or hypnotized or tyrannized" (679) victim.[3] Another example appears while Sabbath is at Norman and Michelle's apartment. After he riffles through their daughter's room, the narrator comments: "The savage license taken here astonished even the perpetrator" (535). Norman walks in on Sabbath being thrilled by a photograph of his adult daughter Deborah, and Sabbath imagines him thinking: "Enter our terrorist" (512). And, while he somehow snuggles with Rosa, the housekeeper at Norman and Michelle's place, he reminds us that, "He had a harassment record a mile long already. They'd string him up by his feet outside NOW. Roseanna would see they did it to him the way they'd done it to Mussolini. And cut off his prick, for good measure" (540). In all of these instances Roth emplots Sabbath as a harasser, a terrorist, and, indeed a "perpetrator." But in all cases Roth unpacks this alignment with perpetration by either having the supposed victim come to his defense or by constructing another perpetrator who turns him into a victim, as is the case with the image of a castrated and strung-up Sabbath, visualizing himself as Mussolini.

While the narrator explains how the whole scandal with Kathy Goolsbee came about in 1989, he makes it clear that whereas Sabbath might think he was fishing for her, "she'd pierced *him* . . . he [was] being craftily landed and that someday very soon now he could discover himself eviscerated, stuffed, and hung as trophy on the wall above the desk of Dean Kimiko Kakizaki" (564). Sabbath also, after his disgrace, reverses the polarity of victimization and perpetration by sarcastically claiming that Kathy had paid "unwanted attention to my *mind!* . . . Help! I've been mentally harassed! Help! I am the victim of mental harassment! . . . Call the dean! My *dick* has been disempowered" (594, original emphasis). As was the case when Sabbath imagined being castrated and hung up like Mussolini, he here plugs into the very familiar Roth trope of castration and impotence. Mussolini recalls the war and Sabbath is vehemently racist against the Japanese, something he justifies by placing the blame on Japan for the death of his brother, shot down over the Philippines in 1944. This anti-Japanese racism is fueled when the Japanese dean weighs in on the Goolsbee scandal.

Roth makes the confusion between victim and perpetrator clear at the level of typography by inserting a series of split pages wherein a recording of the damning conversation between Sabbath and Kathy can be read below the narrative. The conversation was taped by both Kathy and Sabbath for their later delight, and then accidentally left by Kathy in the bathroom and broadcast on a phone line so that hundreds of people could hear it (and, in Sabbath's fancy, enjoy it heartily as just another bit of porn). If this had happened now, the recording would have gone viral. After being made public on the call-in line, the tape was given to the dean. From the transcript (567–85), the affair appears consensual; from the perspective of the "mollycoddling professors" (572), Sabbath had abused his position of power as Kathy's professor and become her "victimizer" (567) while she maintained her "innocence" (567). Sabbath had been keeping tapes of these explicit conversations in a locked file cabinet and knew full well the disgrace that would befall him if any were to be made public: "Sabbath knew the danger of what he had in those shoeboxes yet he could never bring himself either to erase the tapes or to bury them in garbage at the town dump. That would have been like burning the flag. No, more like defiling a Picasso. Because there was in these tapes a kind of *art* in the way that he was able to unshackle his girls from their habit of innocence" (566, original emphasis).

The image of the flag as uncanny object will reappear later in the text, when Sabbath drapes himself, shroud-like, in the flag that graced his brother's coffin. And here, the reference to "defiling a Picasso" conjures up the Nazi take on "degenerate art" where modernists such as Picasso produced art unsavory to fascist taste. Another such moment where the war figures subtly in this text appears when Sabbath and Norman are laughing together and then Sabbath thinks unkindly of his friend: "Another sentimental Jew. You could fry the sentimental Jews in their own grease" (506). By here alluding to human grease as lubrication for frying, Roth conjures up the (probably apocryphal) ghoulish accounts of Holocaust victims' fat being used for this and other purposes.

Returning to Roth's recounting of the Kathy Goolsbee scandal, Sabbath's anti-Japanese racism is focused on the dean, whom he terms the "midget Jap dean" (562) and whose name he consistently mangles (she appears as Kakizaki, Kakumoto, Kamizaki, Kuziduzi, Kamizoko, Kakizomi, Kazikomi [566–96]). Roth explains that Sabbath "hated her fucking midget guts, not for her leading the coven that cost him his job. . . . [but for] loosing those girls that killed him, a dozen of them a year, none over twenty-one, and always at least one" (562–63). Roth uses "killed" in a triple sense here. First, this reverses Sabbath's imagined killing of his first wife, Nikki. Second, the disgrace kills not him exactly, but his employability as a teacher. Third, it recalls the proximity of sex and death of which the coming on the graves never fails to remind us. In these moments Roth makes it virtually impossible to have any sympathy for Sabbath. His blatant racism and clear flattening of these students simply into "girls" with whom he can engage in play blocks identification with and sympathy for our main character. But Roth also makes into prudes and scolds the women who denounce Sabbath. In Roth's parodic take on feminism, a group is formed that identifies itself with the acronym SABBATH: Women Against Sexual Abuse, Belittlement, Battering, and Telephone Harassment (567). The third sense (that of meeting with the Devil) of his titular character's name appears here, as the reference to a "coven" makes clear. One of the group's cochairpersons announces in a "clinical" voice that she is about to play the tape of the explicit conversation between Sabbath and Kathy. She concludes by noting, "in his psychological assault on an inexperienced young woman, Professor Sabbath has been able to manipulate her into thinking that she is a willing participant. Of course, to get the woman to think that it is her fault, to get her to think that she is a 'bad girl' who has brought her humiliation on herself by her own cooperation and complicity . . ." (568, ellipses in original). The transcription that appears below in the split page, meanwhile, makes it perfectly clear that Kathy is not only "complicit" but is in fact the instigator—it is she (and not Sabbath) who turns the conversation sexy. And, while Sabbath heatedly discusses his disgrace with Kathy while they sit in a car on Battle Mountain, Kathy, sobbing, repeats, "I want to suck you" (569), thus furthering the text's contention that she is not the victim.

In all cases, the novel argues, what may look from the outside like an older, more experienced man exploiting a younger, naïve woman, what may look like sexual abuse, is in fact sex and/or sexual play between consenting adults. A minor character, Gus Kroll, asks Sabbath if he can "take a joke that's not too appreciative of women," to which Sabbath replies: "The only kind I *can* take" (407). Indeed, *Sabbath's Theater* makes fun of the feminists who are up in arms about Kathy Goolsbee's debasement, but it also makes fun of Sabbath. As David Greenham notes, "Sabbath is masculinity ironized."[4] In a chatty little book about *Portnoy's Complaint* whose cover announces its sympathy for Roth's 1969 novel by mimicking the original bright orange and red of the first edition, Bernard Avishai declares: "all men are created equal, but with a little porn clip running in the back of our minds, which can turn life, liberty, et cetera into a rough ride."[5] Claudia Roth Pierpont, at the conference in honor of Roth's eightieth birthday, held up Drenka as a marvelous example of a strong female character in Roth's world. But Sabbath reveals perhaps the most salient feature of her character near the outset of the novel: "Inside this woman was someone who thought like a man. And the man she thought like was Sabbath. She was, as she put it, his sidekicker" (379). In other words, at least in Sabbath's view, they both have a porn clip (and of course there's nothing little about it) running in their minds all the time. Unlike the women Roth's characters problematically convey as prissy people who turn them off—think of Kepesh's Claire Ovington, who can't stand to swallow Kepesh's come (*The Breast, The Professor of Desire*)—Drenka drinks it all in, literally and figuratively. Drenka revels in poring over sexual exploits, enjoys pretending to be a whore (and getting paid by a Sabbath, who can ill afford it), and initially eschews monogamy. In being, in Sabbath's construction, like a man she becomes certainly one of the strongest and most memorable of Roth's female characters; but why does she need to be configured as male-ish for this to be so?

Sabbath's Theater ultimately expresses the confusion between perpetration and victimization through the anxiety around sexuality that Sabbath goes to such great lengths to identify and detonate. Kathy cannot be seen as a victim of Sabbath and nor can he be seen as a perpetrator; and yet it is within Sabbath's dialogue with Kathy that he aligns himself with Nazis and thus with perpetration: "If they send me up for sodomy, the result could be death. And that might not be as much fun for you as you may have been led to believe. You may have forgotten, but not even at Nuremberg was everyone sentenced to die" (586). In other words, even some Nazis were let off. It's a telling revelation for Sabbath, who had also compared himself to Mussolini, but who generally argues against the demonization of what he maintains is the "delightful Dionysian underlayer of life" (587)—and therefore against viewing him as akin to one of the perpetrators on trial at Nuremberg. By using this analogy Roth cracks open the divide between German and Jew, between victim and perpetrator. Sabbath simultaneously identifies across the ravine with victims. As I discussed above, Sabbath imagines himself being buried next to a Holocaust survivor, which contrasts sharply with his self-analogizing to Nazis. This again underscores Roth's central concern with the relationship of victim and perpetrator arrayed as a continuum.

As Roth digs in with all these graves, he reinforces the importance of death to *Sabbath's Theater*. Roth dedicates the novel to two friends, Janet Hobhouse and Melvin Tumin, who died in 1991 and 1994; Tumin will be the inspiration for *The Human Stain*'s Coleman Silk. The epigraph to the novel, from *The Tempest*, is, "Every third thought shall be my grave" (act 5, scene 1). As it turns out, the graves of Morty, Sabbath's mother, Nikki's mother, Drenka, and Linc take up more thought than his own grave. He does finally invest in a plot bought with some of the cash stolen from Michelle but left uninhabited by his body at the close of the novel, whose final paragraph includes, "He could not fucking die" (787). Indeed, Roth would formalize this theme that had been present throughout his work, with his final cluster of novels that center on death as their explicit focus. Roth has Sabbath reflect:

> no evidence had ever been offered Sabbath to persuade him that the dead were anything other than dead. To talk to them, admittedly, was to indulge in the most defensible of irrational human activities, but to Sabbath it was alien just the same. Sabbath was a realist, ferociously a realist, so that by sixty-four he had all but given up on making contact with the living, let alone discussing problems with the dead. Yet precisely this he now did daily. His mother was there every day and he was talking to her and she was communing with him. Exactly how *are* you, Ma? (385)

Within the context of the novel we can read this passage as echoing the long scenes of Sabbath's lost first wife, Nikki, sitting over her mother's body in absolute communion with the dead to the exclusion of the living (469–88). When Roth ends the passage with Sabbath's direct address to his mother, we can imagine Nikki asking her mother the same question. Adhering to no particular religious creed, Nikki feels no need to bury the parent to whom she remains unwilling to bid farewell. Sabbath notes, "I was a Jew accustomed to the dead's being buried when possible within twenty-four hours, but Nikki was nothing" (475). Although Sabbath's mother may have been buried in a timely manner, she never stops haunting him. During moments when Sabbath talks to her he often questions his own conversation with the dead:

And just who did he think he was talking to? A self-induced hallucination, a betrayal of reason, something with which to magnify the
inconsequentiality of a meaningless mess—*that's* what his mother was,
another of his puppets, his last puppet, an invisible marionette flying
around on strings, cast in the role not of guardian angel but of the
departed spirit making ready to ferry him to his next abode. . . . His
mother had by now draped her spirit around him, she had enwrapped
him within herself, her way of assuring him that she did indeed exist
unmastered and independent of his imagination. (474–75)

Similarly, a ritual of one-sided dialogue between Amy and the deceased
Lonoff is a daily occurrence in *Exit Ghost*. All of these ghosts circulate
throughout these novels and perform differently in each instance. The
memory of Sabbath's brother Morty, for example, haunts Sabbath in ways
that illuminate the continuum between victim and perpetrator.

Sabbath considered Morty's death in the Philippine theater of the Second World War in terms of his national rather than cultural identity: "But
he didn't die because he was a Jew. Died because he was an American"
(744). In contrast to the many European Jews who were killed for being
Jewish, despite the assimilation (and indeed in part because of it), Morty's
death can be attributed to the very patriotism that Sabbath mocks when he
"desecrates" the flag. In a decaying seaside house belonging to Sabbath's
almost one-hundred-year-old cousin Fishman, Sabbath discovers Morty's
uncanny objects in a box containing an American flag and a yarmulke.
Freud's derivation of the uncanny came on the heels of war, in 1919, and
it is not accidental that these objects of Morty's are relics from war. Freud
tells us that "the uncanny is that class of the frightening which leads back
to what is known of old and long familiar" (825), and this certainly happens
with these objects from the dead. When Drenka's son, Matthew, finds Sabbath at her grave, he decries him: "You desecrate my mother's grave. You
desecrate the American flag. You desecrate your own people. With your
stupid fucking prick out, wearing the skullcap of your own religion!" (782).
Sabbath's "prick" is merely incidental and rendered useless here in light of
the desecration launched by his use of these uncanny objects from the war.
When Sabbath first reflects on this combination of flag and yarmulke, he
notes: "He remained wrapped in the American flag. Never take it off—why
should he? On his head the red, white and blue V for Victory, God bless

America yarmulke. Dressing like this made not a scrap of difference to any-thing, transformed nothing, abated nothing, neither merged him with what was gone nor separated him from what was here, and yet he was determined never again to dress otherwise. A man of mirth must always dress in the priestly garb of his sect" (751).

In further elaborating on the uncanny, Freud notes that "this uncanny is in reality nothing new or alien, but something which is familiar and old-established in the mind and which has become alienated from it only through the process of repression" (833). Looked at through this lens, the repressed is here not only the memory of Morty but also a return of the repressed contents of Sabbath's identity as American and Jewish.

Roth has always been invested in the confluence and divergence between Jewishness and Americanness, and here in the final tragicomic mode of the novel he combines them through these tattered objects belong-ing to the beloved brother killed precisely for being American rather than Jewish. While imagining that Roseanna is pleasing herself rather than being pleased by the young Christa, Sabbath would like to cheer her on; when he fantasizes Roseanna's climax, he lifts his "God Bless America yarmulke in admiration of the crescendos and the diminuendos of the floating and the madness" (770). These disremembered cloth objects of Morty's remind us that on the other side of the Atlantic he could have been killed for being Jewish, and this is an alternative reality that is never far from the thoughts of many of Roth's characters (and many characters in Jewish American fic-tion, and many diaspora Jews). By simultaneously having Sabbath wear the flag and yarmulke, Roth in one sense brings together these modes of iden-tification; but by being ridiculous in this garb, by pissing on Drenka's grave in this garb, by lifting the yarmulke as a toast to the "floating and the mad-ness," Roth of course makes deep fun of the very project of hyphenated identities.

The donning of the flag and the yarmulke resonates with Eli, from *Goodbye, Columbus*'s "Eli, The Fanatic," who, in a moment of either mad-ness or clarity, dons the garb of the Hasidic man who he had previously been trying to kick out of the assimilated little town in which he lives.[6] Wearing the "Jewish" clothes comes to stand in for a Jewish identity forged through the more quotidian forms of community identification. Virtually all of Roth's male characters, not least because of their onanism and *shiksa*-love, are configured as outside the hallowed and somehow cleaner imagined monogamous Jewish homes with the wife and husband (homes in fact much like the one in which Roth was reared in Weequahic). When Sabbath recalls Drenka's final moments, the pair of them relive the strangely emotionally laden scene of golden shower fun, and also prefigure the yarmulke and the flag together: "'My American boyfriend.' 'Shalom'" (755). This (sarcastic?) response of Sabbath's also recalls "Eli" because when Eli says "Hello" to Tzuref, the latter invariably replies "Shalom" (263). This is then reversed when, wearing the black Hasidic coat, an attendant says "Nice day" to Eli, to which he responds in a whisper, "Shalom" (288). Sabbath wears these garments while he remembers visiting Drenka on the night that she died: "Driving Morty's things north for safekeeping, wrapped in the flag and wearing his yarmulke, driving in the dark with Morty's things and Drenka and Drenka's last night" (288). By configuring Sabbath as driving with "Morty's things and Drenka," Roth leaves open the possibility that his character is hauling around Drenka's ghost . . . or is it merely the memory of Drenka's last night? Roth underscores the importance of these uncanny objects of Morty's by indicating that they helped prevent Sabbath from killing himself (746). Drenka hails Sabbath in his Americanness, and he responds with Jewishness ("Shalom") as though he were then wearing the flag and the yarmulke as he is in the moment of remembering but not during his last night with Drenka in the hospital.

In keeping with the Rothian pattern of inserting black characters at strategic moments to serve as plot turners, as Sabbath leaves Fischel Shabas's house with the stolen flag and kippah he encounters, again, the young black woman who had told him to keep banging on Fischel's door—and Sabbath, naturally, sexualizes this: "That black girl from across the street coming over for dessert. Don't stop bangin'. Wouldn't mind hearing that from her every day" (725). But as he leaves the house he sees her again and not only does he examine her racially ("features that could be part Indian. . . . Admixture of races, always mystifying" [740–41]), but he also Jewifies himself by replying, when she asks his name, "Rabbi Israel, the Baal Shem Tov—the Master of God's Good Name" (741). It is almost as though he were responding to his own stereotyping and/or delimiting of the complexities of other subjectivities to racial identities by performing a similar such preemptive stereotyping on himself.

It can be so tricky to discuss the race and gender politics of Roth's writing. Yes, the women often come across problematically sexualized, stereotyped, lambasted; the feminists appear as sexless prudes; and yet the men are jokes as well. Greenham argues that Roth "is so far from being a misogynist that it is inexplicable why he has been read this way. Roth charts the crisis of masculinity."[7] Although I disagree that it is "inexplicable" that Roth has been charged with misogyny, I do agree that he is a most excellent purveyor of the trials and tribulations of masculinity and that this is often threaded through the blurring of aggresee and aggressor. But one does not preclude the other. Tracing the "crisis of masculinity" does not mean one is free of misogyny; in fact, one could say that some crises of masculinity include a denigration of women in order to construct a counterpart that is figured as more powerful.

The formulation that Stuart Hall uses to describe the articulations between race and class could also apply to race and gender. Hall notes that, "Race is, thus, also the modality in which class is 'lived,' the medium through which class relations are experienced, the form in which it is appropriated and 'fought through.'"[8] We could say that gender and race are inextricably lived one through the other as well. As I discussed in the introduction, there is a substantial difference between Roth's careful fleshing out and detailing of white (mostly Jewish) characters and the skeletal sketching (mostly black) characters receive when they appear in order to offer a plot twist. Apart from Coleman Silk (who "passes" for Jewish), there are no major black characters in Roth's oeuvre. But figures such as the woman across the street from Sabbath's aged cousin repeatedly drop in willy-nilly. A minor character, a little boy who loves Gauguin and who befriends Neil in "Good-bye, Columbus," offers a moment of attempted identification between black and Jew that recedes as Neil becomes more like a racist character he initially resisted. The movement between victim of oppression and perpetrator of racism is often dramatized in Roth through the vicissitudes of these thwarted identifications. As Debra Shostak has argued, Roth can be seen at once to be exploding and in some case reproducing misogynist stereotypes; perhaps the same can be said for these seemingly random and incidental appearances of characters of color.[9] By their very profusion coupled with the light outlines they receive from Roth's pen, can we not say that Roth is in fact implicitly commenting upon the way white privilege can imagine that race itself is peripheral—even though this very marginality is itself an enduring fiction?

Moments of touching on questions of race without delving into them proliferate in *Sabbath's Theater:* at the instant that Sabbath picks up Christa, the young German woman with whom he and Drenka have a threesome and who then reappears at the close of the novel as Roseanna's gorilla-like lover, Sabbath puts on some jazz in the car.[10] "'Are they black?' the German girl asked. 'No. A few are black but mainly, Miss, they are white. White jazz musicians. Carnegie Hall in New York. The night of January 16, 1938.' 'You were there?' she asked. 'Yes. I took my children, my little children. So they would be present at a musical milestone. Wanted them beside me the night that America changed forever'" (421). That Roth places the question of racial identity in the German girl's mouth is obviously loaded on the eve of war. Sabbath locates the change and the "milestone" as a musical one but of course 1938 was also arguably the year when, five years into Hitler's dictatorship, the world realized the depth of the violence behind the virulent anti-Semitic rhetoric that had always been on the surface of his many speeches. In November 1938, Kristallnacht made the headlines all over the world.[11] Sabbath, who was born in 1929 (four years before Roth), then lies to Christa by telling her he was at Carnegie Hall with his children (he would have been nine at the time and furthermore was childless). Roth then tells us in an aside that, as Sabbath plays at being "Father Time," "There is no other way to play it (422), thus prefiguring racial play that characterizes *The Human Stain.* This echoes the conversation about the musicians' race—as they play they are mostly not black but mixed. In the same scene Christa goes on to tell Sabbath that she left New York for the village of Madamaska Falls because people in the city only wanted to use her. Sabbath queries: "'People in New York are worse than people in Germany?' 'History would seem to some to tell a different story'" (422).

Indeed, Roth is careful here to reverse the usual association of Americanness with the apple-pie happiness that is so meticulously destroyed in *American Pastoral.* As Christa and Sabbath drive on through the quiet, wooded night, as Sabbath thinks through how best to seduce this young woman found on the road cross-dressed (more playing) in a tuxedo, he wonders that she finds this odd reversal between New York and Germany and marvels that he "could take her up to Battle Mountain and strangle her to death in her tuxedo. Painting by Otto Dix. Maybe not in congenial Germany but in cynical, exploitative America she was running a risk out on the road in that tuxedo" (423).[12] Like the moment I cited above when Sabbath aligned himself with a Nazi, he here plays at being a perpetrator of a violent crime—murder, as he also imagines murdering Nikki. As Christa recounts for Sabbath her former life as a club girl in the city, she tells him that "Lots of black men" were into her club scene (425). Sabbath was terrified that if his musical tape switched from jazz to klezmer, his hunt for her cunt would be over: "All she had to hear was Elman's klezmer trumpet oleaginizing 'Bei Mir Bist Du Sheyn' and she'd leap from the moving car, even out in the middle of nowhere" (425). Black people, Christa is used to, even though she insists on labeling her fellow club-goers racially; Jews, on the other hand, no way. If klezmer, marked like the yarmulke or the utterance of "shalom," were to begin spooling out of the car, this would frighten the "German girl."

These scenes between Christa and Sabbath underscore how, in Roth's novels, the Holocaust is an ever-present, if only sometimes explicit, theme. Here, Sabbath notes that the "history" of Germany would indicate that people there might not be "worse" than those in New York. Roth's repetition of the phrase "the German girl" to describe Christa and the understanding that if Jewish music were played she would escape further thickens the referential web. The scene also highlights the play or the continuum between victim and perpetrator that is at the heart of my reading of Roth. Here we have a woman whose German ancestors likely perpetrated crimes related to the Holocaust herself figured here as the object of Sabbath's manipulative tendencies. Meanwhile, the Jewish Sabbath envisions himself as a murder, Mussolini, or on trial at Nuremberg.

Another in a long chain of totemic and immensely underdeveloped black characters appears to Sabbath as he vainly searches for Nikki. Having discovered someone with her first initial and last name in the phone book in Baltimore, he knocks on the address listed there in the hopes of finding his lost first wife, Nikki: "It's Mickey, Nikki" (495). When there is no answer save that of the bark of an unseen dog, Sabbath raps on the neighbor's bungalow door. She turns out to be "an alarmingly thin and wrinkled elderly black woman" (495) who assumes that Sabbath had beaten his wife and this is why she had run away. She offers no confirmation that Nikki is her neighbor and, after making her pronouncement, abruptly slams the door on Sabbath. As he returns to New York after this encounter, Sabbath reflects, "It had taken that blind old black woman to get him to understand that he had been jilted, discarded, abandoned!" (496). Here Sabbath trades in Oedipean mythologies of blindness as knowing, of blackness as mystery. But again by choosing to feature so many of these characters as plot-drivers, is he exposing and critiquing their very marginality? These characters are marginal in that their consciousnesses are almost never disclosed, and yet they remain simultaneously crucial as presences that preside over key moments of various protagonists' anxiety-filled transitions.

A persistent thematics of unmasking runs throughout Roth's oeuvre and is manifest in the revelation offered to Sabbath by this unnamed woman. Sabbath meditates that his finances are in shambles due to the combined forces of arthritis (his twisted, gnarled fingers having arrested his ability to perform as a puppeteer) and his "unmasking . . . as a degenerate" at the college (378). The title of the Roth documentary resonates with exploration of the veil drawn back: *Philip Roth: Unmasked*. All of this unmasking and unveiling reveals that the perfect American family is always already corrupted and that the Mickey Sabbaths of the world merely manifest the latent content of every household.

Notes

This is a slightly different version of chapter 4 of my book *Jewish Anxiety and the Novels of Philip Roth* (New York: Bloomsbury Academic, 2015); printed here with permission.

1. *Oxford English Dictionary*, Compact Edition, vol. 2 (Oxford: Oxford University Press, 1971), 2613.

2. Philip Roth, *Sabbath's Theater* (New York: Library of America, 2010); hereafter cited parenthetically.

3. Similarly, at one point Christa accuses him of exploiting her, to which Sabbath replies, "I don't think either of us [i.e., Sabbath and Drenka] exploited you any more than you exploited either of us" (*Sabbath's Theater*, 419).

4. David Greenham, "The Concept of Irony: Jane Austen's *Emma* and Philip Roth's *Sabbath's Theater*," *Philip Roth Studies* 1, no. 2 (fall 2005): 165.

5. Bernard Avishai, *Promiscuous: "Portnoy's Complaint" and Our Doomed Pursuit of Happiness* (New Haven: Yale University Press, 2012), 207.

6. Philip Roth, "Eli, the Fanatic," in *Goodbye, Columbus*, by Roth, 247–98 (New York: Vintage International, 1993).

7. Greenham, "The Concept of Irony," 173.

8. Stuart Hall, "Race, Articulation and Societies Structured in Dominance," in *Cultural and Literary Critiques of the Concepts of "Race,"* ed. E. Nathan Gates (New York: Garland, 1997), 341.

9. Debra Shostak, "Roth and Gender," in *The Cambridge Companion to Philip Roth*, ed. Timothy Parrish (New York: Cambridge University Press, 2007), 111–26.

10. "Under his eyes, Christa and Rosie developed complete gorilla personalities—two of them living in the gorilla dimension, embodying the height of gorilla soulfulness, enacting the highest act of gorilla rationality and love" (*Sabbath's Theater*, 774).

11. For a précis of these headlines, go to the website of the Center for Holocaust & Humanity. which covers the local and national responses to the *Reichskristallnacht*: www.holocaustandhumanity.org/kristallnacht/local-and-national-responses/

12. Some of the editions of *Sabbath's Theater* feature Dix's painting *Sailor and Girl* (1926) on the cover. I am grateful to Ira Nadel for confirming the title and date of the painting since Dix seems to have created several works with the same title.

11

Philip Roth and the American "Underclass" in *The Human Stain*

Andy Connolly

This essay discusses the much-overlooked issue of class in Philip Roth's *The Human Stain* and its significance to the broader questions of race and identity politics that the novel explores. My argument focuses on Faunia Farley's status as a member of a much-maligned "white underclass" in contemporary America and how her beleaguered social position contrasts with the committed belief held by Roth's protagonist in the novel, Coleman Silk, that he has transcended the historical boundaries established by his racial origins. Through a detailed examination of Faunia's embattled life, I argue that her largely inescapable sense of belonging to an unregenerate underclass provides new ways of understanding the historical limitations involved in Coleman's passing from one racial category to another.

Contrary to certain critical responses that have read Roth's treatment of passing in the novel as an affirmation of the creative potentials of selfhood over the determining influences of social categories, my discussion concentrates on how Coleman's quest for self-authorship is constrained by his need to acculturate to a certain model of "white" middle-class identity. Drawing upon Roth's thematic of a "human stain" that confounds our efforts to make life coherent in terms of moral or ideological certainties, I explore how Faunia's unseemly existence on the social margins calls into question the wholesome notions of self-completion and propriety that define Coleman's whiteness. In doing so, my argument also draws attention to how Faunia's life of hardship and toil serves to tarnish the pristine moral outlook of other characters in the novel who seek to speak authoritatively about her social position. Faunia's conscious awareness of her "stained" humanity serves not only as a rejection of the belief in self-transformation that Coleman's passing invokes but also to undermine the shallow moral positioning of proponents of political correctness in the novel who make facile claims about the historically determinate basis of identity. In this sense, Faunia's class experiences symbolize a particular type of historical "stain" that cannot be wiped clean by willful acts of individual self-reinvention, on the one hand, and more compensatory efforts to sanctify the vulnerabilities and sensitivities of the underprivileged on the other.

Perhaps even more significant, as I argue, is how this idea of historical experiences that cannot be comfortably assimilated within the neat ideological perspectives of others reflects back upon complex questions about the relationship between history and literature in Roth's writing. As I will discuss immediately below, *The Human Stain* reexplores particular ideas of personal and aesthetic liberation from notions of historical origin that have been so well documented throughout Roth's fiction, particularly in relation to Jewish ethnic identity. Yet in spite of how the novel's obvious fascination with Coleman's passing appears to uphold a firm belief in the individual's ability to detach himself or herself from inherited influences, Roth's characterization of Faunia works as a counterthrust against any simplistic idea that the self can transcend history and exceed all externally imposed limits. As the remainder of this essay explores in greater detail, Faunia's unglamorous life of work and social degradation serves to underline the extent to which the "stain" of history continues to leave its trace upon Roth's self-reflexive concerns with issues of creativity and subjectivity.

The Peculiar Problem of Literature and History in the Zuckerman Novels

Scholarly efforts to situate Philip Roth's fiction within a political or historical framework, of which there have been relatively few to date, can prove arduous and difficult. Indeed, Roth's writing is so rich in formal innovation and literary self-reflection that any attempt to foothold his work within such

broader contexts demands great care and elaborate persuasion. The present
volume should prove a fruitful addition to the recent growth of valuable
scholarship on Roth's engagement with wider issues of social and political
relevance. However, in attempting to illuminate further his concern with
such "worldly" matters, it remains vitally important that we continue to
acknowledge how Roth's literary career has been characterized, to a considerable extent, by his declared belief in "the independent reality of [. . .]
fiction" from considerations of authorial context.[1] Roth's close relationship
to high-minded principles about literature's outright formal separation from
the nonliterary realm of "real" life finds repeated articulation and exploration in the Zuckerman novels. As Roth's literary surrogate, Nathan Zuckerman expresses a committed belief in the imagination's power of dissociation
from and "reinvention of the real."[2] By labeling his writing as an attempt
to "sweep away the limits on life" (*Counterlife*, 235), Zuckerman affirms a
deep faith in the affective power that literature holds, for author and reader
both, in terms of its ability to defamiliarize the prosaic details of everyday
existence and transform them into something newly imagined. This demi-
urgic concept of the literary author as one who re-creates the world afresh
in terms of his singular aesthetic vision is succinctly encapsulated in *The
Facts* by Roth himself, who informs us of how fiction serves as his creative
means "to wield the whip over the facts [in order] to make real life amazing"
(7).

As leading scholars like Ross Posnock argue, Roth's adherence to formalist concepts about the strict separation of the work of literature from the
social involvements, ideological entanglements, or personal attachments of
the author provides a serious challenge to those of us who would attempt to
carry out a "redirection of scholarship from author to context."[3] However, as
I will argue in relation to questions of race and class in *The Human Stain*,
Roth's clear affinity with formalist aesthetics is not entirely irreconcilable
with a historical reading of his work. In fact, it is only by offering a clear
recognition of the powerful influence on Roth's fiction of such rarefied ideas
about the aesthetic sanctity of the authorial subject and the literary artifact
that a valid argument in favor of reading his work in a broader contextual
light can be made.

Roth's fictional exploration of ideas about "the impenetrable line divid-
ing fiction from reality" and the adversarial relationship of the authorial
imagination to external influences and origins is perhaps most notable in

the Zuckerman novels' dramatization of the conflict between the Jewish writer and his ethnic community.[4] Finding in literature what he calls his means "to spring myself from everything that had held me captive as a boy," Zuckerman expresses a committed desire for aesthetic liberty that opposes itself to insistent pleas for ethnic loyalty that are voiced by important members of his Jewish readership.[5] This tension between the writer's dedication to his art and the opposing arguments made by others that he write in ways that are sensitive to the needs of his ethnic group is explored in detail in *The Ghost Writer*, where the young Zuckerman is faced by accusations that some of his earliest published stories may serve to reinforce anti-Semitic stereotypes among a Gentile audience. Zuckerman ultimately swears full loyalty to the prerogatives of his art over the demands made by a stringent sense of ethnic particularism on his writing. As the events of *The Ghost Writer* and later novels clearly indicate, Zuckerman's career as a writer— much in parallel with that of Roth himself—is, from its inception, defined in terms of a necessary "betrayal" of received wisdoms and protective caveats about his vulnerable social identity.[6]

The Zuckerman novels involve many such examples of this broader contestation that the writing self and the fictional text are not subject to the censoring judgments or imposed criteria of others but to the playful and "independent reality" of the literary imagination. In this sense, writing serves as a mode of self-authorship for Zuckerman, through which he is able to unfetter himself from the various aspects of his social and personal facticity. Throughout the Zuckerman books, and in other notable Roth novels like *Portnoy's Complaint*, this connection between principles of aesthetic autonomy and ideas about the individual subject's relative freedom from the determining factors of history and origin finds repeated emphasis and exploration. Such parallels made between the literary text and the individual as a self-authoring subject find, as I will examine below, particular emphasis in Zuckerman's fictional exploration of the life of Coleman Silk in *The Human Stain*.

This aesthetic idea about the individual's ability to escape the snares of historical situatedness is, however, one that is always subject to moments of frustration and limit in the Zuckerman novels. In *The Ghost Writer* and throughout the further eight novels in which he appears, Zuckerman's determination to remove himself and his writing far from the insular purview of his community is complicated by the mixed sense of guilt and self-defensiveness that inheres in his fiction as a result of damning accusations that he has betrayed his Jewish past. Despite his defiant sense of freedom to subject "real" life to the internal workings of the imagination, Zuckerman is never able to ignore and rise above the scorn of those readers—Jewish or otherwise—who repeatedly charge him with an unethical dereliction of duty to what they claim are certain unimpeachable "facts." As a result, Zuckerman's writing remains entangled in an almost endless conflict with those who set out to challenge both its moral and verisimilar credentials. In novels such as *The Anatomy Lesson* and *The Counterlife*, for example, Zuckerman demonstrates an acute sensitivity to criticism through his serious-minded attempts to respond to the many cheap demands that are made by others that he stop distorting the "facts" and start exercising a greater fealty to perceived notions of what is decent and "true." In ways that tend to put something of a hold on his otherwise playful subversion of what passes as given or acceptable, Zuckerman's earnest efforts to defend the sovereignty of his art provide something of a distorted mirror image of the prudish voices of opposition to his writing. His rejection of the pious moral and ideological values that others attempt to impose upon his fiction is, in this regard, spurred by Zuckerman's own highly ethical and intractable position on the sanctity of certain lofty literary principles.

Zuckerman's well-intentioned attempts to reassert the uniquely speculative purpose of his fiction as a means of exploring "what-could-be" over what constitutes life as it "actually is" (*Counterlife,* 247) thus forges a closer connection between his writing and its detractors than he had originally wished to countenance. What the earlier novels particularly demonstrate is that, by feeling the need to repeatedly defend the formal possibilities inherent within fiction against the scandalized and irate reactions of certain Jewish readers, Zuckerman's writing is brought uncannily back to the very questions of ethnic belonging and moral responsibility from which he had sought an escape through literature in the first place. As Roth's comments on his own literary development in the essay "Writing and the Powers that Be" suggest, Zuckerman's life in writing is defined by a paradoxical sense of both detachment from and attachment to extraliterary notions of the "facts" and authorial origins: "I have greatly refashioned my attachments through the effort of testing them, and over the years have developed my strongest attachment to the test itself."[7] As with Roth, Zuckerman's life and career has been characterized by an unrelenting fixation with the complex tensions that characterize "the test itself," rather than any untrameled liberation of the author from the extraliterary pressures that attempt to shape his art.

Coleman Silk and the Snare of American Racial History

In *The Human Stain,* Zuckerman sets out to recount the highly complex biography of his late friend Coleman Silk. While attending Coleman's funeral, Zuckerman is made surprisingly aware that Silk was in fact African American by birth and that his racial origins had been concealed to the wider world by his single-minded decision, made some fifty years earlier, to "pass" as a white man. The two men initially become acquainted following an incident of considerable irony and pathos, in which the aged Coleman—by now a successful professor and former dean of Greek classics at Athena College—has been accused of using a pejorative epithet to describe two African American students whom he has never met and whose racial identities, as a result, are unknown to him. Despite arguing that his use of the word "spooks" to describe these students was intended as a jocular means of calling into doubt the corporeal existence of two people who had never attended his class, Coleman incurs the zealous wrath of a number of politically correct faculty members at Athena. Although fully aware of the ironies involved in such an accusation, Coleman refuses to relent in his lifelong quest to define himself on his own terms by informing others about his concealed racial heritage. Having spent his life in a defiant attempt to liberate himself from both racist prejudice and corollary efforts to find compensation in modes of racial self-awareness, Coleman is angrily unwilling to overcome the charges that he faces by submitting to the new wave of moral thinking about such things as race and gender that has become the official discourse of his colleagues at Athena.

Declaring that Coleman's "art was being a white man," Zuckerman draws close parallels between what he sees as Silk's dedication to reimagining the "individual as real apart and beyond the social determinants defining him" (*Stain*, 333) and his own struggle to find release from the restrictions put in place by his Jewish origins.[8] Zuckerman's enthrallment with Coleman and the "beautiful calibration of his deceit" (334–35) is driven by his own obsession with how acts of narrative masking and self-disguise serve to distance the writer from claustrophobic judgments about his personal responsibility for the moral and social implications of his art. As he explains in *The Counterlife*, Zuckerman finds in fiction a playful means of "impersonation" (320) and "imposturing" (321) under different narrative guises, by which he is aesthetically liberated from the limiting demands of staying true to the presumed "facts" that attach themselves to any sense of "real, authentic, or genuine life" (320). "The sliding relationship with everything" (*Stain*, 108) involved in Coleman's self-propelled passage from the African American "we" (108) into "the boundless, self-defining drama of the pronouns we, they, and I" (109) somewhat mirrors the fluid movement between voices and viewpoints that defines Zuckerman's skillful art of narrative impersonation. According to Zuckerman, both he and Coleman are empowered to invent and adopt new disguises by a fearless ability to disabuse themselves of demands that they remain faithful to core notions of self, family, and race.

Zuckerman finds clear resonances in Coleman's pillorying by the proponents of political correctness at Athena of the narrow-minded charges of ethnic betrayal and anti-Semitism that his writing had faced forty years previously. Not only is political correctness looked upon as a reductive closing off of the creative possibilities of the self in the novel, but it is also presented as a form of moral prurience that seeks to dampen the sense of sexual vitality that finds shared expression in both Zuckerman's and Coleman's efforts to defy the inherited "facts" of their social origins. In the earlier Zuckerman novels and in works such as *Portnoy's Complaint* and *Sabbath's Theater*, Roth characterizes what he sees as the aesthetic relationship between acts of individual self-determination and literary authorship in terms of a longing for erotic fulfillment and potency that defies the impositions by which society seeks to render the individual as a weak and impotent by-product of his external environment. Although he himself claims to have renounced the unsettling yet stimulating effects of the "sexual caterwaul" (37) in *The Human Stain*, Zuckerman is fascinated by intimate revelations that the aged Coleman makes about his lustful affair with Faunia Farley, an Athena College janitor who is half his age. Zuckerman ponders the extent to which Silk's late foray into the world of sexual abandonment marks a return to "the oldest adult Coleman there ever was [. . .] [whose] considerable talent for conscientiousness was spent garnering pleasure alone" (20). On listening to Coleman's candid tales about his early sexual encounters, Zuckerman speculates upon how Silk's burning ambition to overcome the steep limitations set by his racial background was fueled by an insatiable erotic urge to explore the libidinal possibilities of "the raw I with all its agility" (108). What he labels the "transgressive audacity" (37) of Coleman's youthful erotic adventures thus serves as Zuckerman's focus for revisiting the deep connections that he had explored in previous novels between desire and the individual's efforts to affect a radical estrangement from the established "facts" about the self.[9]

There is a considerable convergence of agreement among many scholars as to the ways in which *The Human Stain* prioritizes a creatively performative idea of subjectivity over more historically rooted concepts of social identity. Such readers have tended to emphasize how Roth's interest in the individual as a revisable text or cluster of variable signifiers touches upon postmodern ideas of subjectivity.[10] Insofar as Zuckerman identifies with Coleman as someone who shares in his own belief that the self can be reconceived in terms that are radically removed from the determining factors of race, there is a great degree of merit to these assessments of *The Human Stain* as a tour de force for ideas about the fluid makeup of social identity. However, I would contend that this consideration of identity in *The Human Stain* as a form of masquerade that is blissfully liberated from fixed notions of social belonging is somewhat limited.[11] As Zuckerman's tortured relationship with his Jewish past indicates, the exhilarating sense of freedom to reinvent the self in terms that are completely different to its inherited social origins that Roth's fiction explores is sharply attenuated by a certain level of failure to completely master and surpass the intransient "facts" that impose themselves on the individual. Although this does not involve any consideration of outright social determinism or cohesive group identity in the Zuckerman novels, it does mark, as I have suggested above, a paradoxical sense of how efforts to detach the self from the past carry with them a persisting degree of unshakeable attachment to external notions of lineage and influence.

In ways that reflect this quandary, Coleman's "trajectory outward" (135) in search of an unbounded sense of self is stymied by the limitations and anxieties involved in his need to authenticate his postracial identity. By drawing upon contemporary debates on the formation of "whiteness" in American culture and history, I wish to look at how Coleman's self-invented identity in *The Human Stain* is in fact shaped by a socially acceptable model of white subjectivity that predicates itself upon a rejection of race as a perturbing marker of what is "nonwhite." Such an understanding of the wider imperatives that shape Coleman's remodeled identity helps to illustrate the extent to which he is limited by the societal pressures inherent to his act of passing from one racial category to another. In turn, I will examine how Coleman's confident disguise as a white man is made uncomfortable at certain moments in the novel by incidents in which he becomes refamiliarized with the lack of self-possession that he had once associated with his African American heritage. Such moments of anxiety over his achieved social stature are most tellingly evident in his relationship with Faunia, whose perceived existence as a "nonwhite" subject forces Coleman to revisit the buried trauma of his own racial past.

Coleman, Faunia, and the Problem of "White" Subjectivity

David Roediger traces the construction of a racially inflected ideal of "whiteness" as the basis of social inclusion in America to nineteenth-century ideologies of slavery, according to which the masculine independence of the self-determining white subject was contrasted with the perceived emasculated characteristics of a servile and dependent racial other. Roediger discusses the flexible shifts in the demarcation of this "color-line" by explaining how certain European immigrant and industrial working-class communities in the nineteenth and early twentieth centuries, who were as yet to achieve a level of economic self-sufficiency or sociopolitical status worthy of the free white male, became labeled as wage-dependent and impoverished "nonwhite" people.[12] Roediger's work is part of a broader field of research on race, class, and whiteness that has emphasized how the delineation of concepts of nonwhite identity in American history has involved eschewed ideas about the causal relationship between perceived racial deficiencies and socioeconomic immiseration. As Karen Brodkin explains: "When immigrants were seen as a necessary part of that working class which did the degraded and driven labor, they were constructed with stereotypes of blackness—stupid, shiftless, sexual, unable to defer gratification."[13] Remarking upon the way in which behavioral patterns of "preindustrial permissiveness [were] imputed to African-Americans" both during and after slavery,[14] Roediger also mentions how "white" bourgeois virtues of industrious individualism and moral self-control developed in counterpoint to perceived character weaknesses among nonwhite subjects.[15]

Roediger underlines the contemporary relevance of his historical analysis by arguing that the markedly racial and gendered configuration of purportedly deracinated concepts of whiteness in the American past continue to find currency in recent conservative ideas of a postracial society, according to which the social and economic opportunities for middle-class achievement are available to anyone who is willing to embrace necessary values of hard work and self-discipline. Roediger tells us that, while such a vision of national inclusion claims to put an end to anxieties and debates about the persistence of racial and class exclusion in contemporary American life, it in fact works to consign those who have yet to achieve a certain degree of economic self-reliance and middle-class success as inferior, nonwhite subjects who are unwilling to fully accede to the competitive rigors that the American free market demands. Such scholarship on the continuing relevance of historical concepts of whiteness is highly informative of broader conservative opinions that have emerged since the 1970s about the gendered and racial makeup of an impoverished "underclass" in American society.

For conservative opinion and policymakers, the underclass is defined as a group that is plagued by a toxic mixture of poverty, moral torpor, social disintegration, and a devirulent waning of the work ethic. Their lowly social position is not shaped by material conditions, according to this viewpoint, but rather by a human failing to function efficiently within a liberal capitalist system that demands submission to values of self-denial and competitive individualism. According to Michael Katz, this increasingly popular way of ignoring "the structural conditions that [have] generated poverty" is part of a longer history in America,[16] through which "some poor people are [seen as] undeserving of help because they brought their poverty on themselves."[17] Rather than a collection of vitalized and active citizens, the underclass have become reviled in the popular conservative imagination as an amorphous and deindividuated mass that is characterized by the inertia of passivity and laziness, on one hand, and volatile impulses toward violence, crime, and general licentiousness on the other. In this sense, the "lower-class person" is defined by what is classically perceived as a racial and gendered tendency to be "impulsive"[18] that not only contravenes the rigors of bourgeois life but, as Brodkin and Roediger suggest, marks him or her as irremediably nonwhite in character.[19]

Despite early pretensions to being an artist and living a bohemian lifestyle in Greenwich Village, Coleman soon discovers that the unrestrained potential of the deracinated self loses most of its aesthetic and libidinal reach in the imperative to become unobjectionably white and bourgeois. Coleman finds that his determination to shape his life solely on his own terms is "co-opted" (*Stain*, 110) by a model of white identity that offers little more than "the pleasure of being conventional unconventionally, but that wasn't really the idea" (110). While Coleman's passing may, to a certain degree, give expression to a desire for self-mastery (potency), the erotic economy of his concept of the individual as unconditioned by broader historical forces is also dependent upon a vertiginous idea of the self as somewhat amorphous and lacking any clearly formed sense of social identity (impotence). Coleman's unbounded longing to author and control his own personal destiny is thus inscribed by a sense of lack or incoherence that is potentially detrimental to the highly individuated ideal of whiteness to which he must conform.

Yet although he has remained concealed within the "protection of the walled city that is convention" (335) for most of his adult life, Coleman is reintroduced to "the perpetual state of emergency that is sexual longing" (32) in his affair with Faunia. Such a return to the life of libidinal excess that he had earlier led "before the serious things took over completely" (25), however, carries a peculiarly double bind for Coleman. His erotic pursuits provide him with a certain experience of liberation from the staid life of convention and decorum that he has come to inhabit as a respectable white man. However, such erotic self-abandonment also reintroduces him to a chaotic and indeterminate space of desire within which his rigorous disguise of whiteness is faced by an unnerving sense of dissolution. The extent to which this late erotic encounter leaves Coleman anxious and uncertain by threatening to exile him from his well-formed social identity is particularly dramatized in the novel by the manner in which Faunia is presented as lacking the sense of coherent subjectivity and individual self-possession that underwrites "socially sanctioned whiteness."[20]

Coleman's lawyer, Nelson Primus, makes an appeal to what he believes to be his client's sense of class and civility by describing Faunia's turbulent existence on the social margins as "everything that is the antithesis of your own way of life" (*Stain*, 157). In trying to make Coleman realize the severity of the dangers posed by the "wild grievance" (78) of her obsessively jealous ex-husband, Les Farley, Primus insists upon making clear the disorder that Faunia's underclass environment will bring to the well-fashioned life of his more genteel client: "Faunia Farley is not from your world [. . .] [but] a world where nobody's ruthlessness bothers to cloak itself in humanitarian rhetoric" (80). However, Primus's values of "professional reward and bourgeois success" (79) constitute a world devoid of "rash compulsions" (78) or any other types of "incriminating impurity" (79) that Coleman has begun to find new quarrel with in his later life. As far as Coleman is concerned, the nuts of wisdom imparted by Primus embody just another example of the "coercions of propriety" that have "tyrannized" (153) his life in passing, and from which he now longs to find escape through Faunia. Reawakened to his more youthful impulses of rage and desire following the "spooks" incident, Coleman offers a speech of angry rebuke to the younger man's prudent advice. By climaxing his diatribe with a reference to his lawyer's "smug fucking lily-white face" (81), Coleman reveals awareness, at least in an unconscious sense, of the nexus of race and class perceptions at play during this interaction. Departing his lawyer's office, Coleman quickly realizes that the vitriolic words he directed toward Primus are an exact repetition of the pejorative statement his own brother, Walter, had used against him following the announcement to his family of his decision to pass some fifty years earlier. His use of Walter's exact words to attack Primus's "lily-white" sense of decorum underlines the extent to which Coleman has, in similar fashion to Zuckerman, deeply internalized the harsh judgment against his perceived betrayal of familial and racial loyalties for acceptance into the world of white privilege. Coleman's harsh disavowal of the sober warnings offered to him about his continued relations with Faunia further serves to underscore how his renewed sexual vitality inspires a desire to be unwhitened: a burning wish to reject the world of pristine manners and conventions that have long since dampened his youthful longing to exist beyond social limits and moral dictates.

Outraged by having been first brought to heel by the dominating influence of "white" social convention only to be subject much later on in life to the racially sensitive codes of moral judgment exercised by his colleagues at Athena, Coleman appears to find in his partnership with Faunia an exhilarating experience of personal release from the strictures associated with public forms of "de-virilizing . . . virtue mongering" (153). In their private refuge, Coleman finds in Faunia "the *least* repellent person he knows, the one to whom he feels drawn because of having been aimed for so long in the opposite direction—because of all he has *missed* by going in the opposite direction" (164). However, the sense of rejuvenation that their sexual encounters bring is ultimately made difficult by the contrasting ways in which Coleman's relationship with Faunia serves also to restore to conscious recognition deeply interred feelings of distress over his concealed origins as a racially marked, nonwhite subject. In this fashion, the sense of transcendent ecstasy that places the lovers outside of what Faunia disdainfully refers to as "[a]ll the social ways of thinking" (229) serves only as a momentary salve for Coleman's anger over his failure to disentangle himself from the knot of shifting historical definitions of race. Outside of the erotic moment, his late search to loosen himself from the suffocating categories and definitions of race in America comes at a difficult personal cost for Coleman, insomuch as the sexual partnership with Faunia also serves to reintroduce him to the trauma of his prior exclusion from the social register of whiteness.

Faunia as Social Misfit

A variety of shifting perceptions in the novel of Faunia as someone who works in three low-paying jobs serves to underscore the symbolic connection between her class identity and the contradictory effect of the erotic function that she performs for Coleman. For example, while Zuckerman expounds upon the "stupefying power" of "an enamored old man watching at work the cleaning woman-farmhand who is secretly his paramour" (51) during a scene in which both men take pleasure in the spectacle of her milking cows, Faunia later deeroticizes this image by emphasizing the sense of economic struggle and social alienation that it involves: "the dairy farm is a lot of fucking work, to you it sounds great and to you it looks great, Faunia and the cows, but coming on top of everything else it breaks my fucking hump" (227). At other stages in the novel, Faunia repeatedly makes clear to Coleman why the liberating effect of sex cannot completely suspend "the matter-of-factness of [their] being separated by unsurpassable social obstacles" (47). Her determination to dispel any delusions about their erotic courtship is restated during a scene in which she dances at the request of the watching Coleman. Undergoing what is described as a "formal transfer of power" (227), the dance moves from being an act controlled and authored by Coleman's male gaze into an erotic ritual in which Faunia makes clear to him how the restorative effects of desire are predicated upon an equally powerful understanding of loss and mutability. She attempts in this instance to show him how sex affords only a temporary respite—"[t] hat slice out of time" (229)—from their social differences and problems, canceling out briefly what she derisively calls "[e]verything the wonderful society is asking" (229). While desirous of its sense of euphoric release, she holds no illusions about the possibility of eternalizing the erotic moment that she shares with Coleman by giving in to "the indulgence of the fantasy of forever" (236). By contrast, Faunia is keen to remind him of how the painful experiences of her economic struggle and class status persist outside of the ecstatic pleasures of their sexual union: "Last night? It happened. It was nice. It was wonderful. I needed it too. But I still have three jobs. It didn't change anything. That's why you take it when it's happening, because it doesn't change a thing" (235).

While Coleman's "greedy fascination appropriates" (51) the image of Faunia milking the cows that was mentioned above, a later scene where he secretly watches her during a break from her job as an Athena College janitor has a much different effect. In this particular instance, "his vantage point" (157) affords no sense of an erotic spectacle. Instead, his idealization of Faunia as a "Voluptas [who] makes virtually anything you want to think come true" (157) is corrupted by a jarring realization of her social (and racial) otherness. Watching Faunia sitting on the grass and joking with her fellow janitors, Coleman ponders how: "without him to take her cues from, she took cues instead from the gruffest example around, the coarsest, the one whose human expectations were the lowest and whose self-conception the shallowest" (157). Outside of her role as his "Voluptas," Faunia no longer "takes her cues" from Coleman's instruction but instead appears to be shaped by a particular social environment in which his "white" notions of a purposeful life based on principle of disciplined self-reliance are glaringly absent. References in the narrative to spontaneous outbursts of coarse laughter and the littered detritus of pizza boxes and Coke cans all serve to signify Coleman's estrangement from the janitorial staff's lunch-hour camaraderie. From his superior distance, Coleman spies in on what appears as a world of impulse gratification and aimless leisure—what Roediger describes as the perceived "careless style" of the nonwhite subject—that contrasts greatly with the life of intellectual pursuit and mannered refinement to which he has long been accustomed. The sudden alarm that Faunia's alien environment causes Coleman is made evident by how "this scene of no great moment on the lawn back of North Hall [which had] exposed him at last to the underside of his own disgrace" (157). Perturbed by what he sees when witnessing Faunia at ease in the context of her menial labor, Coleman quickly calls his son, Jeff, in order to tell him that "my affair with this woman is over" (171). Contrary to the actual explanation that he gives for this decision, Coleman contemplates privately that it might be solely "[b]ecause she works as a janitor" (171). This "scene of no great moment" thus becomes enlarged into a sense of personal catastrophe for Coleman, who, on being suddenly made aware of the full extent of Faunia's lowly social position, is once again faced by the harrowing specter of nonwhite marginality that he had previously left behind in his determination to pass as a white man.

In contrast to Coleman's intermittent bouts of apprehension and revulsion over her nonwhite status, Faunia appears to willingly embrace her marginal social position. On discovering after her death that Faunia was originally born into wealth and also that she left behind a written diary, Zuckerman describes how she disguised herself as lower class and feigned illiteracy in order "to impersonate a member of a subspecies to which she does not belong and need not belong but to which . . . [she] [w]ants herself to believe she belongs" (146). This performance in social disguise is designed, according to Zuckerman "to spotlight the barbaric self befitting the world" (297). In this fashion, Faunia serves as a choice vehicle for the novel's overriding theme of an inerasable "human stain" that reminds us of "why all the cleansing is a joke" (242). Faunia's determination to be "[r]econciled to the horrible, elemental imperfection" (242) of life by estranging herself from the world of "whitened" bourgeois niceties that has circumscribed Coleman's existence may thus be construed in terms of *The Human Stain*'s broader interest in creative acts of passing and how they involve a forceful assertion of the self against suffocating forms of public morality and social respectability. Faunia's intimate awareness that "[t]he fantasy of purity is appalling" (242) does involve a certain vitality that makes her appear immune to the cheap forms of self-delusion and grand moralizing by which other characters in the novel live. At the same time, however, Faunia is made extremely vulnerable by the fact that she has disbarred herself from the forms of moral, social, and intellectual capital by which other people seek to armor themselves against the contingent and misshapen aspects of mutable existence. As Zuckerman explains, she "mistrusts everyone, sees the con in everyone, and yet is protected against nothing" (146). Faunia's disguise is therefore a means of disinvesting herself of any protective sense of masking. It involves a paradoxical notion of individual agency that is predicated upon a sense of the self as unguarded, amorphous, and directionless.

Faunia's outright disillusionment with all types of social and moral pretenses is thus characterized by her willing acceptance of powerlessness and immobility. In fact, the novel reveals how the psychic scars left by acts of repeated sexual abuse have helped to *determine* Faunia's decision to live as a member of the underclass. As Zuckerman explains, beneath the coarsened facade that she presents to the world, the immiserated life of social degradation adopted by the adult Faunia is traumatically connected to the younger "[k]id whose existence became a hallucination at seven and a catastrophe at fourteen and a disaster after that, whose vocation is to be neither a waitress nor a hooker nor a farmer nor a janitor but forever the stepdaughter to a lascivious stepfather" (164). Insomuch as Faunia *acts* by rejecting the world of clean and wholesome things, then, it is in a way that reflects her deeply disillusioned awareness that *acting* is itself somewhat futile; that there is no social, moral or psychological means of escape from her early exposure to life's sense of "impurity, cruelty, abuse [and] error" (242).

In this sense of how her *passing* reflects her *passivity* in the face of life's irremediable hardship and disappointment, Faunia is largely defined by certain intransigent "facts" relating to economic struggle, female victimhood, and nonwhite alienation that cannot be transformed into more desirable terms by either the compensatory language of identity politics or Zuckerman/Coleman's purported faith in the bright possibilities afforded by acts of individual self-reinvention. As one who disavows the forms of propriety and self-guardedness that give a semblance of coherent shape to other lives, Faunia leaves herself open to the judgments of people like Nelson Primus who see her as a disdainful and abject sore on an otherwise pristine New England landscape of middle-class respectability. She is, in this sense, unreconstructed in terms of her social identity. The material, psychological, and cultural aspects of her class status are somewhat fixed to the extent that she refuses to see them as amenable to uplifting forms of transformation and "cleansing."

Rituals of Purification

Yet while her lack of social armor leaves her subject to the prejudices and manipulation of others, Faunia's rejection of any appealing type of "cleansing" serves to also challenge the ways in which others seek to anchor their lives in socially meaningful terms. Faunia, in this regard, is a troubling marker of excess within a world obsessed by notions of purity and order. As a source of uncleanliness, she must be either repelled or subject to purification in order not to contaminate the neat ideological perspectives of other characters who come into contact with her. However, Faunia lives in a way that most authentically reflects the novel's fascination with the human stain that cannot be simply made sanitary and clean. Just as her "impure" life as an unregenerate member of America's working poor serves to destabilize Coleman's sense of whiteness, the "mayhem, the jumble, the mess" (3) of Faunia's underclass experiences also works to challenge the sanctimony of other significant moral and ideological positions in the novel.

One notable example of this clash between the disorder of Faunia's existence and the ordering ambitions of other characters in the novel is evidenced by the novel's treatment of Delphine Le Roux, the politically correct zealot who leads the campaign to charge Coleman as a racist. For someone who attaches such value to the determination of social and cultural origins in the formation of experience and identity, Delphine's internal mode of self-identification is described as being far closer to that of Coleman than might first appear: "I will fight *against* the given, impassioned subjectivity carried to the limit, individualism at its best" (273). Yet in contrast to Coleman, whose credo of individualism is inspired by his humanist education in literature, Delphine attributes her belief "that she's unclassifiable" (271) to her tutelage in phenomenology and poststructural theory. However, Delphine is decidedly less interested or willing to extend this notion of complex internal subjectivity to those whom she sees as the perpetrators and victims of historical oppression. In particular, Delphine's view of Faunia as "the hapless thirty-four-year-old illiterate woman" (284) who is the final target of Coleman's ruthless exploitation renders the former not only as a passive object of pity but also as a cipher in her maneuvering for moral authority over others. What is further significant is how Delphine's canned language of victimhood misses entirely the deeper layers of socioeconomic struggle that materially structure the racial, gender, and class exclusions involved in Faunia's underclass status. In this sense, Delphine's uncorrupted sense of moral righteousness is typical of what people like John Patrick Diggins have described as an anemic academic politics that has "no social constituency beyond the college campus" and that portrays the historical divisions of "the contemporary world not as the story of class struggle . . . but as the systematic victimization of people as 'object.'"[21]

Delphine's flirtatious yet sexually unconsummated relationship in the novel with Arthur Sussman symbolizes the extent to which her politics are more that of a spectator of suffering than of a person who is fully engaged in the sociomaterial struggles of others.[22] Although she parries his neoliberal theories with her own leftist arguments, Delphine finds an important degree of sustenance in the fact that Sussman is the only person with whom she can have a "real conversation" (*Stain*, 267) on Athena's campus. As an antagonist, Sussman allows Delphine to exhibit her enlarged sense of personal engagement with social and political issues in ways that she cannot with the more softly liberal people at Athena, who tend to shun her radical theories. Delphine responds to Sussman's neoliberal equation of "radical personal liberty" with "radical sovereignty in the market" (268) by explaining that "for most people there isn't enough money to make choices and there isn't enough education to make educated guesses—there isn't enough mastery of the market" (268). Yet while she virulently opposes his economic interpretation of individual liberty, Delphine shares with Sussman a deep commitment to "personal sovereignty, personal freedom" (268) in terms of how her sense of intellectual privilege separates her from those more lowly people who she describes as being entrapped within the murky aspects of market relations. Ironically, Delphine valorizes her own role as an independent-minded intellectual in her ability to objectively discuss the sense of dispossession that defines "most" people's relations to impersonal economic forces. Delphine's assumed "mastery" of knowledge about the greater forces and conditions of socioeconomic life in America thus marks her as an embodiment of the classic leftist intellectual whose sense of her own historical agency triumphs over that of the masses whose participation in the drama of history she claims to understand and serve as a spokesperson.

Despite her deep attraction to him, Delphine's determination to resist Sussman's sexual overtures ensure that the political distinctions between them are not capsized within what Zuckerman describes throughout the novel as "All that craziness desire brings. The dissoluteness" (242). She explains to Sussman her unwillingness to take their flirtations to a level of physical intimacy by stating: "[I]t is a question of 'a frame of mind.' 'It's about who I am'" (269). There is an unwitting admission here to the fact that Sussman and his belief system—as well as Coleman and all others whom she opposes—serve as the "frame" within which Delphine's personal portrait is developed. Just as Zuckerman is peculiarly attached to his conflicts with those voices of criticism that he sets himself against, Delphine's politics appear to rely more upon their antithetical relationship with someone like Sussman than to spring from any intimate experience or knowledge of the disenfranchised populations that she claims to represent. Indeed, Delphine's fear that the man who responds to her personal ad may end up being of a racial minority "or on Medicare" (261) would appear to betray her hidden level of revulsion for marginal subjects who, she believes, could never be her equal in terms of intellectual understanding and cultural sophistication. Conversely, her unconscious longing for Coleman's sexual attention in the novel suggests how a deeper level of pathological need undergirds Delphine's combative political rhetoric. Through Zuckerman's imaginative exploration of the wants and anguishes that motivate her but that she hides from public view, we get a picture of Delphine as someone who has found in an academic discourse of moral and political certainties a means of sublimating the erratic and irrational impulses of her deeper desires, thereby empowering her with a more coherent and masterful sense of self than she might otherwise attain.

The degree to which the turmoil and "vagrancy" of Faunia's embattled life as a member of the American underclass serves as a critical rejection of the "astringent rituals of purification" (2) enacted by others in the novel is made particularly evident by a number of critically overlooked passages in *The Human Stain*, in which Zuckerman makes scornful reference to the owners and customers of the dairy farm on which she serves as a resident worker. In parodic fashion, Zuckerman describes how "Organic Livestock" is presented by the "college-educated environmentalists" who run it as "a unique operation, nothing like what was going on at the big dairy farms, nothing impersonal or factory-like about it" (45). Selling "raw milk" that is "uncompromised by pasteurization and unshattered by homogenization" (45), Organic Livestock thrives upon a contemporary nostalgia for the perceived virtues of an earlier epoch, in which modes of small-scale agricultural production once flourished. Zuckerman comically derides how the hyperbole used to promote this brand of agrarian idealism is reinforced by the self-congratulatory attitudes of local customers who seek to distance themselves, by dietary means of consuming "whole rather than processed food" (46), from the putrefying aspects of modern life: "The farm has a strong following, particularly among the numerous people tucked away up here, the retired as well as those raising families, in flight from the pollutants, frustrations, and debasements of a big city . . . in reverent tones mention will be made of Organic Livestock milk, not simply as a tasty drink but as the embodiment of a freshening, sweetening country purity that their city-battered idealism requires" (46).

As his critical narrative commentary in works such as *The Counterlife* and *American Pastoral* fully emphasizes, Zuckerman rails against such cosseted notions of pastoral simplicity and wholesomeness. By ridiculing the unquestioning idealism of Organic Livestock, Zuckerman subtly draws our attention in *The Human Stain* to Faunia's social struggle as the unseen and repressed "pollutant" that contaminates its Brook Farm style of utopianism. The farm's local reputation as an unmechanized agrarian haven from the ugly disorders of modern life, and glorying in the undivided unity of sentiment between its earnest producers and well-heeled clientele, is undermined by the alienated labor of Faunia, for whom "the farm is [just another aspect of the] fucking hard work" that her three low-paying jobs entail.

The honorific outpourings made by local community members about how "body, soul, and spirit are getting nourished as a whole" (46) by Organic Livestock milk is completely forgetful of how Faunia's labor is invested and extracted in the farm's production. This convenient form of amnesia is further evidenced by the speech that Sally, one of the farm's co-owners, makes at Faunia's funeral. Aghast at the outpouring of sentiments that "made it just about impossible for me to stay focused" (286), Zuckerman ridicules Sally's proclamations about Faunia's undivided sense of belonging within the Organic Livestock "family" as just another maudlin example of what marks the "Purifying Ritual" (to borrow from the title of the novel's final section) of the funeral eulogy genre. Explaining to the graveside listeners how "she [Faunia] helped to try to keep the family dairy farm alive in New England as a viable part of our cultural heritage" (286), Sally takes the opportunity to portray the farm as less of a model of business and consumption than as a moral crusade against a culture that has been corrupted by the impersonalizing forces of industrial capitalism. Zuckerman's sensibilities, by contrast, make him indignant toward this "environmental Rousseauism" (286), particularly to the extent that it seeks to render the chaos and confusion of Faunia's actual life as a member of America's "hidden" poor in terms that are more palatable to Sally's wistful reverie.

The nonmechanically sourced and chemical-free "raw milk" that the farm sells represents a wholesome connection to nature that involves a commitment to not subtracting any "raw" essentials or adding artificial substitutes. However, this "natural" process does indeed involve an extraction in terms of Sally's acquisition of the surplus labor carried out by Faunia. As Zuckerman's biting allusions help us to understand, it is possible to radically reconceptualize the metaphorical association of "raw milk" with the unmediated, "back-to-nature" idealism that so inspires Sally, her business partner, and their customers. The silences and omissions regarding the many "impurities" associated with Faunia's belonging to an embattled underclass world can be understood in terms of how they situate her unglamorous work at the farm as an example of the unmentioned, excess fat that is skimmed off the top in order to make Organic Livestock and its trademark commodity appear fully clean and pure.

Zuckerman, Writing, and the Stain of History

Faunia's willful inhabitation of the lower strata of American life is one that is denuded of the appealing mask of moral propriety and disarmed of all feigning means of social empowerment. In this sense, she embraces her social role so as to give an external embodiment to her deeply internalized sense of a human stain that cannot be removed by efforts to make life whole and clean. Delphine, Sally, Nelson, and, to some extent, Coleman all seek to position Faunia in ways that attempt to either neutralize or repress the dangerous sense of excess that her unruly life poses to their varying efforts to offer a pristine and coherent facade to the world. Yet despite such efforts to sideline Faunia and render her as harmless to the adroitly composed worldviews held by others, Zuckerman's narrative brings into detailed focus the impurities and disorder that hallmark her existence. As a result, Faunia's presence in the text serves as a reminder of the irrepressibility of certain unwholesome experiences of class, gender, and racial exclusion that are blanched by the neat portraits of life that Coleman's whiteness, Nelson's bourgeois propriety, Delphine's academic leftism, and Sally's environmentalism all seek to project.

The difficulty that Faunia poses in terms of other people's efforts to confidently define her in ways that are palatable to their own sensibilities is reflective of the role that questions of historical experience and social identity perform in the Zuckerman novels. Zuckerman's writing is motivated by a longing to find in literature a "transcendent calling" (*Ghost,* 4) that will liberate him from the "facts" of his biographical context. Yet despite such efforts to "spring the historical lock" (*Stain* 335) and reinvent the self within fiction, Zuckerman is tied to his past insomuch as he has been unable to disencumber himself of the very conflicts and self-divisions that he has experienced in relation to his Jewish heritage. His Jewish origins thus act as the unwashable stain in Zuckerman's quest for artistic purity. No matter how much he attempts to overcome the sullying influence of social attachments through the releasing valve of the imagination, Zuckerman's Jewishness continuously returns to haunt him in the form of an unending conflict and entanglement with his "unliterary origins" (*Ghost,* 3).

Indeed, Zuckerman has sought in the later trilogy of novels, for which *The Human Stain* is the final installment, to remove his personal battles from the scene of his writing in a way that will, at last, set him and his art free from any embroilment with the world outside of literature. However, this self-effacing narrative strategy involves another example of passing as purification that is evidenced by Coleman's adoption of the mask of whiteness. By *passing* over the inner tensions that have beset his own life and writing in *The Human Stain,* Zuckerman attempts to conceal from view the debilitating effects that his Jewish origins have had upon his efforts to reinvent himself as a detached literary aesthete, unmoored from the corrupting influences of social involvements. Yet while he appears to successfully bury all traces of his conflicted sense of self in the novel, Zuckerman's fraught relationship with his Jewish past finds a distorted lens through his examination of Coleman's life. As a kind of surrogate or double for Zuckerman—who, in turn, is Roth's surrogate—Coleman provides his friend with a means of both detaching from and revisiting the painful conflicts that have beset his past. In this fashion, Zuckerman fictively examines the euphoric joys and dreaded limitations involved in Coleman's passing as a way to further explore, yet also keep hidden, his ongoing preoccupation with the collisions between his aesthetic sensibilities and the sense of ethnic particularism that defined his Jewish upbringing. It is this sense of an irrepressible "stain" of the historical—whether it comes in the form of Zuckerman's Jewishness, Coleman's racial background, or Faunia's squalid life of class poverty—that rears its head in *The Human Stain* in such a way that places limits and frustrations on the novel's ostensible celebration of the creative separation of both the literary text and the individual self from history.

Notes

1. Philip Roth, *The Facts: A Novelist's Autobiography* (London: Penguin, 1988), 4; hereafter cited parenthetically.

2. Philip Roth, *The Counterlife* (New York: Vintage, 1986), 247; hereafter cited parenthetically.

3. Ross Posnock, *Philip Roth's Rude Truth: The Art of Immaturity* (Princeton: Princeton University Press, 2006), 51.

4. Philip Roth, *Exit Ghost* (London: Jonathan Cape, 2007), 267.

5. Philip Roth, *The Anatomy Lesson* (London: Vintage, 1983), 368.

6. Philip Roth, *The Ghost Writer* (London: Vintage, 1979), 69; hereafter cited parenthetically.

7. Philip Roth, *Reading Myself and Others* (London: Corgi, 1977), 9.

8. Philip Roth, *The Human Stain* (London: Vintage, 2000), 345; hereafter cited parenthetically.

9. A pointed example of this thematic can be found in Zuckerman's reflections in *The Counterlife* of his brother, Henry's "impotence . . . [as being] like an artist's artistic life drying up for good" (35). Having learned that the failing libido caused by Henry's heart medication has brought about an abrupt and tormenting end to a secret affair with his dental assistant, Zuckerman contemplates how his brother's impotence induces a newly contented state of *"living* with the facts . . . letting them inundate him" (234). For Zuckerman, by contrast, the "chasing [of] erotic daydreams" (235) holds a symbolic kinship with the imaginative quest by which both the private individual and the literary artist can seek a "an escape from the facts" (234).

10. Derek Parker Royal, for example, extends his interesting discussion of the relationship between death and aesthetics in *The Human Stain* by pointing out how Coleman re-creates his identity *ex nihilo*, following the passing into death of his African American self. Explaining how "with the negation of identity comes the possibility of subject re-creation" in the case of Coleman, Royal concludes that *The Human Stain* "gets to the heart of Philip Roth's (post-modern) project of signifying American identity, ethnic or otherwise" (Royal, "Plotting the Frames of Subjectivity: Identity, Death, and Narrative in Philip Roth's *The Human Stain*," *Contemporary Literature* 47 [2006]: 138). Francoise Kral adds to Royal's claim by suggesting that *The Human Stain* places "identity [a]s interstitial" in a way that allows for a type of postmodern exploration of new and highly mutational subject formations (Kral, "Frictions of Identity in *The Human Stain*, *Philip Roth Studies* 2, no. 1 [2006]: 48). For Kral, Roth's novel playfully allows for "a negotiation between different existing definitions, which, in turn, forms a new one and contributes to an infinite spectrum of identities, thus calling for new interpretative

patterns that should prove able to take account of the fluidity, the complexity, and the provisionality of identity" (54). Mark Maslan has added to this view of subjectivity in the novel by indicating the ways in which Coleman's "passing reveals the performative nature of supposedly natural categories of identity" (Maslan, "The Faking of the Americans: Passing, Trauma, and National Identity in Philip Roth's *Human Stain*," *Modern Language Quarterly* 66, no. 3 [2005]: 381). Unlike Royal and Kral, however, Maslan does reserve criticism for what he sees as Roth's decision to locate Coleman's "performative" act of passing within a wider notion of "historical commonality" (381) by linking it to a distinctly American tradition of individualism and self-fashioning. By making Coleman's rejection of an assigned racial identity as "merely the precondition for embodying a national one" (381), according to Maslan, Roth goes some way to reinscribing yet another, even more encompassing notion of "natural" or historically inherited identity.

11. In addition, I would take issue with Anthony Hutchinson's view that Roth's treatment of Coleman's passing involves a rejection of entrenched notions of identity politics in favor of a commitment to an older liberal idea of inclusive citizenship that is based upon a pragmatic flexibility with regard to the conditions of subjectivity and the possibility of social advancement. According to Hutchinson, Coleman's rejection of fixed racial categories is supportive of a liberal progressive belief system, according to which: "the 'identity' of individuals and social groups is . . . seen as contingent and malleable—a product, primarily, of unequal economic relations that has in the past and can continue to be in the future reshaped by egalitarian political movements" (Hutchinson, *Writing the Republic: Liberalism and Morality in American Political Fiction* [New York: Columbia University Press, 2007], 160). Yet, as my ensuing argument claims, this idea of citizenship and belonging is one that does not readily extend to a character like Faunia. In Coleman's case, as I suggest, this idea of the self as malleable is also one that comes at a great cost and involves a certain need to exclude any lingering signs of attachment to his racial past.

12. David Roediger asserts that "ideas of freedom for the mass of white males developed in tandem with notions and practices that ensured that those who were not white could not pursue happiness effectively in political, social, and economic realms" (Roediger, *Colored White: Transcending the Racial Past* [Berkeley: University of California Press, 2002], 123).

13. Karen Brodkin, *How Jews Became White Folks and What That Says About Race in America* (New Brunswick, NJ: Rutgers University Press, 1998), 71.

14. David Roediger, *Wages of Whiteness: Race and the Making of the American Working Class* (London: Verso, 2007), 106.

15. David Roediger discusses the relevance to working-class immigrants in the nineteenth century of the Protestant work ethic of moral self-regulation in

the following terms: "the white working class, disciplined and made anxious by fear of dependency, began during its formation to construct an image of the Black population as 'other'—as embodying the preindustrial, erotic, careless style of life the white worker hated and longed for" (Roediger, *Wages of Whiteness*, 14).

16. Michael Katz, *The Undeserving Poor: America's Enduring Confrontation with Poverty* (New York: Oxford University Press, 2013), 203.

17. Katz, preface to *The Undeserving Poor*, x.

18. Katz, *The Undeserving Poor*, 26.

19. As James Patterson has mentioned, the slew of perspectives about the breakdown of community and family structures among "underclass" black Americans since the publication of the Moynihan Report in August 1965 have fueled the persistent flames of old racial myths "about [how] the amoral and overheated sexuality of black people" leaves them less likely to comply with the values of moral self-control and industrious self-discipline readily exercised by America's thriving middle class (Patterson, *Freedom Is Not Enough: The Moynihan Report and America's Struggle over Black Family Life—from LBJ to Obama* [New York: Basic, 2010], 95). This negative association of poverty with deep-seated notions of racial deficiency serves to strengthen what Michael Sweig describes as "the misconception that the face of poverty is black or brown, not white." While such a popular misreading of economic inequality works to ignore the existence of poor whites, it also has the effect of maintaining the fiction that the unsightly conditions and cultural depravities associated with underclass poverty are exclusively nonwhite properties (Sweig, *The Working Class Majority: America's Best-Kept Secret* [Ithaca: ILR, 2001], 88).

20. Brodkin, *How Jews Became White Folks*, 41.

21. John Patrick Diggins, *The Rise and Fall of the American Left* (New York: Norton, 1992), 21.

22. This glaring absence in Delphine's privileged and academically distanced understanding of actual social struggles recalls Richard Rorty's criticism of the cultural Left's role as a removed "spectator" of historical suffering. For Rorty, the particular cultural foci of identity politics tend to exclude considerations of economy and class as certain aspects of poverty and underclass hardship are far too unsettling to its neat range of victim categories: "Nobody is setting up a program in unemployed studies, homeless studies, or trailer-park studies, because the unemployed, the homeless, and residents of trailer parks are not 'other' in the relevant sense" (Richard Rorty, *Achieving Our Country: Leftist Thought in Twentieth-Century America* [Cambridge: Harvard University Press, 1998], 80).

Selected Bibliography

We have selected sources on Philip Roth's work with a focus on his many political themes: the relationship between politics and literature, American liberalism, (American alternate) history, Jewish identity and Israel, race relations, and gender. The Philip Roth Society provides a comprehensive list of resources on its website (www.philiprothsociety.org). In addition, the Society publishes the journal *Philip Roth Studies* and therein offers annually an overview of Roth scholarship.

Philip Roth's Fiction

American Pastoral. London: Vintage, 2005.
The Anatomy Lesson. London: Vintage, 2005.
The Breast. New York: Vintage International, 1994.
The Counterlife. London: Vintage, 2005.
Deception. London: Vintage, 2006.
The Dying Animal. London: Vintage, 2002.
Everyman. London: Jonathan Cape, 2006.
Exit Ghost. London: Jonathan Cape, 2007.
The Ghost Writer. London: Vintage, 2005.
Goodbye, Columbus. London: Vintage, 2006.
The Great American Novel. London: Vintage, 2006.
The Human Stain. London: Vintage, 2001.
The Humbling. London: Jonathan Cape, 2009.
I Married a Communist. London: Vintage, 1999.
Indignation. Boston: Houghton Mifflin, 2008.
Letting Go. New York: Vintage International, 1997.
My Life as a Man. New York: Vintage International, 1993.
Operation Shylock. A Confession. New York: Vintage International, 1994.
Our Gang (Starring Tricky and His Friends). London: Vintage, 2006.

The Plot Against America. New York: Vintage International, 2004.
Portnoy's Complaint. London: Vintage, 1999.
The Prague Orgy. New York: Vintage International, 1996.
The Professor of Desire. New York: Vintage International, 1994.
Sabbath's Theater. London: Vintage, 1996.
When She Was Good. New York: Vintage International, 1995.
Zuckerman Unbound. New York: Vintage International, 1995.

Philip Roth's Nonfiction

The Facts: A Novelist's Autobiography. New York: Vintage International, 1997.
Patrimony. A True Story. London: Vintage, 1999.
Reading Myself and Others. New York: Vintage International, 2001.
Shop Talk: A Writer and His Colleagues at Work. New York: Vintage International, 2002.

Biographies of Philip Roth

David, Thomas. *Philip Roth*. Reinbeck: Rowohlt Taschenbuch Verlag, 2013.
Nadel, Ira B. *Critical Companion to Philip Roth: A Literary Reference to His Life and Work*. New York: Facts on File, 2011.
Pierpont, Claudia Roth. *Roth Unbound: A Writer and His Books*. New York: Farrar, Straus and Giroux, 2013.

Collected Interviews with Philip Roth

Conversations with Philip Roth. Edited by George J. Searles. Jackson: University Press of Mississippi, 1992.
Hage, Volker. *Philip Roth: Bücher und Begegnungen*. Munich: Hanser, 2008.
Savigneau, Josyane. *Avec Philip Roth*. Paris: Gallimard, 2014.

On Philip Roth and the Political Power of Literature

Brühwiler, Claudia Franziska. "A Reluctant Public Intellectual: Philip Roth in the German-Speaking Media." *Philip Roth Studies* 10, no. 1 (2014): 77–90.
Stow, Simon. "Written and Unwritten America: Roth on Reading, Politics, and Theory." *Studies in American Jewish Literature* 24 (2003): 77–87.
Wöltje, Wiebke-Marie. *"My finger on the pulse of the nation": Intellektuelle Protagonisten im Romanwerk Philip Roths*. Trier: WVT, 2006.

Zucker, David J. "Roth, Rushdie, and Rage: Religious Reactions to Portnoy and the Verses." *Journal of Ecumenical Studies* 43, no. 1 (2008): 31–44.

On Philip Roth and Liberalism

Hutchinson, Anthony. *Writing the Republic: Liberalism and Morality in American Political Fiction.* New York: Columbia University Press, 2007. (See the chapter "Liberalism Betrayed," 96–168.)

Neelakantan, Gurumurthy. "Philip Roth's Nostalgia for the Yiddishkayt and the New Deal Idealisms in *The Plot Against America*." *Philip Roth Studies* 4, no. 2 (fall 2008): 125–36.

Vials, Christopher. "What Can Happen Here? Philip Roth, Sinclair Lewis, and the Lessons of Fascism in the American Liberal Imagination." *Philip Roth Studies* 7, no. 1 (spring 2011): 9–26.

On Philip Roth and American (Alternate) History

Abbott, Philip. "'Bryan, Bryan, Bryan, Bryan': Democratic Theory, Populism, and Philip Roth's 'American Trilogy.'" *Canadian Review of American Studies* 37, no. 3 (2007): 431–52.

Alexander, Edward. "Philip Roth at Century's End." *New England Review* 20, no. 2 (spring 1999): 183–90.

Brauner, David. "'What was not supposed to happen had happened and what was supposed to happen had not happened': Subverting History in *American Pastoral*." In *Philip Roth: American Pastoral, The Human Stain, The Plot Against America*, edited by Debra Shostak, 19–32. London: Continuum, 2011.

Brühwiler, Claudia Franziska. "Political Awakenings." *Transatlantica: Revue d'études américaines/American Studies Journal*, 2/2007, *Plotting (Against) America*. http://transatlantica.revues.org/document1702.html.

Charis-Carlson, Jeffrey. "Philip Roth's Human Stains and Washington Pilgrimages." *Studies in American Jewish Literature* 23 (2004): 104–21.

Geraci, Ginevra. "The Sense of an Ending: Alternative History in Philip Roth's *The Plot Against America*." *Philip Roth Studies* 7, no. 2 (2011): 187–204.

Gordon, Andrew. "The Critique of Pastoral, Utopia, and the American Dream in *American Pastoral*." In *Philip Roth: American Pastoral, The Human Stain, The Plot Against America*, edited by Debra Shostak, 33–43. London: Continuum, 2011.

Graham, T. Austin. "On the Possibility of an American Holocaust: Philip Roth's *The Plot Against America*." *Arizona Quarterly* 63, no. (fall 2007): 119–49.

Kaplan, Brett Ashley. "Just Folks Homesteading: Roth's Doubled Plots Against America." In *Philip Roth: American Pastoral, The Human Stain, The Plot Against America*, edited by Debra Shostak, 115–29. London: Continuum, 2011.

Kauvar, Elaine M. "My Life as a Boy: *The Plot Against America*." In *Philip Roth: American Pastoral, The Human Stain, The Plot Against America*, edited by Debra Shostak, 130–44. London: Continuum, 2011.

Kellman, Steven G. "It Is Happening Here: *The Plot Against America* and the Political Moment." *Philip Roth Studies* 4, no. 2 (2008): 113–23.

Kimmage, Michael. *In History's Grip: Philip Roth's Newark Trilogy*. Stanford: Stanford University Press, 2012.

Kinzel, Till. *Die Tragödie und Komödie des amerikanischen Lebens: Eine Studie zu Zuckermans Amerika in Philip Roths Amerika-Trilogie*. Heidelberg: Winter, 2006.

———. "Philip Roth's *Our Gang*, the Politics of Intertextuality and the Complexities of Cultural Memory." *Philip Roth Studies* 9, no. 1 (2013): 15–25.

Kumamoto Stanley, Sandra. "Mourning the 'Greatest Generation': Myth and History in Philip Roth's *American Pastoral*." *Twentieth Century Literature* 51, no. 1 (Spring 2005): 1–24.

McDonald, Brian. "'The Real American Crazy Shit': On Adamism and Democratic Individuality in 'American Pastoral.'" *Studies in American Jewish Literature* 23 (2004): 27–40.

Michaels, Walter Benn. "Plots Against America: Neoliberalism and Antiracism." *American Literary History* 18, no. 2 (2006): 288–302.

Parrish, Timothy. "Autobiography and History in Roth's *The Plot Against America*, or What Happened When Hitler Came to New Jersey." In *Philip Roth: American Pastoral, The Human Stain, The Plot Against America*, edited by Debra Shostak, 145–60. London: Continuum, 2011.

Pozorski, Aimee. *Roth and Trauma: The Problem of History in the Later Works (1995–2010)*. London: Continuum, 2011.

Royal, Derek Parker. "Pastoral Dreams and National Identity in *American Pastoral* and *I Married a Communist*." In *Philip Roth. New Perspectives on an American Author*, edited by Royal, 185–207. Westport, CT: Praeger, 2005.

Tanenbaum, Laura. "Reading Roth's Sixties." *Studies in American Jewish Literature* 23 (2004): 41–54.

On Philip Roth, Jewish Identity, and Israel

Aarons, Victoria. "American-Jewish Identity in Roth's Short Fiction." In *The Cambridge Companion to Philip Roth,* edited by Timothy Parrish, 9–21. Cambridge: Cambridge University Press, 2007.

Cooper, Alan. *Philip Roth and the Jews.* Albany: State University of New York Press, 1996.

Duban, James. "Being Jewish in the Twentieth Century: The Synchronicity of Roth and Hawthorne." *Studies in American Jewish Literature* 21 (2002): 1–11.

Furman, Andrew. "A New 'Other' Emerges in American Jewish Literature: Philip Roth's Israel Fiction." *Contemporary Literature* 36, no. 4 (winter 1995): 633–53.

Kaplan, Brett Ashley. *Jewish Anxiety and the Novels of Philip Roth.* New York: Bloomsbury Academic, 2015.

Miller Budick, Emily. "Roth and Israel." In *The Cambridge Companion to Philip Roth,* edited by Timothy Parrish, 68–81. Cambridge: Cambridge University Press, 2007.

Parrish, Timothy. "Imagining Jews in Philip Roth's Operation Shylock." *Contemporary Literature,* 40, no. 4 (winter 1999): 575–602.

Rothberg, Michael. "Roth and the Holocaust." In *The Cambridge Companion to Philip Roth,* edited by Timothy Parrish, 52–67. Cambridge: Cambridge University Press, 2007.

Sokoloff, Naomi. "Imagining Israel in American Jewish Fiction: Anne Roiphe's 'Lovingkindness' and Philip Roth's 'The Counterlife.'" *Studies in American Jewish Literature* 10, no. 1 (1991): 65–80.

Solotaroff, Theodore. "Philip Roth and the Jewish Moralists." *Chicago Review* 13, no. 4 (winter 1959): 87–99.

Whitebrook, Maureen. *Identity, Narrative and Politics.* London: Routledge, 2001. (See the chapter "Uncertain Identity," 43–63.)

On Philip Roth and Race Relations

Franco, Dean J. "Being Black, Being Jewish, and Knowing the Difference: Philip Roth's *The Human Stain;* Or, It Depends on What the Meaning of 'Clinton' Is." *Studies in American Jewish Literature* 23 (2004): 88–103.

———. "*Portnoy's Complaint:* It's about Race, Not Sex (Even the Sex Is about Race)." *Prooftexts* 29, no. 1 (winter 2009): 86–115.

———. "Race, Recognition, and Responsibility in *The Human Stain.*" In *Philip Roth: American Pastoral, The Human Stain, The Plot Against America,* edited by Debra Shostak, 65–79. London: Continuum, 2011.

———, ed. "Roth and Race." Special issue of *Philip Roth Studies* 2, no. 2 (Fall 2006): 81–176.

Glaser, Jennifer. "America's Haunted House: The Racial and National Uncanny in American Pastoral." In *Philip Roth: American Pastoral, The Human Stain, The Plot Against America,* edited by Debra Shostak, 44–59. London: Continuum, 2011.

Kaplan, Brett Ashley. "Anatole Broyard's Human Stain: Performing Post-racial Consciousness." *Philip Roth Studies* 1, no. 2 (fall 2005): 125–44.

Kral, Francoise. "Frictions of Identity in *The Human Stain.*" *Philip Roth Studies* 2, no. 1 (2006): 47–55.

Maslan, Mark. "The Faking of the Americans: Passing, Trauma, and National Identity in Philip Roth's *Human Stain.*" *Modern Language Quarterly* 66, no. 3 (2005): 365–89.

Morley, Catherine. "Possessed by the Past: History, Nostalgia, and Language in *The Human Stain.*" In *Philip Roth: American Pastoral, The Human Stain, The Plot Against America,* edited by Debra Shostak, 80–92. London: Continuum, 2011.

Parrish, Tim. "Becoming Black: Zuckerman's Bifurcating Self in *The Human Stain.*" In *Philip Roth: New Perspectives on an American Author,* edited by Derek Parker Royal, 209–23. Westport, CT: Praeger, 2005.

———. "Roth and Ethnic Identity." In *The Cambridge Companion to Philip Roth,* edited by Timothy Parrish, 127–41. Cambridge: Cambridge University Press, 2007.

On Philip Roth and Gender

Davison, Neil R. *Jewishness and Masculinity from the Modern to the Post-modern.* New York: Routledge, 2010. (See the chapter "From Klugman to Pipik: Philip Roth and Postcolonial/ Postmodern Old-New Jewish Gender," 162–219.)

Gooblar, David, ed. "Roth and Women." Special issue of *Philip Roth Studies* 8, no 1 (2012): 1–120.

Jaffe-Foger, Miriam, and Aimee Pozorski. "'[A]nything but fragile and yielding': Women in Roth's Recent Tetralogy." *Philip Roth Studies* 8, no. 1 (Spring 2012): 81–94.

Ivanova, Velichka. "My Own Foe from the Other Gender: (Mis)representing Women in *The Dying Animal.*" *Philip Roth Studies* 8, no. 1 (spring 2012): 31–42.

Peeler, Nicole. "The Woman of Ressentiment in *When She Was Good.*" *Philip Roth Studies* 6, no. 1 (2010): 31–45.

Shostak, Debra. "Roth and Gender." In *The Cambridge Companion to Philip Roth,* edited by Timothy Parrish, 111–126. Cambridge: Cambridge University Press, 2007.

Select Other Monographs on Philip Roth

The monographs listed below either touch on several of the subjects above and thus cannot be put under one category alone, or they are more concerned with literary aspects of Roth's work, yet still offer insights for those interested in political debates.

Avishai, Bernard. *Promiscuous: "Portnoy's Complaint" and Our Doomed Pursuit of Happiness.* New Haven: Yale University Press, 2012.

Brauner, David. *Philip Roth.* Manchester: Manchester University Press, 2007.

Brühwiler, Claudia Franziska. *Political Initiation in the Novels of Philip Roth.* New York: Bloomsbury, 2013.

Gooblar, David. *The Major Phases of Philip Roth.* New York: Continuum International, 2011.

Halio, Jay L. *Philip Roth Revisited.* New York: Twayne, 1992.

Hayes, Patrick. *Philip Roth: Fiction and Power.* Oxford: Oxford University Press, 2014.

Ivanova, Velichka. *Fiction, utopie, histoire: Essai sur Philip Roth et Milan Kundera.* Paris: L'Harmattan, 2010.

Masiero, Pia. *Philip Roth and the Zuckerman Books: The Making of a Storyworld.* Amherst, NY: Cambria, 2011.

Posnock, Ross. *Philip Roth's Rude Truth: The Art of Immaturity.* Princeton, NJ: Princeton University Press, 2006.

Safer, Elaine B. *Mocking the Age: The Later Novels of Philip Roth.* Albany: State University of New York Press, 2006.

Shechner, Mark. *Up Society's Ass, Copper: Rereading Philip Roth*. Madison: University of Wisconsin Press, 2003.

Shostak, Debra. *Philip Roth—Contexts, Countertexts*. Columbia: University of South Carolina Press, 2004.

Contributors

Claudia Franziska Brühwiler is lecturer and project coordinator at the School of Economics and Political Science at the University of St.Gallen, Switzerland. She has been a research visitor at the University College Dublin, the University of Virginia, the University of Notre Dame, and Amherst College. She is the author of *Political Initiation in the Novels of Philip Roth* (2013) and has published articles in *Canadian Review of American Studies*, *Journal of American Studies*, *Philip Roth Studies*, and *PS: Political Science & Politics*.

Andy Connolly is assistant professor of English at Hostos Community College, CUNY. He has published several articles on Philip Roth in the *Journal of American Studies* and *Philip Roth Studies*.

Michael G. Festl is permanent lecturer of philosophy at the University of St.Gallen, Switzerland, and president of the Swiss Philosophical Society. He is the author of *Justice as Historical Experimentalism: Justice Theory after the Pragmatic Turn in Epistemology* (2014).

Louis Gordon teaches political science at California State University at San Bernardino and is a member of the National Book Critics Circle. His work has appeared in the *Los Angeles Times*, *Jewish Daily Forward*, *Journal of Israel History*, *Jerusalem Post*, *Jewish Political Studies Review*, and other publications. He is coauthor, with Ian Oxnevad, of a forthcoming book about Middle Eastern politics.

Brett Ashley Kaplan is professor and Conrad Humanities Scholar in the Program of Comparative and World Literature and Program in Jewish Culture and Society at the University of Illinois Urbana-Champaign. She is the author of *Jewish Anxiety and the Novels of Philip Roth* (2015); *Landscapes* *of Holocaust Post-Memory* (2010); *Unwanted Beauty: Aesthetic Pleasure in Holocaust Representation* (2006), as well as numerous articles about Holocaust Representation and modern Jewish literature.

Till Kinzel is lecturer at the Technical University of Braunschweig. He is the author of books on Allan Bloom (*Platonische Kulturkritik in Amerika,* 2002); Nicolás Gómez Dávila (*Nicolás Gómez Dávila: Parteigänger verlorener Sachen,* 2003); Philip Roth (*Die Tragödie und Komödie des amerikanischen Lebens,* 2006); and Michael Oakeshott (*Michael Oakeshott: Philosoph der Politik,* 2007). He is also the editor of numerous books, the latest being on the reception of Edward Gibbon in Germany (*Edward Gibbon im deutschen Sprachraum,* 2015).

Yael Maurer is professor of English and American studies at Tel Aviv University, Israel. She is the author of *The Science Fiction Dimensions of Salman Rushdie* (2014) and has published articles about Holocaust Representation, Jewish American writers, and postcolonial fiction.

Aimee Pozorski is professor of English at Central Connecticut State University and served as president of the Philip Roth Society. She is the author of *Falling after 9/11: Crisis in American Art and Literature* (2014); *Roth and Trauma: The Problem of History in the Later Works* (2011); and editor of *Critical Insights: Philip Roth* (2013) and *Roth and Celebrity* (2012).

Matthew Shipe is lecturer in the Department of English and American Culture Studies at Washington University in St. Louis, Missouri, and the president of the Philip Roth Society. His publications include articles in *Philip Roth Studies, Perspectives on Barry Hannah, Roth and Celebrity,* and *Critical Insights: Raymond Carver.*

Debra Shostak is Mildred Foss Thompson Professor of English Language and Literature and chair of the Film Studies Program at the College of Wooster, Ohio. She is coeditor of the *Philip Roth Studies* journal and the author of *Philip Roth: Countertexts, Counterlives* (2004); editor of *Philip Roth: American Pastoral, The Human Stain, The Plot Against America* (2011); and has published essays on contemporary American fiction and on film.

Simon Stow is associate professor of government at the College of William and Mary. He is the author of *Republic of Readers? The Literary Turn in Political Thought and Analysis* (2007), coeditor of *The Political Companion to John Steinbeck* (2013), and has published articles on politics and public mourning in the *American Political Review, Perspectives on Politics,* and *Philosophy and Literature.*

Lee Trepanier is professor of political science at Saginaw Valley State University, Michigan. He is the author and editor of numerous books, the latest being *The Free Market and the Human Condition* (2014); *A Political Companion to Saul Bellow* (2013); *Dostoevsky's Political Thought* (2013); *LDS in USA: Mormonism and the Making of American Culture* (2012); and *Cosmopolitanism in the Age of Globalization* (2011).

Index

POLITICAL COMPANIONS TO GREAT AMERICAN AUTHORS

SERIES EDITOR
Patrick J. Deneen, University of Notre Dame

BOOKS IN THE SERIES

A Political Companion to Philip Roth
Edited by Claudia Franziska Brühwiler and Lee Trepanier

A Political Companion to Saul Bellow
Edited by Gloria L. Cronin and Lee Trepanier

A Political Companion to Flannery O'Connor
Edited by Henry T. Edmondson III

A Political Companion to Herman Melville
Edited by Jason Frank

A Political Companion to Walker Percy
Edited by Peter Augustine Lawler and Brian A. Smith

A Political Companion to Ralph Waldo Emerson
Edited by Alan M. Levine and Daniel S. Malachuk

A Political Companion to Marilynne Robinson
Edited by Shannon L. Mariotti and Joseph H. Lane Jr.

A Political Companion to Walt Whitman
Edited by John E. Seery

A Political Companion to Henry Adams
Edited by Natalie Fuehrer Taylor

A Political Companion to Henry David Thoreau
Edited by Jack Turner

A Political Companion to John Steinbeck
Edited by Cyrus Ernesto Zirakzadeh and Simon Stow

CPSIA information can be obtained
at www.ICGtesting.com
Printed in the USA
BVOW04*1951050517
482462BV00009B/2/P